GOLIAD

GOLIAD
The Other Alamo

William R. Bradle

PELICAN PUBLISHING COMPANY
GRETNA 2007

Library of Congress Cataloging-in-Publication Data

Bradle, William R.
  Goliad : the other Alamo / William R. Bradle.
      p. cm.
  Includes bibliographical references and index.
  ISBN 978-1-58980-457-9 (hardcover : alk. paper)
  1. Goliad Massacre, Goliad, Tex., 1836. 2. Texas—
History—Revolution, 1835-1836. I. Title.
  F390.B832 2007
  976.4'123—dc22

                                        2007005365

Printed in the United States of America
Published by Pelican Publishing Company, Inc.
1000 Burmaster Street, Gretna, Louisiana 70053

To Sue—
For Everything

Contents

Chapter 1

A Short History of Texas

Tayshas, Meaning "Ally" or "Friend,"
to the Caddos, *Tejas* to the Spanish—Texas

In the early morning of March 6, 1836, a Mexican army of 6,000 soldiers attacked and killed 189 rebel Texans at the Alamo. Exactly three weeks later, 342 Texans were executed at Goliad.

The Alamo has become legend. Goliad has been largely forgotten. But Goliad, more than the Alamo, galvanized the new republic into action that ended with the victory, massacre, and capture of hundreds of Mexicans at San Jacinto. The Alamo was a heroic, if misguided, defeat. Goliad, at least to the Texans, was total war.

The Alamo and Goliad are not isolated, singular events. To understand them and their place in Texas history, it is necessary to know what came before and what would come after.

Obviously, the territory that is now Texas was inhabited by Indians long before anyone else arrived on the scene. But the Indians left little, if any, written history.

When the Spanish first appeared in the territory in 1519, the various tribes had adapted to what their respective geographical areas gave them in the way of resources. The Karankawas lived on the coast between present-day Galveston and Corpus Christi, roaming the area for food that included maggots and, in some cases, other humans. The Karankawas are often described as cannibals, although this assessment is disputed. Most likely humans were not a part of the everyday diet. Only after a battle were bits of the defeated consumed to ingest the strength and courage of the enemy. The Karankawas traveled by dugout canoe, had tattoos, and produced and consumed alcoholic beverages. They were a tall people, the men often over six feet tall.

The Karankawa name means "dog lovers" or "dog raisers," as coyote-type dogs were abundant in their camps.

The Jumanos lived in west Texas, extending into New Mexico and often trading with the Spanish out of Santa Fe. Historians are unsure if the Jumanos were farmers or hunters. They were probably a combination, as west Texans even today know you take what this rough country will give you.

The Tonkawas, defined as "those that stay together," did stay together in central Texas but in rather loosely related clans of nomadic hunters and gatherers. In a unique tradition, they tied pieces of wood to a newborn's head to flatten the forehead.

In south Texas lived numerous tribes lumped together under the title of Coahuiltecans. In the east were the Caddos. The Caddos, who were primarily farmers, lived in east Texas and western Louisiana in the abundance of the piney woods. The Caddos gave the state its name when the Spanish corrupted *Tayshas* into *Tejas*. That, of course, slid into *Texas*. *Tayshas* was Caddo for "friend" or "ally" and it was how the Caddo initially greeted the Spanish.

The Caddos' territory included what is now Caddo Lake and is a good segue into Texas geography. Texas geography explains a lot about Texas history because Texas is a fairly easy place to get around. Get caught in a Texas hailstorm or in the western wastelands without water and a traveler is in trouble. But with food and water, the Indian, Spaniard, Frenchman, or Anglo could travel largely unimpeded. There are no Alps or Rockies to go over or around. There are swamps on the coast that pose dangers, as Santa Anna was to discover, but they are avoidable. The piney woods are navigable. There are no large bodies of water. The only natural lake in Texas is Caddo Lake and half of that is in Louisiana. There are the Colorado, Brazos, Sabine, Red, and Rio Grande Rivers, but they are not in the same league as the Mississippi or even the Tennessee River for width or difficulty in crossing. Texas can be a dangerous place but relatively easy to get across, as Cabeza de Vaca was to find out.

Cortez conquered the Aztecs. His reward was the gold of Mexico. Alvar Nunez Cabeza de Vaca got a seven-year stint in

Texas and no gold. He was originally headed to Florida but the fleet was blown off course. In 1528, Cabeza de Vaca was a thirty-eight-year-old Spanish soldier who had served his king primarily fighting in Italy. His was an old and distinguished, if not overly wealthy, family. The Alvar Nunez part of the name came from the maternal side of the family, honoring an ancestor who had been a prominent naval captain. "Cabeza de Vaca" meant literally "cow's head" in honor of another ancestor who had aided in defeating the Moors. In 1212, Martin Alhaja, a shepherd, pointed out an unmarked pass through a mountain range for King Sancho, allowing Sancho to come upon a Moorish army by surprise and defeat them at the battle of Los Navas de Tolosa. Alhaja marked the pass with the skull of a cow, and the king bestowed the "cow's head" title on the family.

For his service in Italy, Cabeza de Vaca was named treasurer of an expedition that left Spain, wintered in Cuba, and then set off to claim Florida for the crown. They did so on April 15, 1528, landing near present-day Sarasota and heading inland in search of a golden city named Apalachee that some Indians had told them of. The Spanish were always looking for cities of gold. Cabeza de Vaca argued against the expedition but the leader, Panfilo de Narvaez, overruled his treasurer and began thrashing around the coast with three hundred men. The fleet was supposed to parallel his course along the coast but the two forces became separated and the ships were never heard from again. The land expedition found Apalachee but there was no gold. Apalachee was just a village consisting of a few huts and hostile Indians.

Faced with unfriendly Florida Indians and soon down to 250 men because of battle and disease, Narvaez and his men built five barges and set off to sea looking for the mouth of the Mississippi. They overshot their mark due to storms. Two of the barges beached on San Luis Island, just west of Galveston Island. The men on the other three barges were never heard from again. There were eighty survivors on the two barges, but due to disease, drowning, starvation, and Indian attacks there were soon only four survivors. Cabeza de Vaca, Andrés Dorantes de Carranza, an African-born slave

Estevanico, and Alonso Castillo Maldonado. The Spaniards named the island Malhado—"misfortune" in Spanish. Welcome to Texas.

Cabeza fell ill and separated from his companions, became a slave of the Karankawas for four years. Slowly, he began to develop in the eyes of the Indians as a good trader and also as a medicine man. Spanish medicine was crude as any in those days, but it was better than Indian medicine, or Cabeza just got lucky. His fame spread among the tribes and his practice grew. After four years, his wanderings brought him back to the mouth of the Guadalupe River where he was reunited with the three other survivors. The group plotted their escape, setting off from Galveston Island and walking to Culiacán, on the Pacific coast of Mexico. The exact route is unknown, but the distance is over 2,000 miles, with the whole trip taking more than seven years. After the journey, Cabeza and his Spaniard companions wrote about the experience, the Indians, and the topography and geography of Texas.

Along the way, Cabeza saved the life of one Indian by removing an arrowhead from his chest. For this act, the first recorded successful surgery in Texas, Cabeza de Vaca is recognized as the patron saint of the Texas Surgical Society. The logo of the society is a cattle's skull superimposed on the star of Texas.

Cabeza de Vaca went on to serve in Spanish-ruled Paraguay but returned to Spain under a cloud, charged with bad management. Convicted and banished to North Africa, he was eventually cleared. He returned to Spain, where he died sometime in the middle 1550s. The two other Spaniards remained in Mexico and died there.

Estevanico, the African, was persuaded by the viceroy to guide an expedition to Arizona. Scouting ahead he was captured by Zuni Indians and his medicine gourd sealed his fate. The gourd was trimmed in owl feathers, a symbol of death to the Zuni. Debating his fate through the night, the Zuni killed Estevanico in the morning.

Though the four men had varying levels of success at their endeavors, the real accomplishment of Cabeza de Vaca and his group was writing about their adventures. Texas was now on the map.

But being on the map wasn't enough. Spanish exploration was going on all over the world and they were looking for one thing—gold. Texas didn't have gold, at least not gold that was easy to get to, and the oil that was to be the gold of Texas held no interest or accessibility for the Spaniards. There were easier pickings elsewhere, like Mexico and Peru. The search was always on for El Dorado, the city of gold, and expeditions crisscrossed Texas, but no real Spanish settlement was established until new neighbors, the French, moved in next door.

Louis XIV sent Rene Robert Cavelier, Sieur de La Salle, to the New World by the back door, having him lead an expedition down from Canada via the Mississippi to the Gulf of Mexico. Arriving there in 1682, La Salle claimed the Mississippi basin for France and named it, of course, Louisiana after Louis. The purpose of the trip was to establish fur-trapping routes in the middle of the continent. Along the way, La Salle established a fort at what is now Memphis, Tennessee.

La Salle returned to France and then back to the New World in 1684, this time taking the direct route to the Gulf of Mexico with a group of four ships, one of which sank en route. This was especially bad luck as that ship carried the majority of the stores. The remaining ships, like the expedition of Cabeza de Vaca, overshot, missed the Mississippi, and crashed ashore in Matagorda Bay. One of the ships, now run aground, was raided by Indians and La Salle's men shot at them, making enemies of the locals. Another ship, with a crew that had seen enough, sailed for home. The group that stayed built a fort, Fort St. Louis, at the mouth of the Lavaca River and began exploring. A drunken pilot ran the remaining ship aground in 1686 and the French were stranded in Texas.

A group of twenty set out up the Lavaca to find the Mississippi and the French settlements. They shortly turned back but only eight survivors returned to the fort. In March 1687, La Salle and seventeen others tried again but soon got into a fight over food. La Salle was killed by his own men near present-day Navasota, Texas, in Cherokee County. The remaining group split up, with six heading back to the fort and never making it. The others headed to Canada, eventually reaching France in October 1688. In 1689 the Karankawa attacked the fort, massacring the remaining men and carrying off the women and children.

The Spanish didn't know about the French explorers. They only found out about the French fort after capturing French pirates off the Yucatan and gaining the story before executing them. To pinpoint the fort a mapping operation sailed from Havana and surveyed the coast from the panhandle of Florida to Tampico in northeast Mexico. A land force was also dispatched from Tampico, spending four years marching through Texas, Alabama, and Florida looking for the French. In addition, Spanish ships sailed around the Gulf of Mexico looking for La Salle, his camps, and his men. None of the expeditions found them, but they learned a lot about the geography and the people.

The Spanish finally found the fort three weeks after the massacre. La Salle's determined presence alarmed the Spanish enough to make them serious about the occupation of Texas, so they began building mission forts. One of these was Royal Presidio La Bahia, founded in the year 1721 in the vicinity of Fort St. Louis with the duel purpose of converting the Indians to Christianity and keeping an eye out for further French expansion into Texas. La Bahia was to become Goliad. Other missions were founded, failed, moved, and reestablished. The mission at San Antonio de Bexar, the Alamo, was founded in 1717. The Spanish goal of the missions was not to colonize Texas but to use it as a buffer zone between Mexico and the French. The Spanish made this very clear to the French by declaring the town of Los Adaes the capital of Texas. Los Adaes was located inside the border of Louisiana.

This geographical anomaly was resolved in 1762 when France ceded Louisiana to Spain as compensation for its backing France against Britain in the French and Indian Wars. With the issue settled, at least for the time being, there was no need for Los Adaes. The town was abandoned. The capital of Texas was moved to San Antonio, three hundred miles to the southwest. Things settled down in Texas but not in many other places.

Revolution was in the air. While the British had won the French and Indian War, the war had to be paid for. Since the North American campaign had been fought on account of the North Americans, the British figured the North Americans should pay for it. Stamp taxes, tea taxes, and taxation without representation led to the Boston Tea Party, Lexington and Concord, Bunker Hill, and the Fourth of July, 1776. Independence.

The American Revolution seems rather benign for a revolution. Many of the participants knew each other. Though they didn't get along, they had roughly similar backgrounds. The Americans were viewed by the British as country cousins but not in a totally derogatory way. The armies tried to look the same with George Washington's uniform and the uniforms of his officers styled like the uniforms of their opponents except for the color. The uniforms of the common soldiers were different but only because the Americans had no money for such things, while the British had to clothe their soldiers because the majority were not theirs, they were German mercenaries.

Things could get nasty, though. The British suffered over one thousand killed, wounded, and captured at Bunker Hill, a casualty rate of more than 20 percent. This a year before independence was even declared. While almost all Americans know of the British hanging Nathan Hale for spying, most do not know that Washington had Adj. Gen. John Andre hung for recruiting Benedict Arnold. Washington even turned down Andre's request to be shot rather than hung. Finally, those Hessians usually tried to finish things off with their bayonets. But, as revolutions go, it was fairly civilized and well documented, giving the world the Declaration of Independence as a model. It did not result in great numbers of civilian deaths or reprisals or executions, Hale and Andre notwithstanding. It inspired the world.

Unfortunately, the revolutions that followed would be much bloodier than the model.

The French Revolution was a disaster by comparison, with the guillotine executions in the Place de la Concorde and the legislative mess that ended in the dictatorship of Napoleon. About all we got out of it is the origin for right-wingers and left-wingers, for in the first attempts at legislative action, the monarchists (the right-wingers) sat on the right side of the room and the revolutionaries sat, of course, on the left side.

But what does this have to do with Texas? Not much to the Spanish because the Spanish soon had their hands full as well—so full that Texas was very low on their list of priorities. A quick look at the Spanish empire and the stretching of their resources tells the story.

Prior to 1700, Spain had possessions in Belgium, Italy, and current-day Morocco. They had everything in Latin America except Brazil: all or most of Argentina, Chile, Peru, Colombia, Ecuador, Venezuela, Nicaragua, Costa Rica, El Salvador, Guatemala, Mexico, Cuba, and Puerto Rico. They lost Brazil only because of a badly written navigational agreement between Portugal and Spain. In the Pacific, they claimed the Philippines, Guam, and the Mariannas. In North America they claimed Florida, California, Arizona, and New Mexico. And Texas.

The Spanish were spread thin, and they weren't exactly investing in the countries. The colonies were sources of gold and raw materials to be transported back to Spain to pay down debt, sell, or consume. Indigenous peoples that got in the way were exterminated.

The colonists did not like their resources going to Spain. But what they really didn't like was Napoleon conquering Spain and in 1807 naming his brother, Joseph Bonaparte, as king. Charles IV was forced to abdicate while his son, Ferdinand VII, was forced to renounce any claim to the throne. Charles was no favorite (he only got the job because his older brother was an epileptic with mental problems), spending most of his time hunting while his wife and her lover, Godoy, ran the country. Charles and his wife did spend

some time together, however, as they had fourteen children.
While Charles was not beloved by his people, he was at least
family and Joseph Bonaparte was not. The colonies revolted.

Colombia went first, winning independence in 1810, followed by Venezuela in 1811. Argentina went in 1816 and
Chile in 1818. Mexico started in 1810 and Spain was gone
from there by 1821. Peru gained its independence that same
year and Uruguay in 1825. These wars of independence followed the pattern of the American Revolution, and the
Declaration of Independence was often plagiarized whole-
sale. In some cases, like Mexico, it was surpassed, with slavery being banned, at least in the law if not in reality.

Some interesting characters took part in these wars. One of
those, Sir Thomas Cochrane of the British navy, early in his
career captured a Spanish ship with thirty-two guns and over
three hundred sailors. His ship was a sloop with only fourteen
guns and fifty-four men. Other feats followed and he climbed
the ranks to post captain, but he railed against the bureaucracy and corruption of the admiralty and got caught up in, or
was framed in, a stock market scandal. He was imprisoned in
King's Bench Prison when a servant (some claim his wife)
smuggled in a rope. Cochrane opened his window and threw
the rope to the outer wall, secured it, and escaped hand over
hand. He attached the rope to a spike in the wall and started
to descend to the stone road. The rope snapped and Cochrane
fell twenty-five feet to the ground. Somehow unhurt, he continued his escape but was recaptured. A public outcry ensued
and he was released, but his naval career was over, at least for
the moment. Out of work he sailed to Chile to take command
of the rebel navy against the Spanish. Successful militarily, he
argued continuously with the Chilean liberator, Bernardo
O'Higgins, over money and tactics and left after winning independence. He went to Brazil to fight against the Portuguese,
then on to Greece to fight the Turks. As in Chile, he was
successful but made himself unpopular over money and
expenses. Both C. S. Forester and Patrick O'Brian admitted
their fictional maritime heroes, Horatio Hornblower and
Jack Aubrey respectively, were based on Cochrane. Every

year Chilean naval cadets travel to England for the anniversary of Cochrane's death to decorate his grave.

Before the nineteenth century was a quarter gone, the Spanish were out of Latin America except for Cuba and Puerto Rico. It was only a matter of time and they were ousted there, and the Philippines, in the Spanish-American War of 1898.

They were also out of Florida after Gen. Andrew Jackson, chasing runaway slaves and Seminole Indians, neglected to stop at the border. Negotiations ensued, resulting in the Onis-Adams Treaty of 1819. Spain surrendered Florida along with any rights to the Pacific Northwest territory. Spain received no compensation for Florida, although the United States assumed five million dollars in damages done by its citizens living there. What the Spanish did get was a definition of the western boundary of the Louisiana Territory. Put more simply, the United States recognized the sovereignty of Spain over Texas.

This didn't go over well with the majority of United States citizens, as Manifest Destiny was rearing its head and Texas was next. But it could wait, because Spain wasn't going to be around long in Texas or Mexico.

Spain's problems in Mexico began on September 16, 1810, when a priest, Miguel Hidalgo y Costilla, ordered the arrest of all Spaniards living in the town of Dolores. Hidalgo was a fifty-seven-year-old Creole priest, Creoles being of Spanish blood but born in the New World. Somewhat of a second-class citizen but ahead of the local Indians, Hidalgo was also not a total true believer, as he had numerous illegitimate children. Among his seminary classmates he was known as El Zorro, the fox. In addition to the priesthood, he was a good businessman who started trade schools, which he opened not only to Spaniards and Creoles but also to Indians and mestizos, those of mixed Spanish and Indian blood. The one thing that really upset Hidalgo and his followers was having Joseph Bonaparte, brother of Napoleon Bonaparte, as king of Spain.

Hidalgo and a group of confederates had planned to stage a revolt in December but he was found out, forcing him to move up the timing. In the early morning of September 16, Hidalgo entered the town square, waved the banner of the Virgin Mary, rang the church bells, and harangued the crowd. The speech has gone down in history as the "Grito," or shout, and was mostly a harangue against Bonaparte. The mob was whipped up and the revolution was on.

The mob rolled out of the city and snowballed in size. Several cities were captured as the mob marched toward Mexico City. Hidalgo became less of a priest and more of a general, dressing in a bright blue, scarlet, black, and gold uniform. For some reason he turned his mob away from Mexico City and marched on Guadalajara. His revolutionary army dwindled from 70,000 to 40,000, and he was defeated by the Royalists at the battle of Aculco. Undaunted he returned to Guadalajara and built the army back up to 70,000. The Royalists attacked and Hidalgo made his stand at Calderon Bridge—not a good idea, as his forces were bunched up and then chopped up by the smaller but more disciplined Royalist army. A Royalist cannonball hitting and exploding his ammunition dump didn't help either. For his ineptitude, Hidalgo was demoted by other rebel officers to civilian political affairs officer.

Learning of a similar revolt in San Antonio, the rebel army started a march there but was ambushed in the mountains of Coahuila as the result of a traitor's tip. Hidaglo was taken to Durango where he was defrocked and then on to Chihuahua where, on July 30, 1811, he was executed by firing squad. He went out gallantly, directing the firing squad to aim at his right hand, which covered his heart.

Hidalgo was not a great general but he got things started. On the night of every September 15 the current president of the Republic reenacts the Grito on the balcony of the National Palace. Hidalgo also had an immense impact on Goliad. The town name is an anagram for Hidalgo, with the "H" being silent.

After the execution of Hidalgo, a mestizo priest, Jose Maria Morelos y Pavon, took over cobbling together a loose federation of forces across Mexico. A congress was formed, a declaration of independence proclaimed, and a constitution written that, among other things, abolished slavery and class distinctions. But the priest followed in the footsteps of Hidalgo and was soon captured. Taken to Mexico City, Morelos first had to undergo a church trial in which he was defrocked. The church did not call for execution but for banishment to Africa. After the church trial and humiliating defrocking, Morelos was put on military trial. The state asked for execution with his head to be cut off, placed in an iron cage, and put on exhibit in the main plaza. His right hand was to be cut off and displayed in Oxaca. All family property was to be appropriated.

The judge approved the death sentence but not the dismemberment. The body was to be buried whole. Morelos was taken outside the city, said confession with a priest, and then blindfolded. His arms were bound behind him with musket slings and he was forced to kneel in front of an earthen embankment. His final words were "Lord, thou knowest if I have done well; if ill, I implore thy infinite mercy." Four muskets fired but Morelos still moved. Four more shots and he was still.

The mantle then fell to Manuel de Mier y Teran, an engineer by trade, who brought much-needed munitions and artillery efficiency to the young rebel army. With the capture and execution of Morelos the leaders of the revolt had begun quarrelling. The revolution deteriorated into a series of guerilla wars led by territorial warlords. The congress turned selfish, with the members voting themselves large salaries, taking on less revolutionary actions such as addressing each other as "Your Most Honorable." Teran dissolved the congress, arrested the members, and then released them to return to their home provinces. However, Teran could not centrally manage the revolution, and the various warlords went on their own campaigns. The Royalists became efficient at hunting down these groups, but the warlords fought hard since the leaders were usually beheaded upon capture.

By this time, a new viceroy had been appointed by Ferdinand VII. Joseph Bonaparte was gone due to the British conquest of Spain in the Napoleonic War. The viceroy introduced a policy of amnesty for rebels that took most of the fight out of the rebel forces. Teran and his brother took the new viceroy up on his offer and gave up the revolution.

The struggle went on sporadically but not much happened until 1821 when the internal call for more liberty in Spain spilled over into Mexico. An unholy alliance was formed by members of the church, monarchists, and revolutionaries with the only commonality being the desire to see Spain out of Mexico. The coalition picked Agustin Iturbide as their military leader. One officer voting for Iturbide was Antonio Lopez de Santa Anna. Members of the coalition persuaded the viceroy to name Iturbide head of an army to be sent to destroy a rebel army stronghold held by Vicente Guerrero, a particularly effective and elusive revolutionary. Instead of capturing Guerrero, Iturbide and the revolutionary teamed up, declaring on February 24, 1821, the Plan de Iguala, Iguala being the village where the plan was hatched. The plan was based on the Government of the Three Guarantees: protection of the Catholic faith with no competition from other religions, Mexican independence, and equality for all Mexicans.

The government was still to be a monarchy and Ferdinand VII was offered the job with the caveat that he had to move to Mexico. Ferdinand declined. A new viceroy was in passage when the Plan was announced and upon arrival he saw the handwriting on the wall. The viceroy signed the Treaty of Cordova on August 24, 1821, effectively ending Spain's hold on Mexico.

One last act of the Spanish would have a significant impact on Texas. In 1820 the Spanish governor in San Antonio granted Moses Austin permission to found a colony of Anglo settlers in Texas. Moses Austin was born in Durham, Connecticut, in 1761. Married in Philadelphia, he then moved to Virginia, where he operated a lead mine in a town that became known as Austinville. To gain access to more minerals, Moses went to Spanish northern Louisiana Territory, now Missouri. In 1796 Moses sought and received from the Spanish authorities a league of land with lead deposits. In 1797 he received permission to bring in thirty American families as colonists. Moses and his colony prospered. Moses put his net worth in 1810 at $190,000—more than $2.2 million in today's dollars. However, a financial crisis hit the United States in 1818 as a result of banks lending too much to risky real estate deals. Banks collapsed, the Bank of St. Louis being one of them. Unfortunately, Moses was a director of the bank, and he lost his fortune with the collapse. Ruined but resilient, Moses turned to Texas.

Moses traveled to San Antonio. He was initially rebuffed from starting a colony but with some help from the locals he gained approval from the governor on December 26, 1820. Moses left for Missouri in early January 1821 to gather his colonists, but he developed pneumonia from traveling in the rain and cold. In addition, he was robbed and nearly starved to death. Arriving home to Missouri, he neglected his health by working on the Texas project until forced to his bed. His dying words to his wife, Mary, were "tell dear Stephen that it is his dieing fathers [sic] last request to prosecute the enterprise he had commenced." Moses died on June 10, 1821.

Back in Mexico City, Iturbide soon took up where the Spaniards left off by dissolving Congress and declaring himself Augustin I, Emperor of Imperial Mexico. So much for the revolution. Iturbide, or Augustin, was indeed an emperor. His territory stretched from Oregon to Panama and included California, Texas, Arizona, and New Mexico. On January 3, 1823, Iturbide signed into law the existence of Austin's colony after much lobbying by Stephen Austin in Mexico.

Initially, Stephen was not enthusiastic about the project, as he really wanted to be a lawyer. Prodded by the deathbed command, he took up the challenge, traveled to San Antonio where he met with the governor and, like his father, got the green light. He then traveled to New Orleans where he published the offer: 640 acres to the head of a household, 320 acres to his wife, 160 acres to each child, and 80 acres for each slave. Not to the slave, of course, but to the head of the household. As administrator guaranteeing the good conduct of the settlers, Austin would receive 12.5 cents for each acre. The site was to be located between the Colorado and Brazos Rivers. The United States was still in an economic depression and financial panic so the offer looked good to many Americans looking for a new start.

The law signed by Augustin was about the last thing he did as emperor because his ally, Vicente Guerrero, switched sides again and he, along with a group of army officers including Santa Anna forced Augustin—soon to be Iturbide again—into exile on March 19, 1823. He fled Mexico aboard a British navy ship, the H.M.S. *Rowlins.* The ship was arranged by Guadalupe Victoria, an early follower of Morelos's and a republican rather than a monarchist. Iturbide fled to Italy and then to London, where he got wind of a rumored Spanish attempt to retake Mexico. Instead of joining the Spanish, he was convinced by advisors that only he could stop the Spanish invasion and save Mexico. Expecting to be hailed as a liberator, he was instead seized by a military patrol when he landed near Tampico. He was executed by firing squad the same day.

When Iturbide abdicated, the colony law was annulled. Austin went back to lobbying and got it reinstated again, allowing three hundred families into Texas. The new law changed the original land grant and conferred upon each settler a league, or 4,428 acres. Austin completed the first colony and received additional approval to bring in a total of nine hundred families. The main requirements were that the families agree to become Mexican citizens and Catholics.

A political vacuum resulted after Iturbide abdicated until Guadalupe Victoria was named the first president of Mexico in 1824. He was also the first leader in some time who did not end up in front of a firing squad. It was economics that caught up with Victoria: the government was spending twice what it was collecting in taxes. Victoria, looking for a loan, found the British more than willing to help as they were doing in other parts of Latin America. While not colonizing the area, they were loaning money in exchange for access to the large amounts of natural resources needed to fuel Britain's growing economy. The loans bought Victoria some breathing room to oversee projects that would have a long-term impact on the country, including the abolition of slavery, establishment of the national treasury (needed to administer the loans), and the construction of the National Museum.

During President Victoria's term, there was growing tension in Mexico between the conservatives (Centralists) who favored a return to Spanish rule and liberals (Federalists), including Victoria, who wanted to retain independence. The conservatives maintained that the liberals were falling under the influence of the Americans. Americans were personified by Joel Poinsett, the United States ambassador to Mexico, but known now as the man who introduced the poinsettia to the American Christmas scene. He is known to the Mexicans as the ambassador who offered only $1 million for the whole state of Texas. The offer was eventually raised to $5 million but still refused. Victoria survived his term, retiring peacefully in 1828 to his country home, where he died at the age of fifty-seven of natural causes.

After Victoria things really became confusing. In the next election the liberals ran Vicente Guerrero, the rebel who along with Iturbide won independence from Spain, and the conservatives ran Gomez Pedraza. Pedraza won. Guerrero refused to accept the election results, and Leonardo de Zavala, a radical journalist, organized a revolt. Suddenly Guerrero had "won" the election. But Guerrero was more a warrior than a politician. De Zavala was the real power behind the throne and widely thought to be the puppet of John Poinsett. Gen. Anastacio Bustamante, a conservative, mounted a revolt and in 1830 stripped Guerrero of his power, kicking Poinsett out of the country. Guerrero fled to the south and—here we go again—mounted a revolt against Bustamante. Bustamante's minister of war paid a sea captain 50,000 pesos to lure Guerrero onto a ship anchored in Acapaulco Bay. Upon boarding the ship, Guerrero was seized. He was court-martialed, found guilty, and executed on February 14, 1831. By firing squad.

Bustamante is important because he lost to Santa Anna. In 1829 the Spanish had made an effort to take over Mexico again, with the invasion being repulsed by Santa Anna. Thus the young general was a national hero. In contrast,

Bustamante's murder of Guerrero, a bumbling president but revered revolutionary, along with his inability to handle the country's foreign debt problem and economic stagnation made Bustamante politically unpopular. Rumors of him wanting to establish a monarchy didn't help. Santa Anna began his revolt and in 1832 Bustamante beat the firing squad by going into exile.

Antonio Lopez de Santa Anna, born in Veracruz in 1794, joined the army as an infantry cadet at the age of sixteen. Still in his teens, he was wounded in Texas by an Indian arrow. Commissioned a first lieutenant in 1812, he was promoted to captain in 1816. During the revolution Santa Anna remained a loyal Royalist and broke a rebel siege at Orizaba. After Iturbide became a rebel, he convinced Santa Anna to switch as well, but with one condition. Santa Anna had just been promoted to lieutenant colonel by the Spanish and wanted to retain this rank if he joined the rebels. Iturbide agreed.

Iturbide, now Augustin I, and Santa Anna had a falling out when Augustin chided Santa Anna for being too political. Political indeed, as Santa Anna joined Vicente Guerrero in tossing out Iturbide. As noted, Spain attempted a comeback in Mexico in 1829, landing twenty-seven hundred men at Tampico under the command of a General Barradas. More than a third of the soldiers soon succumbed to tropical fever and the rest were on the verge of surrender. When they did so, Santa Anna declared a military victory and was hailed as the "Hero of Tampico." Barradas sailed for Havana.

The Bustamante regime was never without rebellion. Santa Anna joined it in 1832, taking his garrison at Veracruz into battle against General Calderon, and losing. Chased back to Veracruz, the garrison was besieged for the summer, until Santa Anna was finally reinforced. Bustamante went into exile and Pedraza was named a lame duck to serve out the remainder of the term, which ended March 31, 1833. Santa Anna was chosen to replace him. He was elected as a Federalist but in 1834 maintained that Mexico was not ready for democracy and switched to being a Centralist.

More importantly Santa Anna was acutely aware of the

fates of his predecessors and moved quickly to solidify his position. On May 25, Santa Anna disbanded Congress. He put in place the edicts necessary to making himself a dictator. This was not totally unacceptable to his countrymen, as the ten years since independence had not been easy ones.

There was dissent, however. The liberals of Zacatecas rebelled in 1835 when Santa Anna attempted to limit the size and authority of local militias. Santa Anna defeated them on the battlefield, following up with harsh repression. He would be nicknamed the "Harlequin Hangman" because of the numerous executions during his tenure.

As Santa Anna consolidated his power things did quiet down, meaning he was finally free to take on more distant challenges, like Texas.

Throughout the history of Mexican independence, the revolts, rebellions, and repressions were so close to home that the players had no time or inclination to deal with events far away. Texas was far away. Also, the Mexican revolution and that country's path to democracy was not the only rocky one. Less than three years after gaining independence, George Washington had to deal with Shays' Rebellion, when bankrupt farmers revolted against the concept of debtor's prison and a regressive tax system. It also highlighted a problem that Santa Anna would become aware of and address. The United States could not march against the rebels because under the Articles of Confederation such issues were to be handled by the individual states. The rebellion so shook Washington that he became, like Santa Anna would become, a centralist. The Articles made way for the Constitution largely because of Shays' Rebellion.

This led to another revolt when the United States central government accepted the debt of the individual states and imposed whiskey taxes to pay off the debt. With the new constitution allowing federal intervention, Washington used his new powers to send troops into Pennsylvania to squash the tax revolt. Twenty rebels were caught, with two being sentenced to death. Washington commuted the sentences on grounds of insanity and stupidity. The law of unintended consequences set in. Many of the rebels fled to Kentucky and Tennessee, where they set up their stills and founded the whiskey business that is still there today.

Both republics had to go through early traumas close to home, but once such problems were resolved, they both turned their attention to Texas.

Chapter 2

Come and Take It

"While the door of my cottage is open to brave men,
it is eternally shut to cowards."

The first two decades of the nineteenth century were ones of economic stagnation and financial collapse for the United States. The War of 1812 shut down maritime commerce and the recovery was slow. The growing population was looking for an economic safety valve and found it in Texas. The westward push was on and Texas was to be the next big place.

Texas was attractive for another reason. Smuggling was a booming business since the importation of slaves into the United States was banned in 1808. The practice of slavery was not outlawed, just the means of supply. Demand soon exceeded supply, so supply expanded by the smuggling of slaves through Spanish- and then Mexican-controlled Texas, even though Mexico had banned slavery. The law was circumvented by registering the slaves as workers with one-hundred-year work contracts. A subtle, but not very meaningful, difference. At least not to the slaves.

All the factors were in place for a fight over control of Texas: economic stagnation, a restless population, far-away governments with weak central control, free land, and the economic backbone of the South, the system of slavery.

Texas had not been completely quiet during the period of revolt in Mexico, but it was mainly just a backwater—and a nuisance to Spain. Various expeditions and excursions from the United States into Texas took place in the early 1800s making the Spanish nervous. One was led by Philip Nolan, an Anglo but a Spanish citizen, who had lived in Nacogdoches in east Texas for ten years. He traveled around Texas mapping, surveying, and trading horses. Nolan came to the attention of the Spanish authorities when he met in Natchez (at that time under Spanish control) with Andrew Ellicott, the boundary commissioner for the United States. Nolan increased his travels in Texas, sometimes with a passport and sometimes without, and in 1801 led a band of twenty men on an expedition that ended near Waco. The purpose of the expedition was unclear but the Spanish were taking no chances. Nolan was killed by troops dispatched from Nacogdoches to run his party down. The Spanish officer cut off Nolan's ears and sent them to the governor of Texas as proof of Nolan's death.

The twenty survivors of the group were marched to Chihuahua and imprisoned for six years. The king of Spain sentenced half of them to death by hanging. By the time the order got back to Chihuahua, nine of the group had died of disease, so the presiding officer decided only one more had to be put to death. To choose the man who would be executed, the officer ordered the men blindfolded and put before a military drum where each threw the dice. The loser, Ephraim Blackburn, was hanged. The survivors were marched to Acapulco. The final fate of only one is known. Peter Ellis Bean volunteered to fight for the Royalists against the rebels but deserted to Morelos at the first opportunity. He convinced the rebel leader to send him to the United States to get aid and money for the rebels. Now a colonel in the rebel army, Bean arrived in New Orleans in 1814, just in time to fight for Andrew Jackson at the Battle of New Orleans. Bean bounced back and forth between the United States and Mexico, marrying a wife in each country. He eventually committed to Mexico, dying there in 1846.

The exact purpose of Nolan's expedition has never been determined, but he is remembered as the Father of the Filibusters. A filibuster, or freebooter, was a member of a group engaged in unlawful acts against a country. The word comes from the Dutch *vrijbuiter,* then into Spanish as *filibustero,* or pirate, and then into English as filibuster. The pirate designation was to have long-term negative consequences for many Texans, although thirty men at Goliad would owe their lives to the literal definition.

Things were fairly quiet in Texas for the next ten years, until the Hidalgo revolution. The rebels adopted the "enemy of my enemy is my friend" philosophy, sending emissary Bernardo Gutierrez de Lara to Washington and then Louisiana. He solicited aid and volunteers for the rebel fight against the Spanish. Bernardo found his man in Augustus William Magee, an ex-U.S. Army officer who had his career cut short by military politics, failing to get his captain's promotion. Lieutenant Magee resigned from the U.S. Army and decided to start his own, naming himself colonel in his Republican Army of the North. (One might wonder why he didn't name himself general since it was his army. There is no record of his thinking.) Hooking up with Bernardo, Magee went to New Orleans on a recruiting drive.

Magee soon assembled an army of 130 made up of American pioneers, Mexican rebels, French adventurers, and Indians. The recruits were to receive forty dollars a month and a league of land upon successful completion of the campaign to aid the rebels against the Spanish. The army crossed from Louisiana to Nacogdoches in August 1812, and the Spanish garrison fled. Because of their success the army soon grew to over 700. To chronicle and promote their venture, Magee and Gutierrez started the first newspaper on Texas soil, *Gaceta de Tejas.* Gutierrez was the nominal head of the army, but Magee was the commander and his officers were American.

The army marched on La Bahia, a distance of three hundred miles from Nacogdoches. La Bahia is the presidio that guards the town of Goliad, which was founded around the missions Rosario and Espiritu Santo. (The names La Bahia and Goliad will be used interchangeably here unless a specific location is referenced.) The Spanish governor, Manuel Maria de Salcedo, moved fifteen hundred troops out on the road to La Bahia to block the Republican Army of the North but Magee sidestepped them, taking the near-empty fortress by surprise and capturing stores, cannons, ammunition, and the payroll. Salcedo fell back on La Bahia. A siege ensued with the Spanish outside and the rebels inside the fort, but because of the captured supplies, the rebels were able to hold out for four months.

In February 1813 Magee died. There were rumors of suicide and political intrigue but the most plausible cause was disease. Samuel Kemper, a Virginian who had led an abortive revolt against the Spanish in Florida and gone on to run a tavern in Texas, assumed the rank of colonel and the command.

Salcedo made a final, costly attack that failed, then withdrew to San Antonio in March. More rebel volunteers came as a result of positive publicity and the lure of fighting a corrupt, colonial government. A real war of independence was on.

With the help of his reinforcements Kemper chased Salcedo back to San Antonio, caught his army, and defeated them on April 1, 1813, with the colonel leading the charge. Salcedo asked for terms but Kemper demanded and got unconditional surrender. Salcedo's army was disbanded with the officers released on their own parole. Twelve hundred Spanish surrendered and Kemper and his men rode triumphantly into San Antonio.

At that point events took a dark turn. A Captain Delgado, one of the few Hispanic officers in the Republican Army of the North, asked Gutierrez for revenge against Salcedo, who had ordered the execution of Delgado's father. Gutierrez agreed but was wary of the impact of executions on the Americans. Gutierrez told Kemper that Salcedo and his officers were to be sent to New Orleans and paroled. Kemper agreed. The Royalist officers were assembled and began the march to the coast. They never made it. Delgado and his detachment of Mexican rebels stopped the column a few miles out of San Antonio, bound the Royalists, and slit their throats.

The deed did not go undiscovered for long. Revisionist history paints the Americans of the period as racist, slave owning, land grabbing, Indian killing, unbathed brutes. And they were. They were also idealistic, believing that Texas should be part of the United States because the United States was based on a system of equality and justice. The Americans were shocked and outraged at the murder of the Royalist officers. Kemper and most of his officers quit in disgust. They set out for the United States along with thirteen of the Spanish officers who had joined the revolt. Kemper was joined by many of the rank and file. Gutierrez was relieved of command.

Kemper was replaced by his second in command, Henry Perry, and Gutierrez by Jose Alvarez de Toledo. The Republican Army of the North still had more than three thousand soldiers. In May they defeated another Spanish army marching on San Antonio.

Now the Spanish got serious and sent Gen. Joaquin de Arredondo and his army north. They stopped south of the Medina River, less than twenty miles from San Antonio, and waited.

A split occurred in the rebel army. Toledo was no Gutierrez. He wanted operational control of the army. Perry refused. Toledo wanted to wait on the north side of the Medina, forcing Arredondo to come to him. The Americans wanted to cross over the river and flank the Royalists. The Americans won out, crossing and attacking on August 18, 1813. Arredondo ordered his army backwards, faking retreat. The Americans ran into the trap where they were fired upon from each side by the Royalists.

Toledo saw the trap and ordered the retreat, which his soldiers, the Mexicans and Indians, obeyed. The Americans did not. They charged and did a great deal of damage to Arredondo's forces until running low on ammunition. The Americans finally broke under the weight of Arredondo's army of 2,000 men. Of the 850 Americans who charged, only 93 survived, including Henry Perry. Toledo was wounded but escaped, fleeing to Louisiana.

Arredondo knew about the slaughter of the Royalist officers. He took his revenge by hunting down the rebels, offering no quarter. At Spanish Bluff, eighty rebels surrendered, including Captain Delgado. The prisoners were bound, separated into groups of ten, and forced out onto a fallen cypress tree over a mass grave. As they were shot, their bodies fell into the grave. In San Antonio, three hundred rebel sympathizers were sent to the firing squads, their wives and daughters made to prepare food for the Royalist troops. Arredondo's troops marched east to

Nacogdoches and the rebels, both Mexican and Anglo, crossed the Sabine River to safety. A young officer, Antonio Lopez de Santa Anna, took part in the battle and the executions.

It wasn't until six years later, in June 1819, that Dr. James Long, a hero of the Battle of New Orleans and a favorite of Andrew Jackson, started another unsanctioned expedition, a filibuster out of Natchez. He marched for Texas with eighty men that grew to three hundred by the time Long crossed the Sabine River with the goal of establishing a republic. One of the three hundred was Bernado Gutierrez, the nominal commander of the Magee expedition. Accompanying Long was his wife, Jane, and their infant daughter.

Reaching Nacogdoches, Dr. Long organized a government, proclaiming a republic with himself as president. The new president handed out the usual land with each soldier getting ten leagues or 6,400 acres. The doctor traveled to Galveston to enlist the aid of the pirate Jean Lafitte. Lafitte proved a better military strategist than most of his peers, informing Long that a battle for Texas could not be won without a large, organized, and professional army. This observation was lost on Long and most of his successors.

Long returned to Nacogdoches, but in the interim his army had been defeated by the Spanish. His brother was killed in the battle with the survivors, including his wife and child, fleeing back to the United States. The doctor would not give up. He raised the "Patriot Army" and in 1820 sailed from New Orleans for the Texas coast. Landing, the army traveled inland and captured La Bahia. As with the capture of La Bahia by Magee and his men, the Royalists rallied, surrounding the Anglos and forcing their surrender. Long was not executed but transported to Mexico City.

By the time he arrived, the war for Mexican independence was over, with Iturbide on his way to becoming an emperor. Dr. Long died under mysterious circumstances with the official story being that he was shot by accident. Jane remained at a camp on Galveston Bay with a group of soldiers who had not gone on the attack to La Bahia.

She stayed at the camp with now her two children and a slave girl. Jane was twenty years old and the slave girl was in her mid-teens. The small group of females survived the winter of 1820 eating oysters from the bay and scaring off Indians by firing the small cannons left in the camp. A messenger finally appeared telling Jane of the death of her husband. Determined to revenge the death of James Long, Jane rode to San Antonio and then to Monterrey, beseeching the authorities to punish her husband's killers. Realizing that nothing was going to be done, she finally gave up and rode back to Mississippi. Jane returned eventually to Texas and her suitors are said to have included William Barret Travis, Sam Houston, Samuel Austin, and Mirabeau Lamar. She rejected all suitors and died a widow at Richmond, Texas, in 1880. Her gravestone reads "The Mother of Texas."

The failure of the Long filibuster coincided with the culmination of Moses Austin's dream of a legal and sanctioned colony of settlers in Texas. Stephen F. Austin had a difficult time dealing first with the Spanish and then the Mexicans, but he got the deal done and fulfilled his father's dying request.

Others followed in Austin's path, including Haden Edwards, who set up a colony near Nacogdoches, north of the Austin colony. Like Austin, he had to meet the requirements of the government that included answering to a government-appointed land commissioner. The land commissioner wanted to see paperwork showing ownership, so Haden tacked up notices in Nacogdoches informing current landowners that they had to prove their ownership or lose the property to his new, prospective landowners.

Things became confused with accusations of a rigged election, fraudulent land titles, and false arrests. The governor sent 20 cavalrymen and 110 infantry soldiers to sort things out. Haden Edwards cut through the complexities by declaring a new nation, the Republic of Fredonia. Edwards declared independence from Mexico and attempted to enlist the Cherokee nation in the coming battle. In an early bow to diversity, the flag of the republic was parallel bars, one white and one red. The Cherokees declined. So did the United

States and the members of Austin's colony. When the Mexican force reached Nacogdoches, Haden and his brother realized their new country was lost and fled across the Sabine to safety. The Republic of Fredonia was no more. Haden returned to Nacogdoches in 1836 and died there, peacefully, in 1849. He was active in real estate up to his death.

The fate of the short-lived republic did not slow down migration. People came by boat, horse, wagon, and foot. When Austin started his colonies, there were approximately seven thousand people in Texas. That number had grown to twenty thousand by 1831 and topped fifty-two thousand by 1836. Demographics were 7 percent Hispanic, 10 percent black, and 28 percent Indian. The remaining 55 percent were Anglo. The only group that would decrease in representation was, of course, the Indians.

By 1830 the Mexicans had had enough of the Anglo immigration. They passed the Law of April 6, 1830, ending *empresario* contracts and banning immigrants settling on land contiguous to their native land, a not very subtle snub to the Americans. Stephen Austin had become very adept at negotiating with the Mexican government, managing to have his colony and those of a few friends exempted from the new law. Austin also at this time abandoned his support for Santa Anna over Bustamante, thus annoying the general.

The immigrants continued to work within the framework of a state of the country of Mexico, though Texas was not exactly a state, as the area was thrown in with Coahuila, and their concerns often overrode those of the Texans. In 1832 the Texans held a convention developing a petition to the central government to repeal the Law of April 6, 1830, to separate from Coahuila, and to form a separate state government for Texas. The petition never made it beyond San Antonio.

Undaunted, the Texans held another convention in San Felipe in 1833 that went one step further: writing a constitution. The convention also resurrected prior petitions for custom reform, changes in military rule, legal reform, and the reinstatement of legal immigration. The constitution was based on the American model, and the Anglo petitioners assumed they would be the administrators of the new state of Texas. This was standard operating procedure for all states entering the United States starting in 1792. But that was for entry into the United States, not the Republic of Mexico. In a cultural miscue, the Anglos never gave a thought to using something other than the U.S. model. This assumption was taken as a snub by the leaders in Mexico City.

Conversely, the Mexicans, caught up in the internal politics of setting up the new republic and running through a number of leaders, ignored the validity of many of the petitions, most importantly the fact that a state the size of Texas was thrown in with another state and underrepresented. Both groups did agree that Texas was still to be a state in the Republic of Mexico in some form or shape and would follow the requirements agreed upon by Austin and the government at the time the colonies were established. However, the consensus on being a state of the republic would soon be on shaky ground.

The chairman of the constitution committee was Sam Houston. Houston was new to Texas but not an unknown to the frontier Anglo.

Sam Houston was born in Virginia in 1793, the fifth son of Samuel and Elizabeth Houston. The elder Houston, a plantation owner, fought in the American Revolution as an officer and paymaster in the Virginia Rifle Brigade. After the revolution, the father continued to serve as a major in the Virginia militia and was often away from home as his primary duty was inspecting forts along the frontier. The major died suddenly on one inspection tour in 1806 or 1807. Elizabeth sold the plantation for a thousand pounds, moving to less expensive land in eastern Tennessee where she had many family members.

Young Sam attended school until he was sixteen but was largely self-taught, learning to read the Greek and Latin classics. In 1811 his brothers apprenticed Sam to an owner of a dry goods store, but Sam ran away to live with the Cherokee Indians. A Cherokee chief, Ooleteka, adopted

Houston, naming him Kalunu, the Raven. He stayed with the
Cherokees for three years, returning home on occasion to get
new clothes. Sam would return to the Cherokees on and off
during his life when things got rough in the white world.

Sam returned to his family when he was nineteen and took
a job as schoolmaster at a newly founded school in Maryville,
Tennessee. Houston later called this period the most satisfy-
ing of his life, though it lasted only six months. One thing he
did learn was how to speak to a crowd, a necessary skill for
a future politician.

Sam quit his position at the school to join the army in
March 1813. The country was at war—again—with Great
Britain. He joined the Seventh Regiment of Infantry as an
enlisted man, which, given the family's military background,
shocked everyone in the family except his mother, Elizabeth.
She bid him goodbye with the words, "While the door of my
cottage is open to brave men, it is eternally shut to cowards."

Sam Houston was no coward and he did not remain an
enlisted man for long, taking the appointment of ensign in
the infantry of the Thirty-ninth U.S. Regiment, the same regiment of Davy Crockett. Houston was promoted within six
months to lieutenant. He was twenty-one.

The war in the west was against the Creeks, the allies of
the British. The Creeks had massacred nearly five hundred
men, women, and children at Fort Mims, Alabama, when the
defenders for some reason left the gates open. The governor
of Tennessee ordered Gen. Andrew Jackson of the Tennessee
militia to avenge the massacre. Jackson was recovering from
a gunshot wound inflicted in a duel by the brother of Sam's
commanding officer but was soon well enough to lead the
army against the Creeks. Houston's regiment joined with the
militia and the army of two thousand marched on the Creek
camp at Horseshoe Bend on the Tallapoosa River in Alabama.
Horseshoe Bend was just that—a bend in the river with the
open end of the horseshoe barricaded with double-walled
breastworks. A thousand Creek warriors were in the bend.

Jackson deployed his two cannon, beginning a barrage
lasting two hours. Under Jackson's command was a group of

Cherokees who went to the opposite side of the bend where they swam across the river, attacking the Creek camp from the rear. Seeing the Cherokees attacking, Jackson ordered a frontal assault. The Thirty-ninth, commanded by Maj. Lemuel P. Montgomery, led the charge. Montgomery mounted the barricade first but was immediately killed. Houston followed, yelling to his men, leading them up and over the barricade. Houston gained the fort but was hit in the thigh by an arrow. He ordered a junior officer to pull out the arrowhead, ripping and tearing his flesh, yet he rejoined his men charging a Creek stronghold. Houston was wounded again with two musket balls smashing into his shoulder. A doctor removed one ball but could not get the other, and Houston was left for dead where he lay. His men were surprised when he was still alive in the morning. A litter was made and Houston started a two-month journey for home. When he arrived, his mother did not recognize him.

Houston eventually recovered enough to rejoin the army and was assigned to the staff of Andrew Jackson at Jackson's plantation, the Hermitage. In 1818, Houston decided on politics, reading law with a Nashville judge to prepare himself. He also joined the Tennessee State Militia, eventually being elected to the rank of major general by his men. Houston was following in the footsteps of his mentor, Andrew Jackson, who had held the same post in the militia.

Jackson's influence would also exert itself on Sam's future political career. Houston, handpicked by Jackson, ran unopposed for congressman from the Ninth Congressional District in the 1823 election. After two terms in Congress, Jackson urged Houston to run for governor of the state of Tennessee. He did so and at thirty-four years old, he won the 1827 election. Jackson was elected president in 1828.

Though he was gaining political strength, Houston had a weakness that could have hampered his ambitions: a reputation for drinking and womanizing. The solution to this political problem was a wife and Houston went looking. He found Eliza Allen, the twenty-year-old daughter of a plantation owner and Jackson supporter. She was also sister to a fellow congressman from Tennessee. The father and brother were in favor of the marriage; the bride was not. Under pressure, Eliza finally agreed and she and Sam Houston were married on January 22, 1828.

Eliza left Sam in early April. News of the breakup leaked out and a scandal ensued with mobs burning the governor in effigy. Bending to political pressure, Houston resigned as governor on April 23, 1829. No one knows exactly why Eliza left Sam, but there are three theories: Eliza had another lover she wished to marry, Sam frightened her with his unorthodox sexual habits, or Eliza was revolted by Sam's physical wounds. Whatever the reason, Eliza left Sam and he left Tennessee. Sam went to Indian Territory, present-day Oklahoma. Both Sam and Eliza would be silent on the marriage for the rest of their lives.

Sam traveled to the home of his adopted father, Ooleteka, who was relocated in the forced westward movement of the Indians. There he tried to drown the past in alcohol, earning the name Big Drunk from the Cherokees. He married again to an Indian woman, Tiana Rogers. Will Rogers, film star, rodeo star, and wit, would be a distant relative to Tiana. Houston opened a trading post on the Neosho River and gradually worked his way back to the white world, becoming an Indian agent. On a trip to Washington in that capacity, he caned William Stansberry, a congressman from Ohio, over perceived corruption involving Indian contracts. Houston was tried before the House of Representatives. His lawyer, Francis Scott Key, got him off with a reprimand and a fine.

Houston returned to Indian Territory but left Tania for Texas in 1832. Houston, like many others, saw Texas as a second chance for wealth and political rebirth. He reentered politics as the representative from Nacogdoches to the Convention of 1833, where he chaired the constitution committee and wrote most of the resulting constitution. The convention chose Stephen F. Austin to take the constitution and appeal for statehood to Mexico.

Austin was not an enthusiastic proponent of the convention or the constitution, but as the leading citizen of Texas and the face of Texas to the Mexicans, he agreed to travel to Mexico City. The trip was an end run around the regional governors and administrators in San Antonio as well as the governor of Coahuila. This made sense, as the governor could not be expected to support and push a change that would dilute his power and territory.

Austin left Texas in April 1833, arriving in Mexico City in July. By this time both Iturbide (Augustin I) and Bustamante were out and Santa Anna was starting his bid for leadership. When Austin arrived, there was a caretaker government in place under Acting President Gomez Farias. Santa Anna and Farias traded power depending on who was in town. Austin met with Farias and Lorenzo de Zavala, a power behind the politician with strong ties to the United States. Both promised action to change the immigration law. In reality, nothing was done. This was not unexpected given the political turmoil made worse by a summer outbreak of cholera. Austin spent most of his time waiting for meetings that never were realized and getting more frustrated each day with a government that had local rebellions and intrigues to deal with. Texas seemed far away to the lame duck Mexican politicians.

In September, Austin finally had another meeting with Gomez Farias, and tempers on both sides boiled over. Austin was frustrated with waiting and Farias had more things to worry about—like rebellions closer to home—than illegal Anglo immigrants. Austin warned that if there were more delays and nothing was done about statehood, the locals would take things into their own hands, forming a state government. Farias did not take kindly to being lectured about statehood from someone he considered to be a foreigner.

Again nothing happened except that Austin wrote a letter to the magistrates in San Antonio, who favored an independent state, telling them to get started on preparations for separation from Coahuila. The letter was intercepted before it could reach the magistrates and mailed back to Farias, who considered it treasonous.

On November 5, 1833, Austin was granted an audience with Santa Anna, who had returned to Mexico City. Also in attendance at the meeting was Lorenzo de Zavala. Santa Anna was cordial and agreeable to all the petitions of the Texans, except statehood. Perhaps Austin was unaware of the requirement or just hoped it would be ignored, but there was a clause in the Constitution of 1824 requiring that any prospective state have a population of at least eighty thousand people before being granted statehood. Santa Anna pointed out, correctly, that Texas wasn't even close. But he did agree that the immigration ban should be lifted and worked to see it done.

Figuring he had made as much progress as possible, Austin departed Mexico City on December 10, 1833. He stopped at Saltillo, the capital of the state of Coahuila, to meet with the governor. There he was arrested in January and taken back to Mexico City. Farias arrested him but filed no charges; hence there was no trial even though Austin demanded one to prove his innocence. Instead, Austin was thrown into solitary confinement in the Prison of the Inquisition, where he was allowed no visitors and no books, although he smuggled in or hid a small journal that he used to record his thoughts. News of his captivity finally reached Texas, and two lawyers, Peter Grayson and Spencer Jack, traveled to Mexico City to petition for Austin's release. They got him out on bail on Christmas Day, 1834.

For a caretaker, Farias went out with a bang. In the first quarter of 1835, he clamped down on the power of the Catholic Church by forbidding priests to preach on politics and cut into their cash flow by limiting tithes. He cut down the officer list in the military. The law limiting immigration to Texas was eliminated, the state government at Saltillo was ordered to increase Texas representation in the state congress, and the internal Texas government was modified with offices in San Felipe and Nacogdoches as well as San Antonio. English was approved for doing official business, the principle of trial by jury was introduced, and in a final swipe at the church, religious tolerance was allowed. Lastly, any restrictions on land speculation were lifted. The land rush was on.

Austin was released in a general amnesty in July 1835 and

returned to Texas after being gone more than two years. He returned a changed man to a changed land. The land rush brought thousands from the United States and thousands up from the interior of Mexico. The new arrivals from the United States ran head-on into the established Anglo immigrants and a new schism developed. The established Anglo landowners were content, not perfectly content, but content to be a state of Mexico. The key for them was statehood, but they wanted a Mexican state of Texas, a state separate from Coahuila. They were satisfied being nominal Catholics and even, in some cases, supported immigration control, as it meant more land for them and less competition for their crops and products.

On the other hand, the new immigrants were United States citizens who viewed Texas as the next state of the United States. This group was widely known as the War Party or War Dogs. They didn't like Mexican laws, they resented missing out on the earlier, easier land grabs, they disliked the arcane commercial laws that often prohibited them from operating businesses, and they didn't like the reopened customs offices at the coastal towns of Anahuac and Velasco. So James B. Miller, a member of the Coahuila and Texas legislature and head of the Department of the Brazos, joined with other militants in authorizing William Barret Travis to mobilize a force and capture Anahuac.

Travis had come to Texas in 1831. He traveled from his birthplace in South Carolina, read law in Alabama, married Rosanna Cato, had a son, Charles Edward Travis, and then abandoned a pregnant Rosanna and set out for Texas. A persistent story is that he left Rosanna because of infidelity—hers, not his—which may be unlikely since he wrote down and numbered his sexual conquests in a journal. "Conquests" is probably not the right word, for many of the women were prostitutes. Arriving in Texas in 1831 he violated the Law of April 6, 1830, and was thus an illegal immigrant.

His conquest of Anahuac in 1835 would be the second time he captured the custom house. In 1832, Travis was hired by William M. Logan to retrieve slaves whom Logan believed were being held by the Mexican commander of the garrison. The Mexican commander was Col. John Davis Bradburn, a Kentuckian in the service of Mexico. Bradburn took his duties seriously and often butted heads with Travis. In this instance Travis tricked Bradburn into thinking Logan was coming with a large force to take Anahuac. This was not the case, and Bradburn arrested Travis and his law partner, Patrick C. Jack, when he discovered the ruse. The two lawyers were imprisoned in a brick kiln.

A crowd gathered, bringing a small cannon and demanding that Bradburn release the prisoners. He refused. He further incensed the crowd by pinning Travis and Jack to the ground and threatening to kill them if shots were fired. Travis called on the crowd to fire so he could die a hero's death. Jack's comments were not recorded. The crowd did not shoot.

The Mexican commander at Nacogdoches came to the rescue. Realizing that his forces were outnumbered, he convinced Bradburn to release Travis and Jack. He also relieved Bradburn of his command. Upon his release Travis moved his law office to San Felipe, where he was joined by his son, though Rosanna stipulated that Charles live with another family, not in the Travis house.

The Anahuac incident led to the conventions of 1832 and 1833 to which Patrick C. Jack was a delegate. After the revolution, Jack was elected a member of the Texas congress and then appointed district attorney for Houston. He died there in a yellow fever outbreak in 1844. Bradburn fled to New Orleans and then to Mexico, where he had a wealthy wife. He rejoined the Mexican army and was involved in the 1836 campaign, though not at the Alamo or San Jacinto. He retired but was called up again for the Mexican-American War of 1842. Ill health again forced his retirement and he died on his ranch outside Matamoros on April 20, 1842.

In 1835, Travis was familiar with the territory around Anahuac and enthusiastic about a return to action. He raised a small group of twenty-five riders armed with another small brass cannon and they set off via Galveston Bay for Anahuac. Travis set up the cannon to face the gate of the improvised fort and demanded the surrender of Captain Tenorio and his forty-four men. Why Tenorio did not fight is not clear. He surrendered, with Travis paroling Tenorio and his men.

The incident created an uproar—not from the Mexicans but from the Texans. Travis was denounced as an idiot, an adventurer, and a traitor. Even James Miller of the Department of the Brazos, who had authorized the expedition, flipped sides, disavowing the incident and offering to send a commission to San Antonio to clear up the whole misunderstanding. Seven towns passed resolutions condemning the attack. A delegation was dispatched to meet with General Cos, who had been sent by Santa Anna with a small army to investigate the incident at Anahuac. Cos was Santa Anna's brother-in-law.

Cos and Col. Domingo de Ugartechea, military commander of Texas y Coahuila, headquartered at San Antonio, were the Mexican officials in charge of the investigation. Ugartechea was political, trying to be conciliatory to the Texans but at the same time asking the central government off and on for more troops. In contrast, Cos was not in any way ready to placate the Texans. He met with the delegations sent south to explain away the Travis mishap but the general wasn't listening. Before even discussing the matter, Cos demanded the arrest of Lorenzo de Zavala, who had fled to Texas from Mexico City, and the arrest of the leaders of the War Party. He didn't know who they were but Ugartechea did. Someone had given him a list, a list that included, not surprisingly, Travis. It also included a colonist named Robert Williamson, known affectionately as Three Legged Willie. The nickname resulted from the wooden leg he wore from the knee to the ground to compensate for a childhood disease that left his right leg useless and bent at the knee. This physical infirmity didn't slow down Willie, for he would fight at San Jacinto, sire seven children, and serve in the Texas house and senate. He was an advocate of Texas joining the Union and made his feelings known by naming one son Annexus.

Regardless of who was on the list, Cos had made a mistake. He demanded the Texans arrest the renegades and deliver them to him. Calling Travis stupid was one thing, arresting him and handing him over to the authorities was another, especially since most Texans were aware of the workings of a Mexican court-martial. Cos insisted the Texans who were still professing to be good Mexican citizens should do their duty and hand over the criminals. They were good citizens, but nominal ones reluctant to hand over fellow Anglos to the Mexicans.

The call went out for another convention to take place at Washington-on-the-Brazos for October 15, 1835. The name of the town was a dead giveaway for what was going to happen. Austin arrived back in Texas via New Orleans in September after his release from bail under the general amnesty. His frustrated negotiations with the ever-changing Mexican government, his imprisonment, his lack of a trial, and his capricious release had all combined to radicalize Stephen F. Austin. At a dinner in Brazoria honoring his return, he told the crowd, "War is our only resource." In a letter to a cousin, he announced that he was convinced that Texas must separate from Mexico, saying that a vast immigration from the United States with "each man with his rifle" would be the answer to the Mexican army and "nothing shall daunt my courage or abate my exertions to complete the main object of my labors to Americanize Texas. This fall and winter will fix our fate—a great immigration will settle the question."

Austin's timing was perfect. As cries to arms went out across Texas, the Mexicans did what is traditionally done to disarm rebels. They seized, or attempted to seize, guns and ammunition. The British had done the same thing and the result was Lexington and Concord.

Colonel Ugartechea ordered the town of Gonzales to send back what was fast becoming a staple of Texan military operations, a brass cannon, a six-pounder this time. The cannon had been sent to Gonzales by the Mexicans in 1831 in lieu of troops to defend the town against Comanches and Tonkawas. There is no record of its use, successful or unsuccessful, against the Indians but Ugartechea did not want it used against him or his troops. The mayor, Andrew Ponton, refused to surrender the cannon, sending out a call to arms. Then he ordered the cannon buried in a peach orchard.

Gonzales was only seventy-five miles east of the Mexican garrison at San Antonio. Ugartechea ordered Capt. Francisco Castaneda and a troop of less than 200 men to confiscate the cannon. Two hundred seemed more than enough as there were only 18 Texan rebels in Gonzales when Castaneda set out. With the response to the call to arms, soon there were approximately 160 Texans facing off against the Mexicans when the troops arrived near Gonzales on October 1, 1835. The cannon was dug up and cleaned. In addition, the Texans hid the ferry and confiscated all the boats on the Guadalupe River.

Castaneda demanded the ferry be returned to its proper place and the cannon turned over to him. With the cannon sitting about two hundred yards away, the Texans pointed at it and yelled, "There it is—Come and take it." The Mexicans declined. Not much happened except for a cavalry feint greeted by more taunts and yelling from the Texans. Both sides retired for the evening.

The Gonzales rebels elected John Moore the colonel of their small force. Moore was thirty-five years old and a landowner in what was then Moore's Fort and is now the town of La Grange, near San Antonio. He had come to Texas from Tennessee at the age of eighteen to avoid taking Latin in college. Moore decided on a surprise attack at daylight. He ordered a blacksmith to work through the night forging anything that could be used for ammunition for the small cannon.

Moore is also credited with the idea for the "Come and Take It" flag inspired by the earlier events of the day. The ladies of the town quickly produced a flag from two yards of cloth on which they painted a picture of the cannon and those words.

Finally all was ready. Moore's force set out in the early-morning darkness to surprise and attack the Mexican camp, but they became lost and wandered into the Mexican pickets. There was to be no surprise attack. Each side glared at each other as the sun rose. Breaking the tension, Moore ordered the cannon fired. No damage was done and Castaneda requested a truce, wondering why he and his men had been fired upon. Moore shot back that Castaneda was attempting to take a cannon that had been given to the town for its defense. The Mexican offered his sympathies and said he leaned toward republicanism but insisted that as the gun was owned by the government, the Texans as citizens did not need to defend themselves against the owners of the cannon. A pretty good argument.

Moore did not agree. Since Castaneda had declared republican sympathies, Moore invited Castaneda to join the revolution. Castaneda declined, citing his orders, and the negotiations were over. Each man returned to his camp and the rebels opened fire with the cannon. After a brief battle where one Mexican soldier was killed, the Mexicans retreated to San Antonio. The skirmish was a small affair but it had produced the opening shot in the Texas war for independence.

Castaneda reported the defeat to Ugartechea. Though upset and angry, the colonel made one final appeal to Stephen Austin for peace, but with the conditions remaining the same: the return of the cannon that was now mostly a symbol and, more importantly, the arrest of the rebels on his list. The appeal to Austin fell on deaf ears. Ugartechea was running out of time, for Cos had landed at Goliad after a stop in Mexico and was marching to San Antonio with eight hundred veteran soldiers.

Sneaking in behind Cos, a small force of rebels under Capt. James Collinsworth captured the fortress at Goliad. Cos was incensed. The Anglo population was delirious with their easy victories. The next stop for the rebels was San Antonio.

Chapter 3

The First Battle of the Alamo

"Who will go with old Ben Milam into San Antonio?
Who will go with old Ben Milam into San Antonio?"

With easy victories at Gonzales and Goliad, war fever was on. The mathematical formula of one Texan besting five Mexicans was gaining creditability with the rebels. The formula would have disastrous results down the road.

On October 11, 1835, Stephen F. Austin arrived in Gonzales. The inevitable election for officers was held with Austin being named General of the Army of the People. Austin was the first to admit he was not a military man. This along with his health broken by the imprisonment made him a reluctant commander, but he accepted the position, starting the army on the move to San Antonio de Bexar.

He marched his growing army to Salado Creek, a few miles northeast of San Antonio. The Gonzales cannon broke down on the road, leaving Austin with primarily infantry and cavalry. And here we first encounter James Walker Fannin, Jr., the future commander of Goliad and commanding officer of the 342 Texans that would be slaughtered there. Fannin had participated in the skirmish at Gonzales as captain of the Brazos Guard and had brought the guard into Austin's camp. Austin assigned Fannin and the guard to join James Bowie's Los Leoncitos in a scouting mission to the south of San Antonio.

The command set out, camping at Mission Espada, a mission six miles south of the Alamo on the San Antonio River. By this time General Cos had reached San Antonio de Bexar and taken command. He was informed of the Bowie/Fannin group scouting south of town and on October 24, 1835, he sent Colonel Ugartechea, in command of 200 men, to attack the rebel camp. The attack was unsuccessful. In their after-battle report to Austin, Bowie and Fannin asked to be resupplied with 150 additional men and provisions.

On October 27 the Bowie and Fannin command renewed their scouting activity and arrived at Mission Concepion Purisima, a hundred-year-old mission less than two miles south of the city of San Antonio. Bowie made the decision to spend the night. Fannin disagreed, arguing that they should return to Mission Espada in accordance with the orders from Austin. Bowie overrode this, noting the tired condition of the men and horses. They would set up camp on the nearby river and return to Espada in the morning.

Fannin disagreed again. He suggested setting up camp in Mission Concepion given its strong walls and defensible position. Bowie countered that Cos or Ugartechea would think the same thing, and the mission would be the first place they would look for the rebels. He also knew their force was outnumbered (Bowie imagined as many as one thousand Mexicans in the attack), and while the walls of the mission would stop musket balls, they would not stop cannonballs. Ninety rebels boxed up in a mission against 1,000 soldiers with cannon was not good strategy to Jim Bowie. In addition, the weather was foggy, a perfect scenario for a surprise attack on a mission that would be easy to find, fog or no fog. Bowie was a colonel and Fannin a captain, and that settled that.

Plus, Bowie was a legend. Even before the Alamo, Bowie, like Davy Crockett, was a western folk hero. Born in Kentucky in 1796, his family was soon on the move, first to Missouri and then to Louisiana, where his father bought and ran a plantation on 640 acres. It was here that Jim Bowie was introduced to the slave trade. Supposedly, Bowie grew up in the Davy Crockett style, hunting bears and wrestling with alligators. He was described as big boned, six feet tall, and weighing about 180 pounds. He started his military career serving in the army in the War of 1812. Afterwards he set up a slave-running business buying inventory from the pirate Jean Lafitte, then running his business out of Galveston.

It was said Bowie was slow to anger, although he turned ugly when he did get angry, and he did not invent the Bowie knife. This honor usually goes to his brother, Rezin, but Jim marketed it by driving it into the chest of Norris Wright during a duel gone bad. The duel degenerated into a brawl during which Bowie was shot twice, once in the chest and once in the thigh, both shots coming before Bowie impaled Wright. As the story raced through the South, blacksmiths were soon overwhelmed with orders for "that Bowie knife."

In 1830, Bowie left for Texas, meeting Stephen Austin in San Felipe. He became a Mexican citizen. Unlike most Anglos, Bowie went farther west, settling in San Antonio where he courted and married Ursula de Veramendi, daughter of one of the two leading patriarchs of the town. He pledged his properties as the dowry, but they were tangled in legalities and Bowie had to borrow $2,500 from his wife's family to pay for a New Orleans honeymoon. Back in San Antonio, Bowie spent his time in land speculation, prospecting for lost silver mines, and fighting Indians.

On one silver mine expedition to San Saba in November 1831, Jim, Rezin, seven other men, and two boys held off an Indian attack lasting more than thirteen hours. Rezin's recollection of the siege is included here to illustrate the Bowie family fighting skills as well as how sudden violence could erupt on the prairies.

Rezin Bowie's Account of the Indian Attack

Nothing particular occurred until the 19th on which day, about ten A.M., we were overhauled by two Camanche Indians and a Mexican captive. They stated they belong to Isaonie's party (a chief of the Camanche tribe) about sixteen in number, and were on their road to San Antonio, with a drove of horses, which they had taken from the Wacoes and Twowokanas, and were about returning to their owners, citizens of San Antonio. After smoking and talking with them about an hour, and making them a few presents of tobacco, powder, shot, &c., they returned to their party, who were waiting at the Llano river.

We continued our journey until night closed upon us, when we encamped. The next morning, between daylight and sunrise, the above mentioned Mexican captive came to our camp, his horse very much fatigued, and who, after eating and smoking, stated to us that he had been sent by his chief, Isanonie, to inform us we were followed by a hundred and twenty-four Twowokana and Waco Indians, and that forty Caddoes had joined them, who were determined to have our scalps at all risks. Isanonie had held a talk with them all, the previous evening, and endeavored to dissuade them from their purpose; but they still persevered, and left him, enraged and pursued our trail. As a voucher for the truth of the above, the Mexican produced his chief's silver medal, which is common among the natives in such cases. He further stated that his chief requested him to say that he had but sixteen men, badly armed, and without ammunition; but, if we would return and join him, such succor as he could give us he would. But, knowing that the enemy lay between us and him, we deemed it more prudent to pursue our journey, and endeavor to reach the old fort on the San Saba river before night—distance thirty miles. The Mexican returned to his party, and we proceeded on.

Throughout the day we encountered bad roads, being covered with rocks, and the horses feet being worn out, we were disappointed in not reaching the fort. In the evening we had some little difficulty in picking out an advantageous spot where to encamp for the night. We, however, made choice of the best that offered, which was a cluster of live-oak trees, some thirty or forty in number, about the size of a man's body. To the north of them was a thicket of live-oak bushes, about ten feet high, forty yards in length and twenty in breadth; to the west, at the distance of thirty-five or forty yards, ran a stream of water.

The surrounding country was an open prairie, interspersed with a few trees, rocks, and broken land. The trail which we came on lay to the east of our encampment. After taking the precaution to prepare our spot for defence, by cutting a road inside the thicket of bushes, ten feet from the outer edge all around, and clearing the prickly pears from among the bushes, we hoppled our horses, and placed sentinels for the night. We were now distant six miles from the old fort above mentioned. . . . Nothing occurred throughout the night, and we lost no time in the morning in making preparations for continuing our journey to the fort; and, when in the act of starting, we discovered the Indians on our trail to the east, about two hundred yards distant, and a footman about fifty yards ahead of the main body, with his face to the ground, tracking. The cry of "Indians!" was given, and all hands to-arms. We dismounted, and both saddle and pack horses were immediately made fast to the trees. As soon as they found we had discovered them, they gave the war-whoop, halted, and commenced stripping, preparatory to action. Among them we discovered a few Caddo Indians—by the cut of their hair—who had always previously been friendly to the Americans.

Their number being so far greater than ours (one hundred and sixty-four to eleven), it was agreed that Rezin P. Bowie should be sent out to talk with them, and endeavor to compromise rather than attempt a fight. He accordingly started, with David Buchanan in company, and walked up to within about forty yards of where they had halted, and requested them, in their own tongue, to send forward their chief, as he wanted to talk with him. Their answer was, "How de do? How de do?" in English, and a discharge of twelve shot at us, one of which broke Buchanan's leg. Bowie returned their salutation with the contents of a double-barrelled gun and a pistol. He then took Buchanan on his shoulder, and started back to the encampment. They then opened a heavy fire upon us, which wounded Buchanan in two more places, slightly, and piercing Bowie's hunting-shirt in several places without doing him any injury. When they found their shot failed to bring Bowie down, eight Indians on foot, took after him with their tomahawks, and, when close upon him, were discovered by his party, who rushed out with their rifles, and brought down four of them—the other four retreating back to the main body. We then returned to our position, and all was still for about five minutes.

"We then discovered a hill to the northeast at the distance of sixty yards, red with Indians, who opened a heavy fire upon us, with loud yells—their chief, on horseback, urging them in a loud and audible voice to the charge, walking his horse, perfectly composed. When we first discovered him, our guns were all empty, with the exceptions of Mr. Hamm's. James Bowie cried out, "Who is loaded?" Mr. Hamm answered, "I am." He was then told to shoot that Indian on horseback. He did so, and broke his leg, and killed his horse. We now discovered him hopping around his horse on one leg, with his shield on his arm to keep off the balls. By this time, four of the party, being reloaded, fired at the same instant, and all the balls took effect through the shield. He fell, and was immediately surrounded by six or eight of his tribe, who picked him up and bore him off. Several of those were shot by our party. The whole body then retreated back of the hill, out of sight, with the exception of a few Indians, who were running from tree to tree, out of gunshot.

They now covered the hill the second time, bringing up their bowmen, who had not been in action before, and commenced a heavy fire with balls and arrows, which we returned by a well-directed aim with our rifles. At this instant another chief appeared on horseback, near the spot where the last one fell. The same question of "Who is loaded?" was asked. The answer was, "Nobody," when little Charles, the mulatto servant, came running up with Buchanan's rifle, which had not been discharged since he was wounded, and handed it to James Bowie, who instantly fired and brought him down from his horse. He was surrounded by six or eight of his tribe, as was the last, and borne off under our fire.

During the time we were engaged in defending ourselves from the Indians on the hill, some fifteen or twenty of the Caddo tribe had succeeded in getting under the bank of the creek, in our rear, at about forty yards' distance, and opened a heavy fire upon us, which wounded Matthew Doyle, the ball entering the left breast and coming out at the back. As soon as he cried out that he was wounded, Thomas M'Caslin hastened to the spot where he fell, and observed, "Where is the Indian that shot Doyle?" He was told by a more experienced hand not to venture there, as, from the reports of their guns, they must be riflemen. At that instant they discovered an Indian; and, while in the act of raising his piece, was shot through the centre of the body, and expired. Robert Armstrong exclaimed, "D—n the Indian that shot M'Caslin, where is he?" He was told not to venture there, as they must be riflemen; but, on discovering an Indian, and while bringing his gun up, he was fired at, and part of the stock of his gun cut off, and the ball lodged against the barrel. During this time our enemies had formed a complete circle round us, occupying the points of rocks, scattering trees, and bushes. The firing then became general from all quarters. Finding our situation too much exposed among the trees, we were obliged to leave them, and take to the thickets. The first thing necessary was, to dislodge the riflemen from under the bank of the creek, who were within pistol shot. This we soon succeeded in doing, by shooting the most of them through the head, as we had the advantage of seeing them when they could not see us.

The road we had cut round the thicket the night previous gave us now an advantageous situation over our enemy, as we had a fair view of them in the prairie, while we were completely hid. We baffled their shots by moving six or eight feet the moment we had fired, as their only mark was the smoke of our guns. They would put twenty balls within the size of a pocket-handkerchief, where they had seen the smoke. In this manner we fought them two hours, and had one man wounded—James Corriell—who was shot through the arm, and the ball lodged in the side, first cutting away a small bush, which prevented it from penetrating deeper than the size of it.

They now discovered that we were not to be dislodged from the thicket, and the uncertainty of killing us at random; they suffering very much from the fire of our rifles, which brought half a dozen down at every round. They now determined to resort to stratagem, by putting fire to the dry grass in the prairie, for the double purpose of routing us from our position, and, under cover of the smoke, to carry away their dead and wounded, which lay near us. The wind was now blowing from the west, and they placed the fire in that quarter, where is burnt down all the grass to the creek, and then bore off to the right and left, leaving around our position a space of about five acres untouched by the fire. Under cover of this smoke they succeeded in carrying off a portion of their dead and wounded. In the meantime, our party was engaged in scraping away the dry grass and leaves from our wounded men and baggage, to prevent the fire from passing over them; and likewise in piling up rocks and bushes to answer the purpose of a breastwork. They now discovered they had failed in routing us by the fire, as they had anticipated. They then reoccupied the points of rocks and trees in the prairie, and commenced another attack. The firing continued for some time, when the wind suddenly shifted to the north, and blew very hard.

We now discovered our dangerous situation, should the Indians succeed in putting fire to the small spot which we occupied, and kept a strict watch all around. The two servant-boys were employed in scraping away dry grass and leaves from around the baggage, and pulling up rocks and placing them around the wounded men. The point from which the wind now blew being favorable to our position, one of the Indians succeeded in crawling down the creek, and putting fire to the grass that had not been burnt; but, before he could retreat back to his party, was killed by Robert Armstrong.

At this time we saw no hopes of escape, as the fire was coming down rapidly before the wind, flaming ten feet high, and directly for the spot we occupied. What was to be done? We must either be burnt up alive, or driven into the prairie among the savages. This encouraged the Indians; and, to make it more awful, their shouts and yells rent the air—they, at the same time, firing upon us about twenty shots a minute. As soon as the smoke hid us from their view, we collected together and held a consultation as to what was best to be done. Our first impression was, that they might charge on us under cover of the smoke, as we could make but one effectual fire; the sparks were flying around so thickly, that no man could open his powder-horn without running the risk of being blown up. However, we finally came to a determination, had they charged us, to give them one fire, place our backs together, draw our knives, and fight them as long as any one of us was left alive. The next question was, should they not charge us, and we retain our position, we must be burnt up. It was then decided that each man should take care of himself as well as he could until fire arrived at the ring around our baggage and wounded men, and there it should be smothered with buffalo-robes, bearskins, deerskins, and blankets; which, after a great deal of exertion, we succeeded in doing.

Our thicket being so much burnt and scorched, that it afforded little or no shelter, we all got into the ring that was made around our wounded men and baggage, and commenced building our breastwork higher, with the loose rocks from the inside, and dirt dug up with our knives and sticks. During this last fire the Indians had succeeded in removing all their killed and wounded which lay near us. It was now sundown, and we had been warmly engaged with the Indians since sunrise; and they, seeing us still alive and ready for fight, drew off at a distance of three hundred yards, and encamped for the night with their dead and wounded.

Our party now commenced to work, in raising our fortifications higher, and succeeded in getting it breast-high by ten, P.M. We now filled all our vessels and skins with water, expecting another attack next morning. We could distinctly hear the Indians, nearly all night, crying over their dead, which is their custom; and at daylight they shot a wounded chief—it being also a custom to shoot any of their tribe that are mortally wounded. They, after that, set out with their dead and wounded to a mountain about a mile distant, where they deposited them in a case on the side of it. At eight in the morning, two of the party went out from the fortification to the encampment, where the Indians had lain the night previous, and counted forty-eight bloody spots on the grass, where the dead and wounded had been lying.

Finding ourselves much cut up—having one man killed and three wounded, five horses killed and three wounded— we recommenced strengthening our little fort, and continued our labors until one, P.M., when the arrival of thirteen Indians drew us into it again. As soon as they discovered we were still there, and ready for action, and well fortified, they put off. We after that, remained in our fort eight days.

Jim Bowie never found the mine his party had set out for.

In 1833, two years after this dramatic encounter, Ursula and most of her family died in a cholera outbreak while Bowie was in Natchez sick with yellow fever. Despite his loss, Bowie returned to Texas, often traveling to Mexico City to bargain for more land. When Austin issued the call to arms, Bowie answered.

The skills Bowie learned fighting Indians on the plains paid off. At Mission Concepion, Bowie went looking for a site similar to San Saba to hold off the Mexicans. He found it at a bend in the San Antonio River less than half a mile from the mission. The battlefield was a plain bordered by trees that narrowed down to a triangle at the bend with the river protruding into the tip of the triangle. The riverbank was steep, with the river ten feet below. Bowie placed his men on one side of the gradual bend and the Brazos Guard on the other, providing interlocking fire across the killing zone. He then ordered steps dug into the sides of the riverbank so the men could use the bank for protection against cannon and grapeshot. The steps were cut two by two so one line of men could rise and fire while another line could step down and reload. The Texans were outmanned but they outgunned the Mexicans, for the Texans were armed with rifles with an outside range of four hundred yards versus the war surplus muskets of the Mexicans with an effective range of less than one hundred yards. The Mexicans were walking into an ambush.

Fannin didn't think the ambush idea was necessary, as he was from the "one Texan is worth five Mexicans" school of warfare. But Bowie was right in overruling Fannin's preference of defending the mission. On the morning of October 28, General Cos arrived with three hundred infantry, one hundred cavalry, and two cannons. The first thing he did was head straight for the empty Mission Concepion. Losing the advantage of surprise, Cos sent his men through the fog searching for Bowie. They found him. The Mexican troops lined up about two hundred yards from the Texan right flank. By eight o'clock the fog had lifted and the Mexicans opened fire, hitting nothing because of the range and the hidden positions of the Texans. The Texans returned fire with their rifles and the Mexicans started taking casualties.

Cos ordered one cannon forward to within eighty yards of the Texan line. The cannon fired as the Texans ducked below the rim of the bank, the grapeshot passing harmlessly over them. Picking off the artillerymen, the Texans fired back. The Mexicans charged, remanned the cannon, and fired with the same result. Additional cannon shots and four failed charges ensued before Cos retreated, having suffered sixty killed and forty wounded. The artillerymen suffered the most, with all being killed or wounded. As often happens in battle, the Texans, overexcited by the sight of the retreating enemy, dashed from the safety of the river in pursuit. Bowie ordered them back knowing that his force was still outnumbered and would be cut to pieces if caught out in the open by Mexican cavalry. The Texans lost one dead, Richard "Big Dick" Andrews, the first casualty of the Texas war for independence.

Bowie's plan had worked perfectly. Fannin's plan was a signal of bad things to come, as defense of the mission would have been a disaster. It was the first place Cos looked and the Texans would have been trapped inside while Cos's cannon knocked the place to pieces. A forerunner of the Alamo had been avoided by Bowie.

Austin arrived after the Texan success and offered his opinion of the battle, telling Bowie he should have chased the retreating army. Bowie noted that he was still outnumbered. Austin then asked why Bowie had not followed orders and returned to Mission Espada the night before. Bowie let the battle and the dead Mexicans speak for themselves.

Bowie, however, did take a few shots at Austin in his battle report, noting,

No invidious distinction can be drawn between any officer or privates on this occasion. Every man was a soldier, and did his duty agreeably to the situation and circumstances under which he was placed. At the close of the engagement a piece of heavy artillery was brought up and fired thrice, but at a distance, and by a reinforcement of another company of cavalry, aided by six mules ready harnessed, they got it off. The main army reached us in about an hour after the enemy's retreat. Had it been able to communicate with you and brought you up earlier, the victory would have been conclusive, and Bexar ours before twelve o'clock.

The missed opportunity noted by Bowie would prove costly. Austin wanted to attack and take San Antonio de Bexar as soon as possible, but Bowie knew the opportunity had passed. Cos and his army were entrenched behind walls and had cannon to tear holes in any attacking army. The Texans did not have enough men or cannon to dislodge Cos and his men in San Antonio and the Alamo. Austin ignored the facts, ordering the siege to begin.

The Texans who would set the siege were not the stupid, rollicking, racist morons roaming around the countryside looking for adventure that revisionist history has portrayed. They were adventurers but they were also seasoned pioneers who had learned to stay alive in the wilderness, hunt their own food, and defend themselves against Indians, Mexicans, the French, the British, and sometimes their own countrymen. Some, like Bowie, had fought in the War of 1812 and most of their fathers or uncles were veterans of that war or the American Revolution. They were a ragtag bunch of killers who were good at their craft.

One member of this group, Noah Smithwick, in describing the army said, "It certainly bore little resemblance to the army of my childhood dreams. Buckskin breeches were the nearest approach to uniform and there was wide diversity even there, some being new and soft and yellow, while others, from long familiarity with rain and grease and dirt had become hard and black and shiny." He went on, noting, "Boots being an unknown quantity, some wore shoes and some moccasins. Here a broad-brimmed sombrero overshadowed the military cap at its side; there the tall 'beegum' rode familiarly beside a coonskin cap, with the tail hanging down as all well-regulated tails should do." He summed it up as "a fantastic military array to a casual observer, but the one great purpose animating every heart clothed us in a uniform more perfect in our eyes than ever donned by regulars on dress parade."

Most of the Texans carried the long rifle, giving them a massive advantage over their foe. The rifle had one major improvement over the single-shot flintlock firing mechanism of the British-made Mexican muskets. The rifle was just that. It had a rifled (spiral-grooved) 42- to 46-inch-long barrel that could easily project its rotating bullet two hundred yards to hit and kill a turkey and it could hit a horse at four hundred yards. The musket had no rifling. Anyone who has thrown a football and then tried to throw a basketball the same distance knows the difference between a musket and a rifle.

This buckskin army with their deadly long rifles fell upon two parts of San Antonio as Cos had divided his command. He had one division defend the Alamo, the presidio, on the east side of the river. A second division held the town on the west side of the river with the main defense centering on two plazas surrounded by easily defended stone buildings. Each group had their own complement of artillery.

The two armies' roles should have been reversed. The Mexican army greatly outnumbered the Texans and possessed trained cavalry that could run through and cut down a small army. The weight of numbers of the Mexican infantry could have overwhelmed the Texans in the open field. A massed attack would have offset the advantage of the rifles, which could only be reloaded four times a minute at the most. Four times a minute is impressive but difficult to maintain when a large number of soldiers are attacking brandishing bayonets. Cos ignored all this, deciding to hole up and defend the two areas.

Then, nothing happened. Austin came to realize the futility of attacking the walls of the city and the Texas leaders halted any assault, waiting for artillery to come up to lay siege to the defenses. The rebels had no artillery with them at the time. The Gonzales cannon had broken down and was buried on the prairie.

The size of the rebel army is difficult to measure because it kept changing. The timing was right for the "regular" army, made up mostly of farmers, since it was October and they had their summer crop in before hostilities started. But soon they would have to prepare for the winter crop and their two-month enlistments began to run out. As these men left, they were replaced by volunteers from the United States, the spearhead of the massive immigration called for by Austin. GTT (Gone to Texas) was painted on the doors of abandoned farmhouses across the United States. From New Orleans came the New Orleans Greys, who took their name from the gray uniforms obtained from a public armory. The word of revolution spread. The army around San Antonio grew, then shrank as the locals left for their farms, then swelled again with more and more volunteers.

These volunteers grew restive and bored with the lack of action. Days stretched into months. Eventually Austin realized, and the army realized, that he was out of his element. The leaders back in San Felipe realized this as well, relieving Austin of his command. Nobody, including Austin, complained. Austin left the army on November 25, 1835, traveling to the United States to raise money and aid for the cause.

The troops elected Col. Edward Burleson as their new leader. Burleson, thirty-seven years old and from North Carolina, arrived legally in Texas in 1830 just before the Law of April 6. Burleson was eager to attack the Mexicans, but the majority of his officers were not, convincing him to continue to wait for the artillery. When the artillery didn't arrive, Burleson met with his officers and it was agreed to abandon the siege, pack up, and go home. The wagons were packed and the army assembled to begin the march out on December 4, 1835, when a Mexican officer, a deserter, came through the lines and was brought to Burleson, then standing in front of the troops. The whole army heard the officer's story of the Mexican army inside starving. The town was theirs for the taking. The story was, of course, suspect, and

Burleson discounted it. Col. Frank Johnson believed it and he mentioned to Col. Ben Milam that perhaps they should ask for volunteers to man an assault.

Today in the front of the Alamo there is a marker about three feet long set in the ground where Lt. Col. William Barret Travis before the ill-fated final battle of the Alamo supposedly "drew the line," asking those willing to stay to cross it. And they did. There is controversy over whether it ever happened because all the participants were killed, though an eyewitness, Louis Moses Rose, the last man to leave the Alamo, did say it happened. Regardless, a very similar type of dramatic call for action certainly did take place at the first battle of the Alamo.

Colonel Milam was a forty-seven-year-old land speculator who never met with much financial success in his endeavors. But he could fire up a crowd and did so on that December day when he jumped in front of the assemblage, took his rifle butt, and drew a line in the dirt, shouting out, "Who will go with old Ben Milam into San Antonio? Who will go with old Ben Milam into San Antonio?" A shout went up from the army. He then said, "Well, if you're going with me, get on this side." Two hundred men crossed the line and Burleson was out of a job. By three in the morning the next day, when Milam assembled the men again, the group had grown to 301 men ready to take the town.

The assault on the Mexicans began on the east side of the river. The attack was not a charge but a gradual movement into the streets of the town with men running from building to building. The fight would turn into a nineteenth-century mini-Stalingrad with the Texans fighting house to house, engaging in vicious hand-to-hand combat. The massive walls of the houses vexed the rebels, as the walls absorbed bullets and defied breaking and entering. Nevertheless, by the end of the day the Texans had captured the houses of the Garza and Veramendi families, the leading families of San Antonio. The Veramendis, or those who survived the cholera epidemic, were the in-laws of Jim Bowie.

The Texan advance was slow because the Mexicans had guns mounted in the towers of the San Fernando church and could fire down on the attackers. Members of the Greys placed their caps on ramrods to draw fire; when the Mexicans figured out what they were doing, the Greys placed their hats on gourds and pushed them over the top of the walls to waste Mexican ammunition and locate Mexican snipers.

Herman Ehrenberg, a German native, member of the New Orleans Greys, and soon-to-be-survivor of the Goliad massacre, described in his book *Texas und Seine Revolution* the first casualty he witnessed: "The bullet tore the brain out of its cavity and spattered it on the walls and over us who stood near him. His colossal body twitched convulsively for hours in the thick clotted blood that flowed out of the wound. It showed us novices the battle of the body with the parting life." This particular death was the result of friendly fire. The fighting was close, the participants firing at anything that moved. There was more friendly fire before a runner sorted things out with the other groups of Texans.

In an attempt to fortify the morale of his own men and scare the attackers, Cos ordered the red flag raised over the church. No quarter. The Texans laughed and scoffed at the gesture. They wouldn't think it so funny when the flag was unfurled again in March. At the end of the first day, the Texans had suffered a total of one killed and two colonels, one lieutenant colonel, and twelve privates wounded.

The second day of battle was much like the first with vicious combat and little gain in territory by the Texans. The Mexican artillery had the upper hand, hurling cannonballs into each house the Texans captured. The Texans stretched and fortified their lines but were not making any real progress. They were getting better at staying alive: only five Texans were wounded that day.

The third day was decisive because one man literally took things into his own hands. Henry Wax Karnes, a young Tennessee pioneer, got mad at the lack of progress and decided he had had enough. His company was pinned down by Mexicans firing from the windows and roof of the last house that blocked their way to the plazas, the key to the city. Telling his comrades to cover him, Karnes grabbed a crowbar and his rifle and ran the gauntlet of fire to the cover of the house. There, based on conflicting reports, he either smashed in a door or dug a hole in the wall with the crowbar. Whichever it was, Karnes gained access to the building and his company charged after him. The Mexicans went out the back door. The crowbar concept took hold and the Texans pried their way from house to adjoining house. They would bust a hole in the wall, fire their rifles, and then clean out any remaining defenders via hand-to-hand combat. The tunnel made its way toward the center of town. Any women or children found in the houses were sent back through the tunnel to safety.

Also on the third day, December 7, Ben Milam was killed by a sniper's bullet to the head. (The Mexicans did have some rifle companies that were the elite of the army). Suddenly the Texans were leaderless and dispirited. In a Masonic ceremony, Milam was buried in the courtyard of the Veramendi hacienda during a lull in the fighting. As the fighting continued, the volunteers somehow managed to hold yet another election. Col. Frank Johnson was elected as their new leader and Maj. Robert C. Morris of the New Orleans Greys was elected second in command.

Though the loss of Milam and his fighting leadership initially dampened the spirits of the Texans in the war zone, after a time, despair turned to rage and they looked for revenge for Ben Milam's death. The attack renewed with the capture of the Navarro house, one block west of the main plaza, overlooking part of the second, or military, plaza. Another Mexican stronghold was captured less than two blocks from the main plaza. Again, the Karnes method was employed with defenders and attackers often firing through the same loopholes but on opposite sides of the walls.

By the evening of December 8 the Texans, planning an attack on the "Priest's House," had advanced house by house to the main plaza. If the house, on the northern side of the plaza, was captured, the Texans would control the plaza. The Texans charged the fence around the house and scaled and broke it down, chasing the Mexicans from their stronghold. Now it was the Texans' turn to defend and they did so against artillery fire and musket fire throughout the night. With the capture of the Priest's House, the Texans controlled the town. The next day the Texans mopped up any last resistance and planned for the attack on the Alamo across the river.

The Texans had regained their morale and spirit after the death of Milam. The spirits and morale of the Mexicans sank. In questioning their prisoners, the rebels learned that food and ammunition were running low in the Alamo. There were more than eleven hundred soldiers and additional civilians, women, and children packed inside the Alamo with no reinforcements in sight. There were rumors of a mass desertion by the army. The civilians had panicked, thinking they would be left defenseless to the murderous rebels. Even Cos was roughed up as he tried to calm the mob.

Cos sent three soldiers to the enemy lines to negotiate, and they were nearly killed by the exhausted rebels. One officer, thinking quickly, produced a white handkerchief and saved the trio. Negotiations dragged on for almost a full day. In the end, it was decided that the Mexican officers would be allowed to keep their arms and property and would be free to go as long as they agreed to leave Texas, not oppose the resurrection of the 1824 constitution, and not fight again against the colonists. Cos surrendered his eleven hundred men and officers and the Alamo. Along with the surrender came twenty-one pieces of artillery, five hundred muskets, ammunition, food, and clothing. Even with the ferocity and viciousness of the street fighting, Texan casualties were minimal except for the loss of Ben Milam. The accounts of the Mexican death toll varies, but it probably numbered about 150. Colonel Burleson assumed command of the Texans again, while Cos and his defeated army left out for Monclova, across the Rio Grande.

The victory of barely three hundred men over an entrenched force of eleven hundred with artillery was impressive. It wasn't quite one Texan for every five Mexicans, but it was close enough.

By the evening of December 10, 1835, the Mexican troops were heading south out of the territory. The Texans held the two military strongholds, the Alamo and the presidio at Goliad. The majority of Texans, who were farmers and merchants, went home to resume their civilian jobs. The newly arrived adventurers idled; the government existed mostly in a vacuum.

As revolutionaries often come to realize, the fighting is the easy part. Governing is the hard part. In the case of the colonists, there was no real government. Each settlement had an *alcalde,* or mayor, and representatives to the Coahuila/Tejas legislature but these roles were primarily reactionary. New law came from Mexico City. The territory either accepted it or protested it. Now the situation was more complicated. Was Texas a republic? Was Texas still a Mexican state or more correctly, a part of a Mexican state? Was Texas soon to be the next state of the United States? That was probably closest to the truth, and most Anglos, including Stephen F. Austin, thought and hoped for that outcome. But there was no established plan or governing body in place at the time to implement any of these scenarios.

A body named the Permanent Council was put in place on October 11, 1835, although it would not live up to its name, as it lasted only three weeks. The council consisted of a committee of safety with representatives from the largest towns in Texas. Richard R. Royall, the representative from Matagorda, was named president of the government. Though lasting only three weeks, the council got a lot done. It sent money and supplies to the army, formed a navy by commissioning privateers, stopped any new land grants, established a post office, and sent representatives to the United States to borrow $100,000. No government this efficient can be expected to last long and it didn't. The council was replaced by the Consultation of 1835.

The Consultation had been planned before the Permanent Council and was scheduled to meet on October 16, 1835, but was postponed because of the military campaign to San Antonio. Like the Council, the Consultation consisted of representatives from the major districts of Texas. Meeting on November 4, their first act was to dissolve the Permanent Council and that was about it. After that, the Consultation split into three factions. Faction one was the old Austin supporters in favor of lobbying the liberal wing of Mexican politics for statehood. A second faction was for revolt and continued military action, if necessary, against the Mexicans. The third group operated somewhere in between, trying to hammer out compromises with the other two warring factions. A compromise was the result and, while they did not declare for independence, they declared their right to declare independence and voted thirty-three to fourteen the establishment of a provisional government with a governor and General Council. They appointed Sam Houston commander in chief of the nonexistent regular army. Finally, they appointed William H. Wharton, Branch T. Archer, and Stephen Austin representatives to the United States. Many of the original Austin colonists, the old guard, saw these appointments as a way for the war supporters to get the Mexican statehood leaders out of the mix and dilute their power.

Henry Smith, the forty-seven-year-old representative from Brazoria who in his lifetime would marry three women, all three sisters, and father nine children between them, was elected governor. Later in life, Smith would join the gold rush to California, dying in a mining camp near Los Angeles in 1851 at the age of sixty-three. As governor Smith was not much of a diplomat. He assumed Texas was already a free and independent country in fact, if not legally. The factional fighting continued in the General Council. By January 1836, Smith had had enough and dissolved the council. The council fought back, impeaching Smith, although events outran the process and Smith was never put on trial. This lack of clarity at the top would have disastrous implications for future Goliad commander James Fannin.

However, Smith's intention to dissolve the council was not a bad idea, as the council had done something really stupid: they authorized an invasion of Mexico.

Chapter 4

The Invasion of Mexico

"Go in and die with the boys."

Invading Mexico was the brainchild of Dr. James Grant, a Scotsman who landed in Coahuila in 1823, purchasing an estate in 1825. He was elected a representative to the legislature of Coahuila y Texas and like many others started a land development project. The project was planned for eight hundred families on the Rio Grande River but the project failed in 1834. One possible reason for the failure could be the bad blood that developed between Grant and Gen. Don Martin Perfecto Cos, making government approval more bureaucratic than usual. With the collapse of the land deal, Grant relocated to Nacogdoches, though he did travel to Monclova as late as March 1835 to attend sessions of the legislature. In April, Santa Anna exercised his Centralist powers and shut down the local state government.

Grant left town one step ahead of Santa Anna's troops, making it back to Nacogdoches in time to be elected to the Consultation as a representative, for some reason, of Goliad. He did not attend because he had joined a company of volunteers commanded by Capt. Thomas J. Rusk heading for the siege of San Antonio.

Before joining the army Grant was in Goliad, where he came up with the plan to invade Mexico, beginning with the capture of Matamoros. The invasion would do two things—show support for Mexicans opposed to Santa Anna and take the war to Santa Anna. Grant might also have thought that he would get back some of his land holdings that would be lost permanently if Mexico and Texas separated.

The plan was based on discussions Grant had with Augustin Viesca, the Federalist governor of Coahuila and Texas. Viesca had been captured when the Centralists took

69

over but escaped and fled to Texas, where he met with Grant at Goliad. The two discussed the political situation and unrest in Coahuila in a meeting with Capt. Philip Dimmitt, the commander of the fort. Viesca and Grant planted the idea with Dimmitt that the people of northern Mexico expected Texas to invade Mexico and would greet the invaders as liberators. Dimmitt wasn't too sure of this. In a letter to Austin he outlined the good points and bad points of an invasion. On one hand a revolt would tie up Santa Anna in Mexico. On the other hand it would be difficult for native Mexicans to embrace Anglos invading their country. Dimmitt had married into a Mexican family and was therefore sensitive to Anglo-Mexican relations. More practically, he questioned the logistics of an invasion.

Grant set off for the battle of San Antonio, shelving the invasion plan for the time being. During the campaign he ingratiated himself with the troops by telling them tales of the gold, silver, land, and ladies south of the Rio Grande. Grant noted the rebellious nature of the locals and, again, the notion that the Anglo invaders would be welcomed as liberators. He found an interested and enthusiastic audience, although he left out many of the details regarding the size and strength of Santa Anna's army.

Grant also convinced an important member of the army, Col. Frank Johnson. The liberator of San Antonio gladly traveled back to San Felipe with Grant to present the plan to the General Council.

Initially, Governor Smith and Sam Houston did not oppose the idea of a feint or expedition into Mexico, for they saw a chance to connect with the Mexican liberals in an attempt to salvage, even at this late date, the Constitution of 1824. An even better outcome would be a revolt with the removal of Santa Anna. But a full-scale invasion did not make sense to either Houston or Smith. In addition, neither Governor Smith nor Houston considered Johnson and Grant to be great military talents.

If anybody was going to lead the expedition, Houston wanted it to be Jim Bowie. To Houston, Grant was nothing more than a local politician seeking glory and wholly unrealistic about the challenges of mounting a campaign against Mexico. Houston sent a letter to Jim Bowie at Goliad giving him the command of any expedition or feint. However, Bowie had already left for San Antonio.

In turn, Governor Smith mistrusted anyone with Mexican ties and although Grant was a Scot, Smith did not trust him because of his Mexican citizenship, his land holdings, and his membership in the legislature. Smith disliked Johnson because Johnson backed Grant.

Grant's presentation of his plan split the council, but Grant swayed enough representatives for the proposal that on January 3, 1836, they received approval to proceed. Governor Smith railed against the plan, but it passed over his objections, and Colonel Johnson was named military commander to lead the charge. Even though he backed the idea, Johnson didn't want to lead the army due to the governor's opposition, so he declined. The council then appointed James W. Fannin, Jr. to take command. Grant interceded, saying that it was Colonel Burleson's intention that he, Grant, be commander so the council named Grant commander in chief of volunteers. This confused things even further since all the members of the army were volunteers, making Grant and Fannin co-commanders in fact, if not in title. Then Colonel Johnson changed his mind, deciding not to be commander after all. There was so much confusion that some members of the council thought there were four commanders in chief: Johnson, Grant, Fannin, and Houston. Houston was not informed of the appointments of Johnson and Grant.

In addition to the confusion over the commander in chief, there was confusion over who was governor. Smith wrote a note to the council suggesting, "look around your flock; your discernment will easily detect the scoundrels. . . . Let the honest and indignant part of your council drive the wolves out of the fold." He then suspended the council until March 1. In response, the council appointed a committee that called on the governor. Smith refused any challenge to his authority as governor, the committee reported back to the council, and the council issued a resolution:

> Resolved that the governor be forthwith ordered to cease the functions of his office, and be held to answer to the general council upon certain charges, a copy of which was to be furnished him within twenty-four hours, that all public functionaries be notified of his deposition; and, in short, that his message be returned to him, with a copy of the proceedings thereon.

The council then named Lt. Gov. James W. Robinson as governor; however, Smith refused to abdicate the post, seizing the state archives and seal and threatening to shoot "any son of a bitch" who tried to take them away. Moving into January, the council could not raise a quorum, and the government ground to a halt without any clarity as to who was governor or who was commander in chief of the army.

This didn't stop Grant or Johnson or Fannin. The three commanders issued calls for volunteers while the legislative battle waged. Grant and Johnson worked pretty much as a team while Fannin worked on his own. Grant and Johnson won over most of the volunteers at San Antonio, and Lt. Col. J. C. Neill, the Alamo commander, sent a message to Governor Smith saying that Grant and Johnson had stripped the Alamo of cannon and supplies and clothing for use on the Matamoros invasion. This message is what so angered Smith, precipitating his problems with the council and subsequent attempts at removal.

The remaining commander in chief, Houston, made a move to halt the expedition. He was convinced that the defense of Texas, not the invasion of Mexico, was their only hope and rode to Goliad to stop the advance. He then rode to the town of Refugio, twenty-five miles south of Goliad, where Johnson and Grant were camped with their dual command, including part of the New Orleans Greys.

At first Houston got nowhere. The volunteers elected their officers and none of them had voted for Houston. Governor and council appointments meant little to them. Houston eventually gathered a crowd telling them,

So great are my hopes that I firmly believe next summer I shall see the flag of Texas floating over all the harbors of our coast!

But in order to win, we must act together. United we stand, divided we fall. I am told you intend to take Matamoras; I praise your courage, but I will frankly confess to you, my friends, that I do not approve of your plans. The capture of a city that lies outside the boundaries of our territory is useless, and the shedding of Texan blood in such unprofitable warfare is a mistake. You say that you want to harass the enemy; will you not do so more effectively by falling upon his armies after long marches and other hardships have exhausted them and demoralized them? Since our military power is weak, let our strength be our unity! Then we shall show our foes what a nation can do when all its citizens rise to protect their rights and say unfalteringly; "We shall be free." Let us teach these Mexicans that when a nation fights for a just cause, the Almighty Himself bears their standard.

The crowd was not buying it. Houston tried a different angle.

Comrades, I see that my suggestions displease you, and yet my only desire is to help my country. I know that my vote counts only for one, and if you are determined to go to Matamoras, then to Matamoras you shall go. But wait at least until the troops from Georgia and Alabama have arrived. Then, march on to new conquests, for with the help of these friends, what forces of the enemy could hold out against you?

This rare bit of clear thinking didn't have much impact initially. An artillery captain of the Greys, Captain Pearson, rebutted, noting they were tired of waiting, the time had come for action. But Houston swayed many with his argument to wait for troops from Georgia and Alabama. A majority of the officers and men agreed to wait at Refugio rather than head farther south to San Patricio, the staging point for any attack on Matamoros.

It was obvious the men and officers did not consider Houston to be their boss, and Johnson and Grant certainly did not think so. Fannin separately confirmed the same thinking. Houston was totally frustrated. On January 30, 1836, he wrote to Governor Smith (at least Houston assumed Smith was still governor and was loyal to him, as were Colonel Neill at the Alamo and Lt. Col. William B. Travis) informing him that he was taking no responsibility for the Matamoros mess and predicted the expedition, even if successful, would boomerang on the Texans. He said he could not find any logic, military or otherwise, in the conduct of the war. He quit the war against Mexico, taking leave to visit and negotiate with the Cherokees in east Texas.

While the Texas government quit functioning, Houston left for east Texas, the Alamo lay stripped of supplies and men, and Dr. Grant and Colonel Johnson made plans to march on Matamoros, one man was preparing in earnest. With rebellion quashed in Mexico proper, Santa Anna turned at last to the pesky Anglos. They would pay for the failure of his brother-in-law, Cos, to hold off an inferior force from a strengthened fortress. They would pay for disgracing Mexico.

The self-titled "Napoleon of the West" was at his best in the field. And he was prepared. All armies draw up contingency plans so that if and when a decision is made to put the army in motion, the army is ready. The Mexican army had laid out their contingency plan for the invasion of Texas in the summer of 1835. In October 1835, while Santa Anna was relaxing at his hacienda, Manga de Clava, word reached him of the hostilities at Gonzales. He was furious and by the end of the month he had his secretary of war and marine, Jose Marie Tornel, briefing Congress on the invasion.

The contingency plan was put into action. Gen. Joaquin Ramirez y Sesma with his fifteen-hundred-man brigade was ordered out of Zacatecas north to Saltillo to organize the Vanguard Division of Operations as the relief force for Cos at San Antonio. From Saltillo, Sesma was ordered to force march his brigade to San Luis Potosi. He then left San Luis Potosi on November 17, reaching Laredo, a distance of three hundred miles, on December 26. This slow pace did not meet the definition of a forced march but no historical reference remains to explain the lack of progress. Sesma certainly had valid excuses, as he was marching his army at the beginning of winter through semiarid and mountainous terrain with little in the way of water and food supplies. Excuses did not please Santa Anna.

Whatever the cause, the army progressed less than eight miles a day, which was not acceptable to Santa Anna. The average mileage per day for an army loaded down with wagons and supplies was seventeen miles per day so Sesma managed less than half the average. In the end it didn't make any difference, because Sesma reached Laredo on December 26, sixteen days after Cos surrendered in San Antonio de Bexar.

With Sesma slowly on his way, Santa Anna ordered other troops assembled. Gen. Antonio Gaona with his 1,600 men and six guns was ordered to Saltillo. Gen. Eugenio Tolsa and his force of 1,800 men and six guns were ordered out of Monclova. Gen. Juan Jose Andrade and his command of 437 cavalry and lancers rode out. This group made up the majority of the army marching on San Antonio. Then, Gen. Don Jose Urrea was ordered with his force to meet with a battalion coming from Campeche, march up the coast, and squash the Matamoros expedition.

Santa Anna traveled to Mexico City before joining the operation. There he drafted and sent orders to Sesma detailing the way the campaign was to be conducted from a civil and financial point of view. First, any colonist (foreigner) who participated or aided the revolt was in violation of the law. The thinking behind that order was that the colonists had "declared a war of extermination to the Mexicans." Because any "foreigner" who participated in or aided the revolt was in violation of the law, the punishment was death or exile. Death was easier to expedite than exile and the impression was given that execution was the preferred method. The troops were to be so advised.

The decree was finalized and signed on December 30, 1835, by Tornel in his capacity as minister of war and marine. The final version read:

1. All foreigners who may land in any port of the republic or who enter it armed and for the purpose of attacking our territory shall be treated and punished as pirates, since they are not subjects of any nation at war with the republic nor do they militate under any recognized flag.

2. Foreigners who introduce arms and munitions by land or by sea at any point of the territory now in rebellion against the government of the nation for the purpose of placing such supplies in the hands of its enemies shall be treated and punished likewise.

In short, the Texans, and any who joined them, were not to be afforded any of the protections of soldiers fighting in a declared war or under a "recognized flag."

Even colonists who did not aid the rebellion were not off the hook. The decree maintained that they would be deported to the interior. And no more immigration of *norteamericanos* would be allowed. Because Texas was in rebellion, it was all perfectly legal under Mexican law.

Finally, Santa Anna had good intelligence about what the Anglos were up to in Texas. While many Mexicans in Texas supported the rebellion, the vast majority did not. They might be Centralists or Federalists, but they overwhelmingly wanted a Mexican and not a Mexicanized Anglo or illegal immigrant straight from the United States running the territory. These Mexicans were in contact with Santa Anna, and he soon knew the details of the fall of San Antonio and the Matamoros expedition.

Cos and his retreating army met Sesma and his advancing army at Laredo. They were joined there by the forces of Gen. Vicente Filisola. The generals received their marching orders from Santa Anna on January 3, 1836, with Sesma ordered to advance to the Rio Grande and Cos and Filisola ordered toward Monclova. The total army strength was just over six thousand and Santa Anna, unlike Sesma, was going to move fast.

The need for speed reflected Santa Anna's need for revenge, and the Mexican army suffered. The years of various rebellions and civil war had resulted in many casualties, forcing the army into a reliance on convicts and conscripts. The cavalry was an elite unit, but the infantry contained large numbers of untrained troops armed with clumsy muskets.

Somehow the invasion had to be paid for. The decree dealt with this problem by ordering Texas to pay, but that was in the future, after the conquest. Money was needed now to pay for supplies with many officers pledging their own credit to feed, clothe, and arm their men. There was to be no wasting of ammunition on the firing range. Santa Anna insisted the soldiers would get their practice during combat. No fodder for the horses and oxen would be needed as, according to Santa Anna, they would graze on the land along the way. Santa Anna was a disciple of his hero, the real Napoleon, who noted that an army travels on its stomach, but the men who comprised the army languished as their basic needs were neglected.

On February 5, 1836, the army was assembled. Final plans were made with Urrea's smaller force sent to Matamoros to reinforce the troops there, then off to eliminate Grant and Johnson. Then to Goliad to capture the fort. Santa Anna's army of one cavalry brigade and three infantry brigades marched for San Antonio.

This was the first major blunder of the campaign. From his intelligence network in Texas, Santa Anna knew there was not a large Texan force in San Antonio. Only about one hundred Texans remained at the Alamo, the rest having been recruited by Dr. Grant and Colonel Johnson. The Mexicans' knowledge of the situation is evidenced by Santa Anna's decision to send his most capable general, Urrea, to Matamoros to block the Matamoros expedition and hunt down Grant and Johnson. In addition, San Antonio was not the epicenter of the Texas revolution. The revolt was based out of east Texas, the leaders of the revolt were in east Texas, and the Anglo population centers were in east Texas. To have the greatest impact on the resistance, the army should have marched directly toward its base. Third, the major military establishment in the state was at Goliad, not San Antonio. Finally, San Antonio was a long way away. The army would have to march north to San Antonio and then turn right and march due east to force the Anglos across the Sabine and into the United States.

Santa Anna's generals recognized these facts. The Mexican generals suggested a route to the northeast that would wrap up Goliad and lead the army straight into the population areas of the east, with the added bonus of being near the coast where the army could travel by ship or be reinforced and resupplied by sea.

Santa Anna argued that San Antonio was the capital and the largest city in the territory. Goliad was nothing and they would get to east Texas when they got there. The generals did not protest too much because everybody knew the real reason for taking San Antonio and the Alamo. It was revenge for the disgrace Cos has brought upon family and country by surrendering to the rebels. The major problem with a dictatorship is that the dictator makes decisions and no one can disagree—not more than once anyway. If the dictator makes the wrong decision, then everyone suffers. Santa Anna made the wrong decision.

On the morning of February 5, 1836, Sesma and his army moved north. Santa Anna left Monclova on February 8 on horseback with a fifty-man security force. His small mounted group moved a lot faster than the marching army, and they soon overtook the column bogged down with carts pulled by oxen and men marching on foot. The column became strung out with the cavalry in front, then the infantry, then wagons, and finally the artillery. The artillery was the slowest due to the bad roads.

Many men took their chances and deserted. After the army passed the Rio Grande, the desertion rate fell off significantly, as this was Comanche territory. The Apaches were momentarily not at war with Mexico, but the Comanches were not at peace with anyone and raiding was their strong point. They cut into the stragglers, killing the soldiers they came upon and stripping the wagons of what they could carry. Many of the deserters who left the army prior to the Rio Grande were the trained drivers and caretakers of the oxen needed to pull the wagons. Santa Anna solved this personnel problem as he solved most problems: by resorting to untrained soldiers drafted to care for the animals. The animals suffered from lack of food, beatings, and exhaustion as they were driven northward.

Along with bad roads and Indians came bad weather. A blue norther came howling south to hit the army on February 13. The norther brought first rain, then freezing rain, and finally snow. Without adequate clothing and some without shoes, the soldiers, many of whom were Indians from the south, suffered and died. And, of course, the camp followers of women and children were harmed as well, along with the weakened oxen and mules. Armies traditionally did not campaign in the winter to avoid such problems.

The weather and foraging opportunities improved somewhat as they made their way north, but the army was dangerously spread out. If the Texans had had a mobile force in the area, they could have done tremendous damage to the army, but the only Texans in the area were barricaded in the Alamo and there were only one hundred or so of them.

Even with the Texas government in shambles, Houston with the Cherokees, and less than 150 men at the Alamo, the majority of Texans, including Houston, were still not overly concerned about Santa Anna. They all assumed he was coming, but not for at least a month. Conventional wisdom dictated that armies did not advance in the winter. The Texans didn't count on Santa Anna's disregard for conventional wisdom, his lack of concern for his men, or the overriding hatred and humiliation he felt because of his brother-in-law's loss of San Antonio and the Alamo. The Texans also assumed, like Santa Anna's generals, that Santa Anna would take the logical route through the southeast, taking first Goliad and then advancing eastward, pushing the Anglos to the Sabine before forcing them across the border to the United States, never to return. The Texans, like Santa Anna's generals, misread the general. On February 23, 1836, the advance members of the Mexican army, including Antonio Lopez de Santa Anna, entered San Antonio.

Back at Refugio, another man who would not and did not heed the logical advice of those around him was Dr. James

Grant. Though Houston had argued that Grant should stay at Refugio at least until reinforcements arrived, the doctor convinced Colonel Johnson as well as a small group consisting mostly of New Orleans Greys (including Houston's debating partner, Captain Pearson) to ride south fifty miles to San Patricio. What they had in mind is unclear, as even they must have known they could not successfully invade a sovereign country like Mexico with less than a hundred men.

Elsewhere, Fannin had recruited the Georgia battalion, moved them by ship from Velasco to Copano Bay, and then marched inland the few miles to Goliad. His separate command totaled about 450 men.

At San Patricio, Grant and Johnson moved a few miles south of town, keeping their force of less than one hundred men busy during the month of February running down and breaking horses. They eventually had enough horses for one hundred riders, and Colonel Johnson started rethinking his strategy. In a meeting with Grant he suggested they drive the horses back to Goliad. The horses would convince Fannin they had sufficient resources to attack Matamoros. Johnson also maintained, logically, that Fannin's additional men would be useful in the campaign. Grant countered that Fannin had been talked out of the expedition by Houston. Besides, Grant knew of a Mexican ranch nearby that had more horses—horses belonging to the Mexican army—and he wanted them. The two men finally cut a deal, with Johnson taking thirty-four men and the one hundred horses back to San Patricio, where they would wait until Grant could join them with the remaining sixty men and the newly captured horses.

Johnson and his men reached San Patricio, and Johnson, James M. Miller, John H. Love, Daniel J. Toler, and an unidentified Frenchman bunked in an abandoned house while the rest of the men took over a blockhouse that served as the fortifications for the town. They were not worried about being discovered and set no sentries. They should have.

By now the capable Urrea had left Matamoros and the army was on its way to Goliad. San Patricio was in the way of his 601 infantry and cavalrymen. Being capable meant knowing the terrain, and Urrea had scouts out at all times looking for the enemy. They utilized the intelligence network of Mexican ranchers who roamed the countryside reporting the movements of the Texans. The locals reported to the Mexican scouts that San Patricio held only a few of the enemy and security was nonexistent. Urrea's men surrounded the town, along with the thirty-four sleeping Texans.

The lack of Texan sentries can be explained by the blue norther that had whipped through the town during the day. A norther like this one and the one that hit the main force can drop the temperature fifty degrees in an hour. The Texans didn't think anyone would be wandering around in that kind of weather. They were wrong.

The Texans awoke to gunfire followed by pounding on the door of the officer's house. The men in the blockhouse came under fire. The firing stopped and a voice told them that they would be offered a free pardon if they surrendered. Captain Pearson, the artillery officer, yelled out that it was a trap. Ignoring Pearson, the men in the blockhouse opened the door, several stepping outside. They were immediately fired upon and one was killed. The others got back in the blockhouse but eventually all were killed or captured, except two who somehow managed to escape.

Johnson and the four other officers had better luck. The Mexican troops outside their house held their fire and yelled to the Texans to light a lamp so the Mexicans could see inside. Daniel J. Toler, who had been one of Grant's partners in Mexico, kept talking and stalling. Firing broke out in front of the house, and the Mexicans guarding the rear raced around to the front. The Texans saw their chance and raced out the back door. They escaped and the Frenchman hid. Emerging the next day he turned himself in after recognizing some of the Mexican officers from the time he had lived in Matamoros. They treated him well and released him.

The Mexicans put the number of Texans killed at twenty and captured at thirty-two. This contradicts other accounts that put the total men in the party at thirty-four. Casualty reports and reports of enemy strength are often exaggerated, but what is certain is that a majority of the Texans were captured or killed.

General Urrea knew his orders and the decree, which said that captured Texans were pirates to be executed or exiled. Urrea would demonstrate here, and later, an inability, literally, to pull the trigger. Preparing for the execution, Urrea, for some unknown reason, approached the town priest, an Irishman, to determine the appropriate location for the firing squad to do its work. The priest balked, saying that if Urrea executed the men in his town, he would never perform mass in the town again. Apparently this was good enough reason for Urrea, and he ordered the prisoners to Matamoros for execution, effectively passing the buck. Rather than being executed the prisoners were put to hard labor when they arrived in Matamoros.

Urrea and his force left San Luis Patricio heading south after Grant's party. They knew from their intelligence network that Grant and Johnson had split up, with Grant hunting horses. On March 2 the Mexicans caught up with Grant and his force at Agua Dulce Creek. The creek, often dry when without rain, runs forty-five miles through Nueces County and is surrounded by rolling hills supporting mesquite, scrub trees, and cactus. Outnumbered and outgunned, Grant realized their desperate situation. He quickly ordered Capt. Placido Benavides to break through the Mexicans, ride to Goliad, and report their fate and the arrival of the Mexican army to Fannin. Benavides made it to Goliad.

The remaining twenty-four Texans and three Mexicans stayed and fought, badly outnumbered by Urrea's men. Six of the Texans escaped to Goliad, where five would later perish in the massacre. At Agua Dulce Creek an additional six were captured and sent to Matamoros to join their San Luis Patricio comrades. The remainder, including Grant, were killed.

One of those captured was Reuben Brown, who later gave an eyewitness account of the battle and Grant's death. Brown was from Georgia, thirty-eight years old, and part of the mass immigration of illegals flowing into Texas. He and two comrades had traveled to San Antonio, arriving one day after the

Cos surrender. Caught up in Grant's enthusiasm, he joined a company under the command of Capt. B. L. Lawrence to participate in the Matamoros expedition.

According to Brown's account, after Grant and Johnson split, Grant stayed south of San Luis Patricio to raid the Camargo ranches for Mexican army horses. One of the ranches was guarded by men under the command of a Captain Rodriguez. Grant picked Brown to lead the charge of fifteen men, and Brown captured Rodriguez in the attack. Urrea's troops came to the rescue. The Texan company was soon surrounded except for Brown, Grant, and Benavides, who were riding on the perimeter. It was at this time that Grant ordered Benavides to escape to Goliad and alert Fannin. According to Brown, Grant then agreed with Brown that the two of them should "go in and die with the boys."

Riding into the surrounded Texans, Brown's horse was shot out from under him. He scrambled off the ground and caught and mounted the horse of Maj. Robert C. Morris who had been killed earlier in the skirmish, but a lancer thrust his pike through Brown's arm, bringing him again to the ground. He was lassoed and beaten.

Grant was not so lucky. Grant shot the rider who lanced Brown but was soon surrounded by Mexican cavalrymen. Grant was wounded, falling from his horse. Several Mexican officers dismounted and approached Grant. They knew the troublemaker since he had lived in Mexico, at one time had large land holdings, and was a member of the legislature. All this was held against him. The officers advanced, running Grant through with their swords.

There are several versions of Grant's death. One version in H. Yoakum's 1855 *History of Texas* maintains that Grant was not killed on the scene but captured and taken back to San Luis Patricio.

> While Grant was in San Patricio, curing his own wound, and carefully ministering to the wants of the wounded of the enemy, he was promised that, so soon as he recovered, and those under his care were convalescent, he should have a passport to leave the country without molestation. The captain left in command of the town, after the departure of

Urrea, secretly despatched eight men in search of a wild horse. The animal was captured about three weeks after the battle of the 2d of March. Grant was now brought forth, and, by order of the captain, his feet were strongly bound to those of the horse, and his hands to the tail. "Now," said the captain, "you have your passport—go." At the same moment the cords by which the mustang was tied were severed. The fierce animal, finding his limbs unfettered, sprang away with great violence, leaving behind him, in a short distance, the mangled remains of poor Grant.

After the skirmish, Brown prepared for his execution. Again a priest was nearby and, accompanied by a Mexican woman, he pleaded for Brown's life to be spared. As before, Urrea could not pull the trigger. The Mexican woman would reappear later to save more men as the "Angel of Goliad." Urrea told Brown he could go free if he agreed to go to Goliad and talk Fannin into surrendering. Brown refused. He was sent as a prisoner to Matamoros, where he spent his days as a street sweeper.

Brown's parents in the United States found out about his imprisonment and contracted an Irishman living in Mexico to arrange his escape. The escape was successful. Brown got back to Texas, where he rejoined the army and was honorably discharged. He established a plantation at the mouth of the Brazos, married a woman from Georgia, and had five children. He dabbled in politics but was mainly living the life of a prosperous landowner up to the outbreak of the Civil War.

Brown joined the Confederate army as a lieutenant colonel of the Thirteenth Texas Infantry with the primary responsibility of guarding Galveston Bay. He took command of a cavalry battalion in 1862 and was promoted to full colonel of the Thirty-fifth Texas Cavalry. The unit stayed in Texas until 1864, when it joined Walker's Texas Division for the Red River campaign in Louisiana. Brown returned to his plantation after the war and died there, the exact date unknown. He was in his mid-seventies at least, as he applied for and was granted a pension in 1881.

Reuben Brown led a long and exciting life. Dr. James Grant's life was as exciting but not as long. Regardless of how Grant died, the Matamoros expedition died with him.

Chapter 5

Tightening the Noose

"Since you have chosen to elect a man with a wooden toe to succeed me, you may all go to Hell and I will go to Texas."

General Urrea sent a messenger from San Luis Patricio to San Antonio with the news of his victory over Johnson. News of his victory over Dr. Grant at Agua Dulce would soon follow. Celebrations broke out in the army, the bells of San Fernando rang out the news. The red flag of death blew in the breeze generated from the swinging of the church bells. Another red flag was raised on Powder House Hill. The series of Mexican defeats from Gonzales to Goliad to San Antonio was broken. The tide was turning for the Mexicans. Morale shot up. The Mexicans outnumbered the Texans inside the walls of the Alamo forty to one.

Historians have noted that the Alamo was a fort that should not have been defended but was while Goliad was one that should have been defended and wasn't. The Alamo was clearly not defendable by the Texans. Imagine 180 plus men trying to defend against an army of six thousand a crumbling structure covering the space of a modern-day football stadium. But the Texans did defend the Alamo and they went down in history. This is a story about Fannin and Goliad, but the fate of Goliad is intertwined with the glory of the Alamo. That story has to be told to put the events at Goliad in perspective.

The Alamo was in dire straits because of Dr. Grant. He cleaned out the place when he left San Antonio on December 30, 1835. He took most of the men as well as the money, clothing, saddles, and arms. He left the cannon, some food, blankets, and medical supplies along with a few muskets, two trumpets, and fifteen broken carbines. The remaining garrison numbered slightly more than one hundred defenders.

Col. James Clinton Neill was furious at the looting and made the squabbling politicians in San Felipe aware of his plight, writing, "It will be appalling to you to learn and see herewith our alarming weakness. If there has ever been a dollar here, I have no knowledge of it." His command was only 104 men, many down to the clothes on their backs and a blanket. Payday was to be January 14, but payday came with no money for the men. The next day his command had shrunk to 80, comprised of the few colonists who had not left for their farms, volunteers with nowhere to go, and a small number of New Orleans Greys who had not joined the Grant-Johnson expedition.

Not only were the Alamo's defenders weak, but the structure itself was ill suited as a place of defense. Green B. Johnson, lawyer and amateur engineer, summed up the Alamo in a letter to Sam Houston saying, "You can plainly see that the Alamo never was built by a military people for a fortress." The mission and its outbuildings covered an area of over three acres. In the middle the famous chapel with the distinctive roofline sat facing west, but the roofline was different, with the famous "hump" not being added until 1848 by U.S. Army engineers. In front of the chapel was the plaza, a rectangle of dirt packed solid by traffic. The main entrance to the compound was on the south side, which was bordered on each side by the "low barracks," a set of one-story buildings. The west wall faced the town and the river and consisted of adobe huts linked by a strong twelve-foot wall. The north wall, which today would run through the middle of the United States Post Office in San Antonio, was similar in construction to the west wall. On the east side was the "long barracks." The "long barracks" was two stories and solidly built.

The chapel that would become the symbol of the battle was in ruins in 1836. Years of neglect had taken their toll. The roof over the main chapel was long gone, though the roof still remained over the small rooms running on the interior walls of the chapel. Inside the chapel Cos had built a ramp of logs and earth running up to a platform on the east end of the large room. Most of the interior space was taken up with the mass of earth and the platform that was used to place a cannon.

The chapel did not quite reach to the south wall. The gap

of approximately fifty yards was the weakest point of a "fortress" with numerous weak points, including walls four feet thick with no parapets, no firing holes, and no well. Water was supplied by a small stream running through the complex.

The Alamo's major problem was its large square footage and the lack of men available to defend the acreage. Colonel Neill was at a loss after the departure of Grant and Johnson. He called his men together to review the situation. He was surprised when the men passed a resolution stating they felt it "highly essential" that the army, even if it was only eighty men, stay and defend the Alamo.

Colonel Neill was an organized and efficient officer. He was no youngster in 1836, having been born in North Carolina in 1790. He had fought in the Creek War and had been wounded. In 1831 he and his wife and their three children moved from Alabama to Texas, where he entered the Texas militia as a captain of artillery in 1835. Neill had been at Gonzales, reportedly firing the "Come and Take It" cannon at the battle. At the first siege of San Antonio, he commanded the sole cannon in the Texas army, using it on December 8 to stop a Mexican counterattack. With the surrender of Cos, Neill, having been promoted to lieutenant colonel by the General Council, was now in command of thirty artillery pieces. The cannon were about the only things Grant and Johnson did not take with them, as the pieces were too large and bulky and the roads too poor.

With his men supporting a defense, Colonel Neill took actions sealing the fate of the Alamo and the men who would defend it. He improved the defenses enough to make it seem defendable to his men as well as to William Travis and James Bowie, who were yet to arrive. In the few weeks between the departure of Grant and Johnson and the arrival of Travis and Bowie, Neill pushed his men to strengthen the fort by erecting an improvised fence from the chapel to the south wall, clearing lines of fire, erecting parapets, and strengthening gun positions.

On January 17, 1836, Houston, in one of his final acts before leaving for the Indian of east Texas, ordered James

Bowie and twenty-five volunteers to the Alamo to destroy it. Houston did not believe in defending fixed positions. Fixed positions tied up men and materials and were perfect prey for a large, ponderous army like the army of Santa Anna. Houston wanted to fight a war along the lines of the American Revolution, where the outgunned and outmanned rebels picked the spots for battle and guerilla warfare supplemented conventional warfare. Houston continued to be the only voice of reason on either side of the revolution, with the Texans attempting to invade Mexico or trying to hold three acres of land with eighty men, while Santa Anna was picking revenge over total victory. Houston's decision to wash his hands of the mess is understandable.

It would get worse because Bowie disobeyed orders. Bowie had the trust of Houston, who praised Bowie, saying, "There is no man on whose forecast, prudence, and valor I place a higher estimate." Bowie and Neill reviewed Houston's instructions to destroy the fort and withdraw. Clear enough except for the phrase "Much is referred to your discretion."

Bowie inspected the fortress and noted its deficiencies. No horses, no medical supplies, no powder, no cannonballs. Morale was low. There was even a near mutiny with one man being expelled. Bowie wrote, "Our force is very small, the returns this day to the Comdt., is only one hundred and twenty officers and men. It would be a waste of men to put our brave little band against thousands."

Bowie had already shown a dislike, similar to Houston's, for fixed positions. At the battle of Concepion he overrode the objections of Fannin, placing his defenders on the river rather than bottled up in the mission. This ruse worked, as Cos attacked the mission and gave away the surprise. For some reason this logic failed Bowie at the Alamo.

Bowie also did not exhibit his usual forceful personality. He did not order Neill to destroy the Alamo and retreat. Instead he poked around; he stalled. Bowie fell under the spell of the Alamo or Neill's improvements or past Texan victories because he and Colonel Neill came to the misguided conclusion to defend the Alamo. Bowie wrote to Governor Smith,

"The salvation of Texas depends in great measure in keeping Bexar out of the hands of the enemy. It serves as the frontier picquet guard, and if it were in the possession of Santa Anna, there is no stronghold from which to repel him in his march toward the Sabine. Colonel Neill and myself have come to the solemn resolution that we will rather die in these ditches than give it up to the enemy." He added his voice to Neill's asking for food, men, and arms. The only man who could override this logic was no longer on the scene. Sam Houston had left San Felipe and would not return until March.

Having made his decision, which was not his to make, Bowie, along with Neill, went to work on the defense of the Alamo. Using local contacts left over from his days as a member of a prominent local family, Bowie gathered horses that his scouts would use for patrols and pumped friends in the community for intelligence. From them and the patrols he monitored the advance of the Mexican army.

Morale in the Alamo improved with Bowie's accelerating the work Neill had started. Bowie made specific assignments so the officers would know their areas of responsibility. Green B. Jameson, the lawyer turned engineer, took to his new vocation building earthen ramps and gun platforms to hold the massive cannon. He built parapets of wood and earth so the riflemen could fire over the wall. His plans included moats and drawbridges, but he just didn't have the time, men, or materials. He did move the eighteen-pounder up on a platform in the southwest angle of the fort where it could sweep the town—a formidable engineering feat by itself. Sgt. Maj. Hiram Williamson drilled the men, forcing some measure of military structure and training on the independent volunteers. Capt. John Baugh was adjutant to Colonel Neill in charge of reprovisioning, or attempting to reprovision, the garrison. He met with considerable success, bringing in a beef herd of forty-two and a hundred bushels of corn, and somehow finding ammunition for the eighteen-pound cannon.

Politics reached the Alamo as news came of the ongoing fights in San Felipe. On January 26, lawyer James Bonham formed a committee that staged a rally in the Alamo to support

Governor Smith. Bonham was a veteran of politics, having been kicked out of what would become the University of South Carolina for protesting against the cafeteria food in 1823. He apprenticed his legal studies and started practicing law in South Carolina, once caning an opposing lawyer for perceived insults toward one of his female clients. He insulted the judge when ordered to stop the beating and was sentenced to ninety days in jail for contempt of court. He served as a lieutenant colonel in the South Carolina militia but moved to Alabama in 1834, where he was caught up in the Texas cause.

Bonham traveled to Texas to meet Houston. They soon became close friends. On December 1, 1835, Bonham offered his military services to Houston, and he was appointed a second lieutenant in the cavalry. Less than two months later Houston recommended that Bonham be made a major, skipping a few ranks in between lieutenant and major. The promotion was never finalized, however, with Bonham remaining a lieutenant during his time at the Alamo.

On January 26 he was heading the Governor Smith support committee drafting a resolution supporting Smith, asking again for money and supplies, and declaring, "We cannot be driven from the post of honor." Bonham signed first and then Bowie. On February 1, Bonham's political career ended, as he lost the election for delegates to represent the garrison at the constitutional convention. Winning the election probably would have saved his life.

There were politics in San Felipe and there were politics in San Antonio. Col. William Barret Travis arrived at the Alamo on February 3. The small fortress now had three colonels, four if Bonham and his South Carolina militia title is included: Neill, Bowie, and Travis with Travis the junior. Travis had only turned twenty-six years old in August 1835 and had participated in the first battle of San Antonio as commander of a cavalry unit returning to San Felipe prior to the surrender of Cos. After the battle, he presented a plan for raising and arming a cavalry unit to the unorganized government. They reacted to the proposal by offering Travis a position as major in the artillery. Travis declined. He was then offered, and accepted, a position as the army's main recruiting officer and lieutenant colonel in the cavalry. In that capacity, he was ordered by Governor Smith to raise a cavalry unit of one hundred riders and go to the aid of the Alamo defenders. He could only raise thirty-nine, with nine deserting en route. From his camp on the Colorado River, he wrote to Governor Smith asking to be recalled.

> I beg that Your Excellency will recall the order for me to go to Bexar in command of so few men, I am willing, nay anxious, to go to the defense of Bexar, and I have done everything in my power to equip the enlisted men and get them off. But Sir, I am unwilling to risk my reputation (which is ever dear to a volunteer) by going off into the enemy's country with so little means, so few men, and these so badly equipped—the fact is there is no necessity for my services to command these few men. The company officers will be amply sufficient.

In addition, he threatened to resign if his wish were not granted. Smith did not respond and Travis proceeded, obviously reluctantly, to San Antonio. Travis is often portrayed as stubborn and foolish, but his letter to Governor Smith illustrates that he knew a bad situation when he saw one, fully realizing that thirty-nine men were not going to stop Santa Anna.

Colonel Travis soon butted heads with Colonel Neill, but on the morning of February 11, Colonel Neill left the Alamo on twenty days' leave due to a serious illness that had struck his family. Additionally, the command may have become overwhelming for Neill given Bowie's personality and the arrival of the firebrand, Travis. Neill has been portrayed as pedestrian and second rate and he was certainly overwhelmed by the personalities that sparkled more than his, including the famous Davy Crockett, arriving in the Alamo on February 8 at the head of his Tennessee Mounted Volunteers, a potent-sounding force made up of only twelve men. But Bowie praised Neill as a leader, writing that "no other man in the army could have kept men at this post, under the neglect they have experienced." Neill left for home and as his last act appointed Travis commander of the garrison.

Neill stayed home for more than twenty days but was heading back to the Alamo when word reached Gonzales of the fall of the fortress on March 6. He joined with Houston in the retreat after the Alamo, dumping the army's cannon into the Guadalupe River. He stayed an artilleryman without artillery until the Battle of San Jacinto where he command-ed the Twin Sisters cannon in a skirmish just before the main battle. Seriously wounded by grapeshot, he missed the victo-ry at San Jacinto. After the war, he served the young nation as a large landowner as a result of his service, an Indian fight-er, and an Indian agent. He died in 1845.

When Bowie learned that Neill had appointed Travis, Bowie exploded. The command structure at the Alamo is a confusing one with the conflict between Travis and Bowie providing much of the interpersonal drama. Why were there two commanders and where did Davy Crockett fit in the pecking order? Davy, the most famous of the group and a for-mer congressman from Tennessee, was also the most reason-able of the three, offering to be a "high private" in charge of his small command of twelve men.

Davy's humility at the Alamo is remarkable since he was nationally famous as a politician, writer, and stage celebrity. Having him appear at an event today would be comparable to an entertainment celebrity and potential presidential candi-date showing up in the same person. Davy was born in 1786 in what is now eastern Tennessee but was then the semiau-tonomous state of Franklin, an exercise in self-rule following the American Revolution. Before and after the Franklin experiment it was considered part of North Carolina until the area became part of Tennessee when the state was granted statehood in 1796. Davy was the fifth of nine children. His parents ran a not-very-successful tavern and his grandpar-ents had been killed by Indians. At the age of twelve, he was apprenticed to a cattle herder but escaped in a snowstorm, returning home. He left home two years later and worked as a laborer, making his way home again two and a half years later, where he stayed until marrying Polly Finley in 1806. They had two sons and by 1813 had moved westward and southward to the Alabama border.

Davy's military career began when he volunteered as a scout in the militia raised to punish the Creek Indians for the slaughter of five hundred men, women, and children at Fort Mims, Alabama. Davy served in the army under the overall command of Andrew Jackson and participated in the massacre of the Creeks at Tallussahatchee. Davy was not at the decisive battle of Horseshoe Bend, as his ninety-day enlistment had run out prior to the battle.

Davy reenlisted in September 1814 holding the rank of third sergeant. That September, Jackson was chasing Seminole Indians and escaped slaves as well as thwarting British expeditions along the coast of Florida. Florida was part of Spain but Spain was so weakened by revolutionary wars elsewhere that the place, like Texas, was pretty much wide open. Jackson captured Pensacola on November 8 and Davy arrived the next day. Davy scouted for the army and was discharged in 1815. Returning home, he was now the father of a daughter as well as the two boys, but Polly died either just before or just after his arrival home. He was called back into service in late February 1815 but paid for a substitute to take his place as he was needed to tend the affairs at home after the death of his wife. This event has been used in attempts to tarnish Davy's character and reputation, but his reasoning was based on the need to be home to care for the family and the fact that hostilities were all but over.

Davy called Polly's death "the hardest trial which ever falls to the lot of man" but it didn't stop his military career, as he was elected a lieutenant in the militia, nor his domestic life, as he married a widow, Elizabeth Patton, during the summer. With a family of five children, three his and two hers, Davy had to make some money and by 1820, through a dowry and debt, Crockett had 614 acres in western Tennessee, a gristmill and gunpowder factory, a distillery, and an iron ore mine. These were substantial assets offset by substantial financial liabilities.

He also helped organize a civic structure in the wilderness, serving as justice of the peace. He survived—barely—the severe economic recession of the time and decided to run for the Tennessee House of Representatives. Davy was elected and then reelected in 1823. In 1825 he ran for the United States House of Representatives but lost, getting 2,599 votes to his opponent's 2,866 votes.

Davy went back to civilian life, almost losing his life trying to float two flatboats full of barrel staves down the Mississippi. The boats got away from him and his inexperienced crew, nearly drowning all of them when an uprooted tree smashed through the two boats. Davy was trapped below decks and escaped through a hatch used to collect water. Somehow he was able to grab hold of a tree trunk. He clung there, totally naked, for the evening. Rescued in the morning he and his crew were brought back to Memphis where he regrouped, becoming a favorite of the local Memphis politicians. Urged on by them he ran again for Congress in 1827 and won.

Davy's campaign style was unique and irreverent. He, like Lincoln, ignored the long-winded oratory of the day and appealed to the common man. Nervous over one speech, he wrapped it up successfully when he "took care to remark that I was as dry as a powder horn, and I thought it was time for us all to wet our whistles a little; and so I put off the liquor stand, and was followed by the greater part of the crowd." At another rally he did not have the money to buy drinks for the thirsty crowd so he went out into the woods, shooting a raccoon that he traded for a quart of liquor. Mark Twain would say that this story had an influence on his writing style and it is easy to see the connection.

These antics didn't go over well with his opponents, who attempted to smear Crockett. Dirty smear campaigns are not new to American politics and everyone running was an open target. Andrew Jackson was accused of being a drunk, duelist, and adulterer since his wife, Rachael, was still officially married to another man when she married Jackson. The first husband told her their Kentucky divorce was final when it was not. Jackson struck back, calling Henry Clay a drunk, gambler, and "whoremonger." Attacks on Davy concentrated on heavy drinking and portraying him as a hick. One opponent accused Davy of being a gambler, drunkard, adulterer, and liar. Crockett did tell lies about his opponent, but he admitted it to the crowd, saying that he was a liar and his opponent was a liar so they were basically even. The crowd loved it. Davy won with 5,868 votes while his two opponents received 3,646 and 2,417 votes respectively.

One of the issues used against Davy was real, as Davy did struggle with his heavy drinking and wrote about it to his brother-in-law upon entering Congress:

> I have altered my cours in life a great deal sence I reached this place and I have not tasted one drop of Arden Spirits sence I arrived here nor never expect to while I live nothing stronger than cider I trust that god will give fortitude in my undertaking I have never made a pretention to religion in my life before I have run a long race tho I trust that I was called in good time for my wickedness by my dear wife who I am ——— certain will be no little astonished when she gets information of my determination.

In Congress, Davy started out in Andrew Jackson's camp, but they fell out over the granting of land deeds and Jackson's campaign to push the Indians westward. The federal government owned 90 percent of the western land and sold it for $1.25 an acre. Seemingly a bargain, it was actually too expensive for most cash-strapped pioneers. The majority of pioneers were squatters with title to their land ambiguous, their claims always in doubt. Crockett made his position clear in a speech to Congress that "the rich require but little legislation, We should, at least occasionally, legislate for the poor."

Davy proposed that every squatter receive a grant from the government for 160 acres. The idea was very popular with the squatters and Davy was reelected in 1829 with a plurality of 64 percent. But Davy never learned the give and take of Congress. He was independent and stinging in his attacks on fellow congressmen. He also switched sides on issues, making him unreliable to coalition builders. He missed the nuances of national politics, concentrating instead on the issues of his constituents. By not going along on the big issues, he missed the chance to have his local issues addressed.

Finally he fell out with the Jacksonians over Indian policy. Davy had been an Indian fighter and his grandparents had been killed by Indians, but he believed the westward movement was an injustice, overstepping on the part of the federal government. He voted against the policy, saying, "If he should be the only member of that House who voted against the bill, and the only man in the United States who disapproved it, he would still vote against it; and it would be a matter of rejoicing to him till the day he died, that he had given the vote."

The Jacksonians went after Davy. His land bill failed in Congress. His next opponent, William Fitzgerald, came out swinging with the old charges of drinking and gambling along with new ammunition including Crockett's support for the Indians and his failure to get anything material done in Congress. The campaign was ugly and getting uglier by the day. Traveling with Fitzgerald from town to town and engaging in debates, Davy finally had enough. He announced that he would beat up Fitzgerald if his antagonist did not tone down the rhetoric. Fitzgerald, standing in front of a table at the next debate in Paris, announced he had no intention of going easy on the accusations. Davy jumped up saying he was going to let his opponent have it then and there. Fitzgerald whisked his handkerchief off the table, revealing a pistol that he took up and aimed chest high at Davy, now less than a step away. Davy backed down to the taunts of the crowd. He lost the close election, getting 7,948 votes to Fitzgerald's 8,543.

Davy may have lost the election of 1831, but he was becoming a star on stage and in print. His homespun style and the tall tales of his drinking, fighting abilities, and frontier upbringing made him the successor to Daniel Boone. The public embraced a comedy *The Lion of the West* with the hero, Nimrod Wildfire, based on Davy. The role was a thinly disguised caricature. When Davy attended a performance in Washington, the crowd exploded in applause upon his entrance. The Wildfire actor came onstage and bowed to Davy, Davy stood and bowed to Wildfire, and the audience erupted into applause again.

The plot line was country bumpkin colonel saves naive, young New York niece from marrying a phony British lord. Through his antics in Washington and his tall tales and bad grammar, Crockett had become well known compared to most representatives. *The Lion of the West* made him famous nationwide. The play was eventually renamed *The Kentuckian, or a Trip to New York* and would have a run of more than twenty years.

Most importantly, Crockett didn't mind being the model for Nimrod Wildfire. Using his enhanced popularity and Fitzgerald's inability to pass his version of a land bill, Crockett beat Fitzgerald by 173 votes, returning to Congress in 1833. Building on the play, the popular press embraced Crockett, with James Strange French writing *The Life and Adventures of Colonel David Crockett of West Tennessee.* The next year the book came out again but as *Sketches and Eccentricities of Colonel David Crockett of West Tennessee.* The volume portrayed Davy as the consummate pioneer capable of superhuman feats but a flop as a politician. While the work increased Davy's popularity, he didn't like its treatment of his political abilities, and he received no money from the sales. To set the facts straight and cash in on his popularity, Davy wrote an autobiography with the aid of Thomas Chilton, a representative from Kentucky and Crockett ghost speechwriter. Titled *A Narrative of the Life of David Crockett of the State of Tennessee,* the work became a bestseller. The most famous "Crockettism" that came out of the book was "Be always sure you are right— Then Go Ahead."

As a member of Congress, the role model for a hit play, and the author of a best-selling book, Crockett was well known now throughout the country. He was even considered by some Whig politicians, and himself, to be possible presidential timber. Davy became even more of a thorn in the side of the Jacksonian Democrats with his popularity and his speeches attacking Jackson every chance he got. Crockett's independence made him a popular figure with the public but not with politicians on either side of the aisle, who managed by consensus and deal making. Davy could care less for consensus or deal making. He also wasn't paying attention in Congress, as he often wasn't there. Instead, he conducted a tour of the east that included a visit to the New York Stock Exchange as well as Boston and New Jersey. He wowed crowds with his stories in Baltimore, Philadelphia, Pittsburgh, and Cincinnati. Davy wrote another book but it concentrated on politics, not pioneer tales, and was a flop.

Sensing weakness at home due to Davy's lack of attendance in Congress, the Jacksonian Democrats ran Adam Huntsman against the celebrity. Huntsman, a veteran who had lost a leg in the War of 1812, concentrated on Davy's lack of accomplishments in his time in Congress and accused Davy of neglecting his constituents as a result of his nationwide popularity. Davy fell back on his humor and country style but lost a close election by 252 votes out of 9,052 cast.

Having failed in his reelection bid, he was nearly broke as his book did not sell well, he was in perpetual debt because of his land holdings, and he had just lost his job. Davy did what a lot of unemployed and indebted men did at the time. He got Texas fever. On November 1, 1835, Davy headed for Memphis with three companions on their way to Texas. At the bar in the Union Hotel he told the crowd, "Since you have chosen to elect a man with a wooden toe to succeed me, you may all go to Hell and I will go to Texas." The small group traveled down the Mississippi to the Arkansas and then to Little Rock, overland to the Red River, and eventually to Nacogdoches. Crockett was hoping to find Sam Houston in Nacogdoches and inquire about acquiring some land on the Red River, but Houston was out trying to raise an army and fighting over who was commander in chief. Crockett took the oath of allegiance to the Provisional Government and wrote in his last letter on January 9, 1836:

I must say as to what I have seen of Texas it is the garden spot of the world. The best land and the best prospects for health I ever saw, and I do believe it is a fortune to any man to come here. There is a world of country here to settle. . . . I have taken the oath of government and have enrolled my name as a volunteer and will set out for the Rio Grand in a few days with the volunteers from the United States. But all volunteers is entitled to vote for a member of the convention or to be voted for, and I have but little doubt of being elected a member to form a constitution for this province. I am rejoiced at my fate. I had rather be in my present situation than to be elected to a seat in Congress for life. I am in hopes of making a fortune yet for myself and family, bad as my prospect has been.

Another famous military man, Gen. Philip Sheridan, would later have a less flattering opinion of Texas. He summed up the state saying, "If I owned Texas and Hell, I would rent out Texas and live in Hell."

For Davy, Texas was a new opportunity for land and elected office. Texas was to Davy what it is to many others—a new start. He arrived in San Antonio with his dozen or so men on February 5, 1836. He arrived to a party and an internal dispute because William Barret Travis and Jim Bowie were at each other's throats.

The battle between Travis and Bowie over the command of the Alamo was the result of a technicality. Bowie was a colonel of volunteers and Travis was a colonel of the regular army. Neill appointed Travis commander because Travis, like Neill, was regular army, but in reality there was no difference between the regular army and volunteers. There was no draft, no conscription, so every soldier was by definition a volunteer. The only real distinction between the two was that volunteers elected their officers. The regular army officers were appointed by the government. But even Travis was willing to hold an election, which he did, and lost to Jim Bowie. The confusion between who was commander of the Alamo mirrored the confusion over who was governor and who (whether Grant, Johnson, Fannin, or Houston) was commander in chief of the army, volunteer or regular.

To celebrate his election, Bowie threw a party, a drunken party. Travis reported to Governor Smith that "since his election, [Bowie] has been roaring drunk all the time." He went on, "If I did not feel my honor and that of my country compromitted I would leave here instantly for some other point with the troops under my immediate command—as I am unwilling to be responsible for the drunken irregularities of any man." But he didn't leave, saying to the governor, "It is more important to occupy this post than I imagined when I last saw you. It is the key to Texas."

The binge lasted for days with the release of prisoners, both Mexican and Texan, and drunken parades of men in the main plaza. Bowie ordered fleeing Mexican families to be turned around and returned to the city. Travis withdrew his men from the fortress to get away from Bowie. Bowie eventually sobered up and assessed the situation through his hangover. He knew the fleeing Mexicans signaled an army was coming. He knew they had nothing in the way of enough men and supplies to stop the Mexican army and hold the Alamo. He knew he was disobeying Houston's order to blow up the fort and withdraw.

In spite of all this he did not order his men to withdraw or destroy the fort. Instead he cut a deal with Travis. On February 14 the two men agreed to disagree. Bowie would take command of the garrison volunteers, and Travis would command the volunteer cavalry and his original command. All orders and letters would be signed by both men. The arrangement would be in force until Neill returned, at which time it would be revisited. The two commanders kicked off the relationship by sending a message to Smith again asking for men and supplies and money to pay the payroll.

The truce did end the partying for the time being, and the men went back to work improving the fortifications. Within days all but three cannon were in position and the ammunition supply supplemented with cut-up horseshoes and any other metal object that could be crammed down the barrel of a cannon.

Dr. Amos Pollard, aged thirty-two, had set up a hospital and somehow was able to get most of the medicines he needed. From Massachusetts, Pollard was one of six doctors at the Alamo and had practiced in New York but succumbed to Texas fever after his wife died in 1831. He settled in Gonzales and fought in that battle before moving on to San Antonio. Being educated and having lived in New York, he is the only victim of the massacre that had a portrait done while living except for Travis, Bowie, and Crockett.

Green Jameson, the Alamo's makeshift engineer, got even more caught up in his contrivances, writing to Governor Smith about the improvements and deriding the Mexicans, declaring, "They have shown imbecility and want of skill in the fortress as they have in all things else." But for all the progress being made they would still be outnumbered, and outnumbered by a huge amount. Everyone seemed to lose sight of this basic fact as they went about their preparations.

Not all Mexicans were spies for Santa Anna. Some were spies for Travis. One San Antonio family, the Rodriguezes, fed information to Travis on a regular basis, as they had sons and cousins shadowing the Mexican army. The sons and cousins reported back to San Antonio so the family would know when to flee the city. On February 16, Travis was told the Mexican army was at the Rio Grande. Another scout, a cousin of Texan captain Juan Seguin, reported on the twentieth that the army was crossing the Rio Grande. Travis decided not to believe the scouts. Travis was like Houston. He believed Santa Anna would not attempt moving his army until spring, March fifteenth at the earliest. Both Houston and Travis underestimated the rage that Santa Anna felt as a result of his brother-in-law's disgrace.

Santa Anna caught up with his army at the Nueces River on February 17. He was 120 miles from San Antonio. The army had to rebuild a bridge burned by the Texans, but by

February 19 they were camped on the Frio River with only 68 miles left to travel. The next day they reached the Hondo River, only 50 miles distant. On the twenty-first of February, Santa Anna was at the Medina River with twenty-five miles between him and the Alamo.

Chapter 6

The Fall of the Alamo

"The Mexicans are upon us. Give me the babe, and jump up behind me."

At the Medina River, Santa Anna waited for his army, strung out behind him, and worked his intelligence network. Civilians came out to the camp giving details of the fortifications. One told Santa Anna there was to be a party in the city that night, a fandango, attended by the Texans. Santa Anna ordered a cavalry unit forward to raid the party and capture the Texans, but a sudden rain raised the river before the unit could ride out to San Antonio. Santa Anna decided to rest his army for a few days.

By the twenty-third of February, the civilian population was well aware of the proximity of the army and they were fleeing. Fleeing civilians look pretty much the same no matter what war or what campaign—traveling on anything that will move or fleeing on foot carrying all they can and then discarding most of it along the way. Travis ordered the refugees to halt. He threatened arrest but was overwhelmed by the mob. Finally, somebody in the mob told him the truth. The Mexican cavalry had advanced to the Leon River, eight miles away.

Travis and Dr. John Sutherland raced up the stairs of San Fernando Church's bell tower. Reaching the top, they searched the countryside. Nothing. Travis ordered the sentry to ring the bell immediately if he saw anything. It was ten o'clock in the morning on February 23, 1836.

At one o'clock the bell rang. A false alarm. Dr. John Sutherland wasn't too sure, asking permission to ride out with John W. Smith on a patrol. Travis and Sutherland agreed on a signal. If they came back at a walk, then it was a false alarm. Anything else and the sentry was right. The two rode out a mile and a half, up and over a slight ridge. They looked, turned, and raced for the Alamo. Sutherland rode so hard and fast, he was thrown from his horse. Smith stopped and helped him back on, and they started back again. The sentry saw them coming and rang the bell. This was no false alarm.

Soldiers dropped what they were doing and raced for the Alamo. Capt. Almeron Dickinson, a thirty-six-year-old blacksmith from Gonzales who had helped man the "Come and Take It" cannon, rode into town to the house where his family was staying. He yelled to his twenty-one-year-old wife, Susannah, "The Mexicans are upon us. Give me the babe, and jump up behind me." Ushered safely inside the Alamo, Sarah and the daughter, Angelina, were the only Anglo females in the fortress. Mexicans with ties to the Texans raced to the Alamo as well, while the Mexican refugees fled in the opposite direction. The flood away from the Alamo was much greater than the trickle into it.

At the main gate was a sober Sgt. William B. Ward. Ward, an Irishman, was usually drunk but not now. Calm among the panic, he manned the cannon at the gate.

Travis knew he must get word of the Alamo's predicament to the government and Fannin. Immediately, he sent a rider to Goliad with the message to come quickly. He approached Dr. Sutherland and asked him to go to Gonzales as well. Sutherland had severely wrenched his knee when thrown from his horse in the dash back to the Alamo but agreed to make the journey. Travis wrote, "The enemy in large force is in sight. We want men and provisions. Send them to us. We have 150 men and are determined to defend the Alamo to the last. Give us assistance." Travis had no time for flowery language or appeals to freedom and liberty. His message was short and succinct.

Sutherland rode out looking for Capt. Philip Dimmitt, the former commander at Goliad, who had resigned his command in January over an argument with Dr. Grant and Colonel Johnson. After his resignation Dimmitt joined the forces at the Alamo as army storekeeper and scout. Dimmitt was on patrol that day and cut off from returning to the Alamo by the arrival of Santa Anna's forces, so Sutherland missed Dimmitt, but he found John W. Smith out on the trail.

Smith and Sutherland agreed to travel to Gonzales together. Starting out for their destination, they turned and watched as the town of San Antonio filled with Mexican cavalry.

By three o'clock the Texans had abandoned San Antonio, and the town was captured by the Mexican army without a shot being fired. Around four o'clock a chilling sight stopped the panic in the Alamo as all eyes went toward the bell tower of San Fernando Church. A large red flag unfurled. In the Mexican army the red flag meant no quarter to be given. All in the Alamo were to die. The Mexican army was not the only military force to use flags for telegraphing their intentions. Pirates often used a two-flag system—a black flag meant they were going to take prisoners and a red flag meant, of course, they were not.

One dramatic gesture could be matched with another and Travis knew drama. Without consulting his co-commander, Travis ordered the eighteen-pounder fired. It didn't hit anything in town but it took everyone's attention off the flag. Bowie, sick but still mobile, was outraged at the cannon shot. He knew, as did everyone, what the red flag meant and he was committed to defending the Alamo. But he was not above talking first (he had tried it at the Indian fight at San Saba with no success) to see if something could be worked out.

Now Bowie acted without consulting Travis, writing a quick note and handing it to Jameson, the engineer-lawyer. Bowie apologized for the cannon shot, writing,

> Because a shot was fired from a cannon of this fort at the time that a red flag was raised over the tower, and a little afterward they told me that a part of your army had sounded a parley, which however, was not heard before the firing of the said shot, I wish, Sir to ascertain if it be true that a parley was called. . . . God and Texas.

The note sounds like Bowie was writing on the run, apologetically asking if the two sides could talk things over. He probably realized this in rereading the note, and his defiance reasserted itself. The note first ended with "God and the Mexican Federation." He crossed that out and wrote, "God and Texas."

Santa Anna would not see Jameson. He responded

through a Col. Don Jose Batres, who wrote,

> As the Aide-de-Camp of his Excellency, the President of
> the Republic, I reply to you that the Mexican army cannot
> come to terms under any conditions with rebellious foreign-
> ers to whom there is no other recourse left, if the wish to
> save their lives, than to place themselves immediately at the
> disposal of the Supreme Government from whom alone they
> may expect clemency after some considerations are taken
> up. God and Liberty.

Jameson returned to the Alamo. Now it was Travis's turn to
be offended, not so much at the Mexicans but at Bowie for
opening negotiations without consulting with him first. Travis
picked Albert Martin as his messenger. Martin was a twenty-
eight-year-old Rhode Islander who had run a general store in
Gonzales. He had been at the battle of Gonzales and the first
battle of San Antonio. Martin walked out the gate and met with
Col. Juan Almonte on a small bridge near Potrero Street.
Almonte was getting a workout that day for he spoke fluent
English, having been schooled in the United States. Earlier he
had translated for Jameson. Almonte declined Travis's invita-
tion to meet with him personally, saying, "I answered that it
did not become the Mexican Government to make any propo-
sitions through me, and that I had only permission to hear
such as might be made on the part of the rebels." The two men
parted, each heading back to their respective camps.

Almonte would survive the battle to be captured at San
Jacinto. Because of his fluency in English, he was included in
the small group of officers who accompanied Santa Anna to
the United States after the battle of San Jacinto. He returned
to Mexico with Santa Anna in 1837. Almonte later was made
a general, entering the diplomatic service holding posts in
Brussels and Washington. He served as secretary of war during the Mexican-American War and then returned to diplomacy. Disgusted with politics in Mexico, he promoted foreign
intervention that resulted in French involvement and the
placement of Maximilian on the Mexican throne. In 1862 he
landed with French troops at Veracruz. Maximilian named

him envoy to France and he died in Paris in 1869 at the age of sixty-six.

Travis responded to Almonte's dismissal of his proposal with another shot from the eighteen-pounder. There would be no more attempts at diplomacy. The Mexicans settled in for the night to begin siege operations in the morning. The 150 Texans closed the gates of their undefendable fortress.

Travis and Bowie adjourned to iron out the command structure and it took care of itself when Bowie collapsed, totally. It was never confirmed, but Bowie probably had pneumonia, tuberculosis, or typhoid fever. His earlier drinking binge certainly didn't help his condition. Whatever the disease or cause, Bowie realized he was contagious and went into quarantine after informing his men on the morning of February 24 that he was turning his command over to Travis. He was carried to a small room near Dr. Pollard's infirmary, where he was attended by Andrea Castanon Ramirez Villanueva, a faith healer using Spanish and Indian medicines.

The Mexicans started the siege work. Siege strategy was well established in 1836 and the Alamo presented no real problem to Santa Anna's engineers. There were no natural obstacles such as a river or cliffs. There was little in the way of man-made obstacles, Jameson's plans notwithstanding. There was no moat, no drawbridge, and no chance of flaming oil being poured over the fort's walls onto the attackers. All the engineers had to do was get enough cannon close enough to the Alamo to pound it into submission. And the defenders could not waste ammunition, as they had little to spare. The eighteen-pounder alone used twelve pounds of powder every time it was fired.

The Mexican engineers dug a gun position on the banks of the river four hundred yards from the walls of the Alamo, a very extreme rifle range but close enough for the Mexican artillery, and they opened up with two nine-pounders in the early afternoon. The Mexicans kept up their fire throughout the day, but the Texans somehow suffered no killed or wounded.

Travis wrote another note to the government and the world. Albert Martin was the courier. In his most famous message, Travis finally dropped the illusion that Texans were fighting for the Mexican constitution with the salutation, "To the People of Texas and All Americans in the World." He also dropped any further reference to Bowie, writing,

Commandancy of the Alamo
Bexar, Feby 24th, 1836

To the People of Texas and All Americans in the World—
Fellow Citizens and Compatriots:
   I am besieged with a thousand or more of the Mexicans under Santa Anna. I have sustained a continual Bombardment and cannonade for 24 hours and have not lost a man. The enemy has demanded surrender at discretion, otherwise, the garrison is to be put to the sword, if the fort is taken. I have answered the demand with a cannon shot, and our flag still waves proudly from the wall. I shall never surrender or retreat. Then, I call on you in the name of Liberty, of patriotism, and everything dear to the American character, to come to our aid with all dispatch. The enemy is receiving reinforcements and will no doubt increase to three or four thousand in four or five days. If this call is neglected I am determined to sustain myself as long as possible and die like a soldier who never forgets what is due his honor and that of his country.

VICTORY OR DEATH.
William Barret Travis
LT. COL. COMD'T.

No matter what mistakes Travis made in strategy or command, no one reading these words can doubt his bravery.

Travis picked Martin to be the messenger because Martin, like Dr. Sutherland, was wounded. He had cut himself badly with an ax a few days prior while cutting wood and wasn't 100 percent. Travis was keeping his healthy men in the fort. Martin snuck easily through the lines, as the Mexicans had not completed their noose, and rode for Gonzales, passing the note to Lancelot Smither. Martin joined the last group of men leaving Gonzales for the Alamo and would die at the Alamo.

Smither, also a courier and recent Alamo defender, added

his thoughts and wrote on the note, "I hope everyone will Rendevu at Gonzales as soon as poseble as the Brave Soldiers are suffereing do not neglect the powder. is very scarce and should not be delad one moment."

Smither gave a summary to Andrew Ponton at Gonzales then rode through a blinding rainstorm to San Felipe with the original. The letter was transcribed and printed in the local newspapers. The original is believed to have been turned over to Travis's daughter, who passed it on to her daughter, who passed it on to her son, John G. Davidson. Davidson loaned it to the state then offered to sell it outright for $250 as a result of personal money problems. That was too much for the state of Texas, but the two parties eventually agreed on $85. The note remains in the custody of the Texas State Library and Historical Commission in Austin.

The siege continued with the Mexican guns growing closer every day. Feints were made from the fort, but the trenches of the Mexicans snaked toward the walls. The progress had one benefit for the Texans: it brought the sappers and gunners within range of the Texan rifles and marksmen picked off dozens of the Mexicans. Dozens didn't matter to Santa Anna and the work continued. The cannon hammered a breach in the east wall on March 5.

During the thirteen days of the siege, the major activity inside the Alamo was trying not to get hit by cannon fire while shoring up the crumbling defenses. A group from Gonzales, including Albert Martin, was able to fight their way into the Alamo but they numbered only thirty-two. James Bonham made a number of trips in and out carrying desperate messages. The last message he carried back to the Alamo was from Three Legged Willie Williamson urging the men to hold, reinforcements were on the way. Bonham probably knew that the Alamo was doomed but he returned anyway. He is believed to have died manning the cannon on the earthen ramp in the chapel of the Alamo.

On March 3, 1836, Travis sent his last message to the government. He had correctly given up on Fannin and concluded, as in previous messages, that "their threats have had no influence on me, or my men, but to make all fight with desperation, and that high souled courage which characterizes the patriot, who is willing to die in defence of his country's liberty and his own honor."

In the Mexican camp, time was dragging. Santa Anna, having made the decision to revenge Cos, was wasting time and he knew it. His intelligence network told him there was no organized resistance except at Goliad. Every day wasted at San Antonio was a day not spent pushing the Anglos toward the Sabine and out of Texas for good.

Santa Anna gathered his generals. They were split, with one side wanting to attack immediately. The other generals urged Santa Anna to wait for the heavy guns to arrive and pound the Alamo into total submission. The cannon assault would reduce Mexican casualties. Not surprisingly, Santa Anna wasn't concerned about casualties, ordering the assault for the early morning of March 6, 1836. The attack order read:

> The honor of the nation being concerned in this engagement against the lawless foreigners who oppose us. His Excellency expects every man to do his duty and exert to allow the county a day of glory, and gratification to the Supreme Government, who will know how to reward distinguished deeds by the brave soldiers of the Army of Operations.

There was no apology to Lord Nelson for stealing the "England expects every man to do his duty" line and substituting "His Excellency" for "England."

Less than two thousand men, all veterans, would make the attack. It would be a classic attack—columns advancing under fire, storming the walls with ladders, and the defenders being overrun and defeated by the sheer weight of numbers. Those defenders not killed in the initial attack would be hunted down with bayonet. The real Napoleon would have approved, even with the lack of bombardment and the inability to utilize the cavalry except to hunt down any defenders who fled into the open field.

The officers were aware of the damage a rifle bullet could do. Cos had seen the effectiveness of this weapon in the first battle, and the battle of New Orleans, more than twenty years earlier, had been won by some of these Texans or their fathers when they directed their fire from behind cotton bales into the oncoming British columns trapped in a narrow killing field south of the city. The entrenched Americans killed seven hundred British soldiers (including the Duke of Wellington's brother-in-law, Maj. Gen. Edward Pakenham) and wounded two thousand. But the British didn't have ladders and the Mexicans did. The plan was simple: endure the fire, get up the ladders, overrun the defenders, and secure victory.

Cos was ordered to strike the northwest corner of the fortress. Col. Francisco Duque would attack the northeast corner. Colonel Romero and three hundred men would attack the east wall while Colonel Morales and his small group of only one hundred soldiers attacked the palisade. One hundred men should have been able to breach the wooden wall easily. Santa Anna would keep four hundred men—engineers and grenadiers—in reserve under his command.

The attack was set for 4:00 A.M. Ladders, crowbars, and axes were distributed during the day and night before the attack, bayonets sharpened, and muskets checked for flint and fire. One officer, in his diary, asked why "Santa Anna always wants to mark his triumphs with blood and tears?" The troops were moved into their jumping-off positions between seven and ten o'clock the night before the attack. They were instructed to sleep; maybe some did. At midnight the officers and noncommissioned officers started moving, waking their soldiers. The officers drew the men into formation and did an inspection to make sure the weapons were as they should be, the ladders distributed, axes sharp—anything to make the time go faster.

Sometime in the night Travis wrote one last message, giving it to twenty-year-old Jim Allen. The gate opened in the darkness and Allen raced out on his way to Goliad to beg Fannin for help. Allen was the last defender to leave the Alamo alive. He would fight at San Jacinto as a scout with "Deaf" Smith, become a Texas Ranger, serve as mayor of Indianola, and raise cattle and farm. He lived to be eighty-six years old, dying at his farm near Yoakum, Texas, on April 25, 1901.

At midnight, Santa Anna drank coffee in his house on the main plaza. At one o'clock the four Mexican columns started moving into their final positions. At two o'clock Santa Anna arrived at his headquarters accompanied by a servant, Ben, a former American slave, and Colonel Almonte. More coffee. Colonel Almonte noted that it would be a costly battle, with Santa Anna responding, "It doesn't matter what the cost is; it must be done."

By three o'clock, the attackers had approached to within two hundred yards of the walls. Only silence emanated from the Alamo, though Travis and his men were awake, taking advantage of the lull in the bombardment to repair what damage they could. At four o'clock Santa Anna took up position in a battery on the north side of the complex with his reserves.

Travis took time to visit the women and children huddled in the small rooms the size of prison cells running the interior walls of the chapel. Starting to leave, he stopped and removed from his finger a heavy gold ring with a black cat's eye stone in the center. He looped it on a piece of string and put it around the neck of Dickinson's daughter, Angelina. The ring is now on display in the Alamo museum. Travis left, inspected the walls one last time, and ordered the men to get some sleep. He went to his headquarters and fell asleep with his sword, double-barreled shotgun, and servant, Joe, by his side. Capt. John Baugh, officer of the watch, walked the north wall.

At five o'clock the Mexican troops could take the silence no longer. A single cheer rang out, another, and then the whole army was cheering. Santa Anna finally ordered the signal given, and Jose Maria Gonzalez, a bugler in the corps of engineers, brought the men to attention. The soldiers lying two hundred yards outside the walls of the Alamo rose like ghosts.

The Texans had placed at least three pickets outside the walls in holes in the ground to sound the alert. They never did. Capt. John Baugh was the first to see, or hear, the Mexicans outside the north wall, and he raced for the barracks, yelling, "Colonel Travis! The Mexicans are coming!" Travis was jolted awake. He and his servant, Joe, grabbed their weapons, rushing to the north wall to the battery named Fortin de Teran. Running across the plaza, Travis yelled to his men, "Come on, boys! The Mexicans are upon us and we'll give them Hell." He slung his coat over a peg by a cannon and shouted encouragement in Spanish to Seguin's men, all Mexican.

The men of Cos's and Duque's command raced for the wall, now looming ten feet above them. The north wall was the weak point in the Alamo defense, seconded by the wooden palisade gap on the south side defended by Crockett. The north wall had no parapet so the defenders had piled dirt on the inside of the wall, making a ramp up to the cannon. The defenders ran up the ramp to the wall. At the top they were exposed, for there was no upper wall to protect them as they fired down upon the attackers.

Mexican soldiers raced through the grapeshot and gunfire. Colonel Duque was hit in the leg by grapeshot and nearly trampled. Even underfoot he yelled, urging his men forward. Those who made it to the wall found shelter since the cannon could not be depressed to hit them. Defenders, including Travis with his shotgun, fired into them but it was nothing compared to the sawed-up horseshoes and nails that had been fired from the cannon.

While firing down into the mass, Travis was killed. A musket ball found its mark, hitting Travis squarely in the forehead. The musket balls, slightly less than three-quarters of an inch in diameter, sometimes would merely bounce off a target, human or otherwise, if fired at range. This bullet did not and Travis was spun around by the impact. His shotgun fell from his hands and he fell backwards, rolling down the earthen ramp running up to the wall. He raised himself into a sitting position near a cannon. Joe reported that Travis was still conscious and strong enough to run a Mexican officer through with his sword before he died.

Joe raced for the barracks and hid in a small room while the battle raged for the next half-hour. He waited while the firing ceased, to be replaced by patrolling Mexicans looking for survivors to kill after the battle. An officer went through the fortress asking, "Are there any Negroes here?" Joe said, "Yes, here is one." A soldier took a shot at Joe and another wounded him slightly with a bayonet before the officer could stop them. The officer grabbed Joe, marching him off to see Santa Anna.

While Joe hid, at the north wall Travis lay dead. More attackers tried to gain the sanctuary of the wall. Some did but most did not, as the cannons continued to rip apart the lines that were still in the killing zone. The Toluca battalion and the Aldama battalion fell back. Regrouping, they charged again and again fell back under the withering firepower of the grapeshot. Regrouping, they charged one more time.

To the right, on the east wall, the Matamoros battalion under Colonel Romero also was pushed back—not exactly pushed back but forced to their right, intermingling with Duque's command, the Toluca battalion—in their initial attack. On the left side Cos and his column were being forced leftward toward Duque in the middle. The columns disappeared, the battalions mixing together to form a mob that could not go backward. Sergeants and noncommissioned officers were placed around the soldiers to pen the men in and force them forward.

Less than 190 men defending a space covering more than three acres cannot hold back a mob. Surging forward, running the gauntlet of grapeshot and rifle fire, more and more Mexicans gained the sanctuary below the walls. They remained under the fire of the riflemen, but the cannon could not touch them.

The biggest threat to them was now friendly fire as the soldiers behind them fired at the walls. Any musket ball or cannon shot that didn't hit the fort had a very good chance of hitting one of them. There was also a shortage of ladders because many were dropped and discarded during the initial attacks and retreats. But soldiers and officers started finding weak spots, even undefended spots, as there were not enough men to defend every foot of the walls. The Texans flocked to the weak spots, opening up even more weak spots.

To Santa Anna in his barricade, the attack appeared stalled.

He sent in his reserves, including many surprised staff officers who had not anticipated being asked to join in the fighting. The band played the "Deguello," the word meaning throat slitting or beheading, and the tune meaning no quarter.

The reserves charged. Many soldiers started climbing the walls stone by stone. Some climbed up a wooden redoubt in the east wall with many falling backward after reaching the top and a defender. But the wave of soldiers kept coming. The sergeants and junior officers pushed, knowing that it was advance or die. Gen. Juan V. Amador went up the wall and directed the Texan cannon turned inward on the compound.

Cos was able to extricate most of his men from the mob and ordered them to turn and attack the west wall. The wall was more formidable here, but the Texans had cut holes in the wall to fire their cannon rather than placing the cannon on top of the wall. The Mexicans clawed their way into the fort through the holes. The first through were killed by the Texans but the tide could not be stopped. Racing across the plaza the first Mexicans in threw open the main gate and troops flooded into the plaza.

Texans caught in the plaza fought back fiercely with rifle butts, knives, and axes but they were soon overwhelmed, trampled, and bayoneted by the Mexican horde. Susannah Dickinson huddled in the small room in the chapel with her daughter, a slave girl, and the women, boys, and girls of the Mexican families, no more than thirty in all. A young acquaintance from Gonzales, Gabriel Fuqua, ran in, wounded by a shot that had crushed his jaw. He tried to talk but could not and returned to the fight.

Dickinson's husband, Capt. Almeron Dickinson, was able to reach his wife and he told her, "Great God, Sue, the Mexicans are inside our walls. If they spare you, save my child." A hug and he was off to join Bonham at the cannon at the top of the ramp in the chapel. The Texans, as well as the Mexicans, were turning the cannon inward and firing grapeshot. They couldn't miss.

At the palisade Crockett and his men fought off their attackers while the north wall collapsed. The men at the palisade fought alone, too far from the barracks that Travis had designated as the location for the last stand. The other defenders fell back and into the barracks. Mexican sergeant Felix Nunez, as quoted in Walter Lord's *A Time to Stand,* describes one of the palisade's defenders.

> He was a tall American of rather dark complexion and had on a long buckskin coat and a round cap without any bill, made out of fox skin with a long tail hanging down his back. This man apparently had a charmed life. Of the many soldiers who took deliberate aim at him and fired, not one ever hit him. On the contrary, he never missed a shot. He killed at least eight of our men, besides wounding several others. This being observed by a lieutenant who had come in over the wall, he sprang at him and dealt him a deadly blow with his sword, just above the right eye, which felled him to the ground, and in an instant he was pierced by not less than 20 bayonets.

The massacre was on as the Mexicans closed. The Texans fired back but the mob overran the building and hunted them down. Some certainly died fighting; some certainly died cowering and begging for mercy. Susannah Dickinson told of one man—some said it was Bowie, but he was identified by Dickinson as Jacob Walker—hoisted aloft on the bayonets of the Mexicans. Others, especially those near the palisade, ran away from the Alamo to be hunted down in the open prairie by Mexican lancers. Bowie was reported both to have been too exhausted to resist and to have killed two soldiers before being run through with swords. He was certainly shot many times, either alive or dead, as Dr. Jack Shackelford later described the walls in Bowie's room as blood spattered. Davy Crockett either died going down swinging or surrendering and then being cut down by the swords of officers on the direct order of Santa Anna. To the American press, Crockett went down swinging. In his memoirs, Col. Jose de la Pena says Crockett surrendered and was then executed.

It doesn't really matter. An indefensible fortress manned by little more than 180 men had fallen to a vastly superior force totaling 6,000. The bodies were gathered and burned but not before Santa Anna was shown the corpses of Bowie, Crockett, and Travis.

Assessments of the battle range from insignificant to comparisons with Thermopylae of Marathon fame. Casualty estimates for the Mexican army ranged upward of sixteen hundred killed but the most realistic estimate is six hundred killed and wounded. As many of the wounded would die from nonexistent medical care, the number is not insignificant, being 10 percent of the total army and one-third of the attacking force.

Alamo debates occupy books, legends, and movies. Theories come and go, from the valiant, fighting backwoodsmen to the cowards awaiting their fate in some corner of the Alamo. Davy Crockett, James Bowie, and William Travis are either heroes or buffoons or both. Santa Anna remains in character and is rarely rehabilitated.

Without question, the Alamo resulted in a rallying cry, a cry that united the people, the army, and the government: "Remember the Alamo."

Soon they would have another: "Remember Goliad."

Chapter 7

Goliad and Fannin

"He got into a fight in West Point and left school, returning to Georgia where he married. Then he went to Texas, where he lost his life."

With the fall of the Alamo was born the cry "Remember the Alamo." "Remember Goliad" would soon follow. Sometimes the cry was "Remember La Bahia," for Goliad is the town, the fort is La Bahia. The fort was built to protect the nearby missions of Rosario and Espiritu Santo.

Today Goliad is a tiny town a little more than one hundred miles southeast of San Antonio with a population slightly more than two thousand. The town is north of the Mission Espiritu Santo by about a mile, and the fort lies another mile south of the mission on the road to Copana Bay. Running past the fort is the San Antonio River. The mission and the fort are owned and operated by the Catholic Church, directly operated by the Catholic Diocese of Victoria, Texas. Both the church and the fort were founded at their current location in 1749.

In 1721 the Spanish had built a new fort on the ruins of La Salle's Fort St. Louis, overlooking the Matagorda Bay. It would have various names but was popularly known as the Presidio La Bahia. La Bahia, meaning the bay, is short for La Bahia del Espiritu Santo, the Bay of the Holy Spirit. The Spaniards had named the Mississippi River the Rio del Espiritu Santo and anything close by was affiliated by name. (The Spanish, and any other explorers of the time, had trouble with east-west navigation because latitude had been invented but not longitude. They could find something while traveling to the east or west, but it was very difficult pinpointing it on the north-south axis. Thus they granted similar names to locations within a region to denote their proximity.) The fort was moved inland for health and climate reasons at least twice but retained the name although it was no longer near any bay. By the end of the eighteenth century, La Bahia was one of the three largest and most important Spanish outposts in Texas, along with Nacogdoches and San Antonio de Bexar.

In the late 1700s garrisons stationed at La Bahia would go forth to battle English and French expeditions. Troops from the fort joined the forces of Gen. Bernardo de Galvez in operations against British forces in Louisiana and Florida in the American Revolution. The town of Galveston is named for Galvez. By 1758 the fort had been strengthened from wood and mud to stone and mortar, while the Mission Espiritu Santo started the first large cattle ranch in Texas, reporting fifteen thousand branded head of cattle in 1778. Like all things in Texas at the time, La Bahia was a backwater to the Spanish, who were having more trouble elsewhere.

The revolt of 1810 by Father Hidalgo impacted La Bahia and more importantly, the nearby village, which later would take its name from an anagram for Hidalgo. The filibuster by Hidalgo's fellow revolutionary Augustus W. Magee, the disgruntled U.S. Army officer who organized the Gutierrez expedition out of New Orleans, resulted in their capture of the fort. The Royalists responded with a four-month siege, Magee died from suicide or disease, and Samuel Kemper took command. Kemper broke the siege, chasing the Royalists to San Antonio. As noted, General Arredondo defeated the rebel forces at the Medina River, slaughtering the prisoners with the assistance of a young officer, Antonio Lopez de Santa Anna.

The revolution split the community of Goliad, with things settling back down after the Royalists squashed the rebellion. The events of the Mexican Revolution then unfolded, followed by the battle of Gonzales and the fall of the Alamo, twice.

The roots of the Goliad campaign began with the end of the Matamoros expedition on March 2, 1836. Dr. Grant was killed at, or soon after, the battle of Agua Dulce Creek. Colonel Johnson fled for his life from San Patricio. Santa Anna had the Alamo under siege, and General Urrea and his six hundred troops were now as far north as Refugio, only twenty-five miles south of Goliad, with scouts roaming the countryside gathering intelligence. Urrea's target was Goliad.

With the death of Grant, the number of contenders for commander in chief in the Texans' military structure was reduced to three—Houston, Johnson, and Fannin. With his narrow escape at San Patricio, Colonel Johnson was now just happy to be alive and not inclined to press his claim as commander in chief. He dropped out of site, only resurfacing after the battle of San Jacinto. He settled near San Jacinto, married, abandoned his wife, and returned to marry her again after she divorced the man she had married after Johnson left. He was not successful in land or mine deals but did become a historian of the Texas Revolution late in life. He died at the age of eighty-three while on a research trip to Mexico. After a few years his body was returned to Texas, the Texas Veterans Association having raised enough money to pay for shipment.

With the failure of the Matamoros expedition, the death of Grant, the disappearance of Johnson, and the proximity of Urrea, Fannin waited at Goliad, unsure of what to do.

Fannin is an enigma, a man of action but lacking a great deal of insight and luck. There is little history about him or his background, but there is considerable confusion regarding his parentage, education, wealth, even the spelling of the family name.

The original family name was Fanning, and the name change came about as a result of friction between family members. The Fannings were a prominent family in the south for a century before the American Revolution. At the beginning of the revolution, Edmund Fanning was a lawyer in North Carolina and a personal friend of Gov. William Tyron. Governor Tyron was a Tory, loyal to the monarchy, and Edmund's brother, James W. Fanning, was a revolutionary. The two brothers went to war on opposite sides. When the British surrendered, Edmund fled to Canada. He reached the rank of lieutenant general in the British army, serving as governor of Prince Edward Island for nineteen years. James W.

Fanning moved to Georgia after the war to become a wealthy plantation owner. James burned with patriotism for his young country. To disassociate himself from his equally successful but Tory brother, he dropped the "g" from Fanning, reducing the name to Fannin.

James W. Fannin died in 1802, leaving numerous offspring, one being Isham S. Fannin. Isham, a successful plantation owner, had an illicit relationship with the daughter of an employee on his brother's plantation, which resulted in the birth of James W. Fannin, Jr. in or around 1804 or 1805. Isham married Margaret Potter in 1809, having a daughter, Eliza, born near the time of Isham's death in 1817, five years after his participation in the War of 1812 as a major in the milita. Both James W. Fannin, Jr. and his half-sister, Eliza, were present at their father's deathbed.

Now things become more confusing. Isham did not raise James Walker Fannin, Jr. He was raised by his maternal grandfather, James W. Walker. As a result, James Walker Fannin, Jr. took for some time the name James Fannin Walker.

Regardless of who raised the boy, the illegitimacy did not seem to cause this extended family a large amount of distress, as James stayed close with his half-sister and appears to have had a loving relationship with his grandfather, James W. Walker. He also respected his father even though Isham did not raise him. In a letter to Eliza written after their father's death and after James had children of his own, he notes, "Can I, who knows a father's anxieties and witnessed this scene [his dying father], remember this and what he's done for me (which but few fathers would have done), not feel some solicitude for the object nearest his heart?"

The fact that he was illegitimate did not keep young Fannin out of West Point. The military background of his father and grandfather may have helped. If so, he did not readily acknowledge the Fannin side of the family, instead entering West Point on July 1, 1819, at the age of fourteen as James Fannin Walker.

The records at West Point reveal a cadet who attended the academy for two years but never made it out of the freshman class. In his first year he was sixty-second out of eighty-six cadets in mathematics, fifty-seventh in French, and sixtieth in "General Merit." In his second year he was flunking French, which put him back in the freshman class. His academic performance was not great, but some other cadets like George Custer and Ulysses S. Grant would have similar records.

The cause for leaving West Point is not clear. A cousin, Martha Fannin, in a memoir to her children wrote, "He got into a fight in West Point and left school, returning to Georgia where he married. Then he went to Texas, where he lost his life." She describes him physically as "splendid and handsome." Despite the family's account, there is no record of a fight at West Point. Academy archives include a letter from a cousin noting the ill health of the maternal grandfather and grandmother so perhaps Fannin considered it to be a family emergency requiring his presence. The superintendent does not indicate a reason for dismissal or withdrawal, writing simply, "I have the honor to enclose the resignation of Cadets James E. Walker of Georgia and Cyrus Canon and recommend that they be accepted to take effect on the 30th of November." The year was 1821. Never getting past his freshman year, Fannin did not absorb a great deal of military engineering, infantry or artillery training, or strategy. Fannin would find out, however, that in 1835 Texas, having West Point on your resume could get you a long way.

Dropping out of West Point, Fannin moved back to Georgia, probably farming or managing plantations. Little is known of his life in this period except that he moved twice and in 1828 was in Columbus, Georgia. There he met and married Minerva Fort. Their first daughter, Missouri Pinkney, was born in 1829. Now with a family to support, Fannin strove for respectability and standing, and the symbol for prosperity at that time was land. He got his land in 1832 at the expense of the Cherokees when their land went into a lottery upon their expulsion from Cherokee territory. A second daughter, Minerva, was born in that year. Minerva was severely mentally ill and her life ended in a Texas asylum.

Land ownership may have meant respectability but the real cash flow was in humans, the slave trade, and Fannin, with a wife and two small children, needed cash. In April 1832, he was in the port of Charleston, South Carolina, waiting for a packet ship to take him to Havana. He describes the situation in a letter to his half-sister, Eliza. He writes her that he is sailing to Havana for a cargo of sugar and that he will "keep a vessel in the trade." He promised her he would sail for New York in the summer and visit her in New Haven, Connecticut, where she was attending boarding school.

The "sugar" was slaves, but he did not want to reveal that fact to his younger half-sister. The United States allowed the practice of slavery but had banned the importation of new slaves in 1808. Rules that are illogical—allowing the practice but not allowing for the labor to run the practice—are very often broken, and the illegal slave trade was doing its business out of the Mexican territory of Texas. The Mexicans skirted their rules against slavery by having the slaves "sign" one-hundred-year work contracts.

Details are scarce as to Fannin's trading activities. It is also not clear when he first entered Texas, but it is known that he made a trip with a small cargo of slaves to the mouth of the Brazos River in June 1834. The trip started on May 26 in Havana, where Fannin bought the schooner *Crawford* for five thousand dollars, paying for the ship by drawing on a draft of E. W. Gregory of New Orleans. The original of the draft was recorded in Brazoria County, Texas, and notes the actual owners of the ship being two men named Thompson and Henshaw of New Orleans. The draft noted,

> It is to sail from Havana on June 12, coming with a cargo of 16 free negroes which is shown and made manifest by the oath of James W. Fanning, Jr., before the United States consul at Havana, together with some two or three gentlemen passengers for the port or roadstead of the Brassos in the Province of Texas on the coast of Mexico, where the blacks are to be landed and the schooner is to proceed at once for New Orleans.

Fannin was to pay for the ship in New Orleans. Apparently

he did not net enough from the slave sale because in August he was in Mobile, Alabama, writing to Thompson to ask for an extension on the debt and assure Thompson he had more sales in the works. If the future sales were not enough to cover the debt, he offered to sell Thompson a pack of mules.

Thompson went along with the extension then and again in September 1835. Fannin wrote Thompson from Texas that he had been "ill—nay, nearly dead." He assured Thompson that he was much better, and "I have since made a good trip, having brought for myself and others 152 negroes in May last [1835], but then can not realize any cash for them until March or April, when you shall be fully paid every cent I owe you. You need not be concerned about the present state of affairs in Texas. There is no serious danger for us." No prediction could have ever been so wrong. By April, Fannin would be dead.

He finished his letter to Thompson with "Tho' we may have to fight some little—but success will certainly follow our efforts. . . . I am settled on Caney Creek, midway between Brazoria and Matagorda."

Thompson wasn't the only one Fannin had borrowed money from, with one historian noting that Fannin had a "leaky pen." Portions of his debt dated back to 1828 in Georgia. In April 1835, Fannin was arrested in New Orleans for owing Theopholus Hyde three thousand dollars and had to borrow fifteen hundred dollars from a man named Kenan to procure his release. Kenan would file a claim against Fannin's administrator for the fifteen hundred dollars and other debts. An additional note covered gambling losses.

Before leaving for war, Fannin entered into one final Texas business deal, a farming partnership with Joseph Mims of Brazoria. Fannin was on the hook for $25,000, of which he funded $17,250—not in cash but in slaves. The remaining $7,750 was to be paid in cash in five equal installments with the proviso that "should the tranquillity of the country authorize it, said Fannin is at liberty to pay the whole of said debt in negroes at fair valuation." The "tranquillity of the country" did not materialize.

In the summer of 1835, Austin landed in Texas after his

release from Mexico and spoke at a banquet at the mouth of the Brazos. Fannin attended. Inspired by Austin's speech and the rumor that Cos had landed at Copano Bay below Goliad and was on his way to San Antonio, Fannin put forth the idea of raising a mounted brigade. The brigade would swoop down and destroy Cos and his command near Goliad. Fannin sent riders out on the plain and up and down the coast to spread the word to recruit volunteers. No recruits materialized and the idea was dropped.

Instead, Fannin gathered a small company christened the Brazos Guard and in October 1835 marched them to Gonzales. The exact number of men in the guards at the "Come and Take It" battle is not known, but Fannin's presence was noted. He and other Texans taunted the Mexicans across the Guadalupe River. After the battle, Fannin was made Captain Fannin of the Brazos Guard.

The victory over the Mexicans at Gonzalez led to the campaign against San Antonio, with Fannin and the guard joining Col. Jim Bowie at the battle of Mission Concepion. Even though Bowie and Fannin argued over strategy and tactics with Bowie prevailing, Fannin became known in some circles as the "Hero of Concepion."

From Gonzales to San Antonio, James Walker Fannin, Jr. had made a great amount of progress in becoming a force in Texas military and political circles. This is even more remarkable given that less then nine months before he had been under arrest for bad debts. He was now linked to Jim Bowie as a result of Mission Concepion and had come in third in the voting for regimental commander in San Antonio, losing out to Edward Burleson. Fannin received 13 percent of the votes. He traded correspondence with Austin and Houston and was on the par, he thought, with Bowie.

In a letter to Fannin dated November 13, Houston offered Fannin the post of inspector general in the regular army. Fannin responded on November 18. While not declining the administrative post, he bargained.

> I would prefer a command in the line. . . . Having elected one Maj Gen—Will they not also make two Brig Genls? If so,

would not my claims be equal to any other? If I can get either—I would prefer it—and I respectfully request your influence for one—otherwise I will accept of the appointment you tender me, provided I can have furlough, to bring on my family, in case I am not required in the field—.

Fannin cannot be accused of shyness in asking to be made a brigadier general, quite a step up from captain. Houston did not respond to the request for promotion or the furlough.

Undaunted, Fannin wrote to Austin and received more than just a furlough.

Head Quarters before
Bexar Nov. 22, 1835
    Capt. J. W. Fannin having represented to me that the absolute necessity of returning home, I have granted to him an honorable discharge and have to say that he has uniformly discharged his duty as a soldier and as an officer.
S. F. Austin
Comdr. In Chief

Just before the first battle for San Antonio and the Alamo, Fannin left for his home in Brazoria. At home he wrote a memo to Governor Smith outlining a Texas army of the future based along the same lines as the United States Army. While the proposal was orderly and well planned, it didn't catch the attention of Smith, who had his hands full with the politics and confusion emanating from the Grand Council. Fighting impeachment was more important to Smith than planning for the army of the future. However, one fan of the plan was William Barret Travis, who wrote to Smith and the General Council, "I approve cheerfully the views and reasoning on the subject of the Regular Army, expressed in the Communication of Capt. J.W. Fannin."

In the meantime Cos surrendered San Antonio in December 1835. The focus of the council now changed to consider Fannin's army, or at least recognize that an army, whether regular, volunteer, or a mix, was needed. Everyone knew Santa Anna wasn't going to let the fall of the Alamo and the disgrace of Cos pass, although they did not think anything would happen until at least April—March at the earliest. Armies didn't march in the winter.

On December 10, 1835, the Grand Council issued a call for Texans to establish an army to defend Texas against the armies of Santa Anna. The call included Fannin.

> Be it further resolved, that J. W. Fannin, junior, and Thomas J. Rusk be appointed, and they are hereby appointed by the General Council aforesaid, forthwith to proceed, the one upon the east side of the Trinity, the other upon the west side, for the purpose of collecting reinforcements, and have them enrolled for service. . . .
>
> J. W. Fannin, jr., and Thomas J. Rusk, be and are hereby constituted agents or contractors for supplying ammunitions, provisions and other necessaries for carrying into effect these resolutions, and they or either of them are hereby vested with full powers, to purchase any and all articles necessary for said volunteers. . . .
>
> Be it further resolved, that the preceding report and resolutions be printed and circulated throughout Texas.

The orders did not include brigadier general rank for Fannin. The position was more like chief recruiting and logistics officer. He was made a colonel and addressed as such—he was referred to as Col. J. W. Fannin, Jr., First Regiment Artillery—in an order from Houston dated December 20 directing Fannin to "upon receipt of this proceed without delay to Matagorda" to establish a recruiting headquarters. In addition, Fannin was instructed to form an officers' corps to be ready by March 1, 1836.

Fannin began his recruiting with the Georgia Guards under William Ward upon their arrival in Texas. The Georgia Guards were natives of Fannin's home state. On November 10, 1835, a rally had been held in Macon, Georgia, as a fundraiser and recruiting opportunity for the formation of the unit to go to the aid of Texas liberty. Twenty-nine men led by William Ward volunteered to go to Texas. The group voted to leave Macon on November 18, 1835, and $3,141 was raised to pay the expenses. The amount was not insignificant, exceeding

$60,000 in today's dollars. The group left on time, stopping at Columbus, Georgia, to join with another volunteer unit and then marching on to Montgomery, Alabama. It was part of the massive American immigration called for by Austin upon his return from imprisonment in Mexico.

At Columbus the volunteers were presented with a white silk flag. In the center was a single blue star. Embroidered on one side of the flag was "Liberty or Death"; on the other, "*Ubi libertas habitat, ibi nostra patria est,*" "Where liberty resides, there our country is." The flag would eventually make its way to Goliad to be raised over the presidio when word was received of the signing of the Texas Declaration of Independence. Lowered at sunset, the flag became entangled in the ropes and shredded.

The volunteers boarded ship at Montgomery for Mobile and then New Orleans. There they changed ships and set out for Velasco, at the mouth of the Brazos River. Arriving on Sunday, December 20, 1835, on the schooner *Pennsylvania,* they were greeted by a group including Austin, Branch T. Archer, William H. Wharton, and Fannin. Austin, Archer, and Wharton were going the other way, to the United States, to raise funds and supplies. Austin was ill and would be dead of heart failure within a year. Archer and Wharton were moderates, hoping Texas could attain statehood and remain part of Mexico. The mission of Austin, Archer, and Wharton is often viewed more as a way of getting them out of the decision-making process by those advocating war with Mexico than any needed mission to the United States.

When it reached Texas, the Georgia battalion was composed of three companies totaling 117 men. The rosters listed 154 names, but some men had lost their enthusiasm, deciding against the trip. The men were armed with United States rifles "borrowed" by William Ward from the arsenal of the State of Georgia.

Ward's acquisition of the rifles would have repercussions for more than 150 years. In 1855 the State of Georgia billed Texas three thousand dollars for the arms and ammunition lost at Goliad. The bill was not paid and the two states negotiated, agreeing in 1857 that Georgia would cancel the bill if and when Texas erected a suitable monument costing three thousand dollars to honor the sacrifice of William Ward and his men. Again nothing happened, until 1976, when Albany, Texas, dedicated a memorial fountain to the fallen Georgian volunteers. Albany, Texas, 375 miles from Goliad, has no historical connection to the battle site but has a sister city in Georgia. The town fulfilled the lapsed Texas promise by adding the memorial as a tourist attraction alongside its preexisting activities, which included the Fort Griffin Fandangle, an outdoor cowboy musical presented each June since 1938. The memorial was finally recognized by the Georgia General Assembly in 2005 in House Resolution 997. The only other monument to the men from Georgia is in Lawrenceville, Georgia, honoring Capt. James C. Winn and Sgt. Anthony Bates, citizens of Lawrenceville killed at Goliad. The monument honors Winn and Bates on one side. The other side of the monument honors eight citizens killed in a Creek Indian battle, also in 1836.

The Georgia recruits were realistic about their lack of military skills, making good choices in naming John S. Brooks as adjutant and Joseph M. Chadwick as sergeant major. Brooks had one year of experience in the United States Marine Corps, and Chadwick had spent two years at West Point. Fannin was recognized for his two years at West Point, and the three company leaders—Ward, Brooks, and Chadwick—wrote a joint memo hailing him.

> Be assured Sir, that a welcome from any other source, however kind or respectful, could not have given rise to prouder feelings. As Americans we hail you as the Champion of liberty, as Georgians we have you as a brother—Actuated by that inborn love of liberty and detestation of tyranny peculiar to the American character, and recently so eminently developed in you, we paused not to calculate the cost, but with arms in hand at once resolved to unite with our brethren in Texas, and share their destiny.

Fannin responded with this advice about their new country.

Engage not in the political affairs of Texas. Leave that to those who have learned. Mistrust anyone who attempts to engage you in political discussion. A residence of one year and acceptance of your headright makes you a citizen with the privilege of one. I trust that no member of the Georgian Battalion would assume these rights sooner.

They wouldn't.

The Georgia battalion was joined by the Lafayette battalions with Fannin assuming overall command as colonel of the regiment.

Put in perspective, by mid-February 1836, Santa Anna's army was at the Rio Grande beginning their crossing. They were also one day into a freezing blue norther that caught the army in the open with no protection. The blue norther turned into a blizzard, causing many soldiers and their camp followers to freeze to death, though no accurate count of the dead was taken. At Matamoros, General Urrea and his command of six hundred were on the banks of the Rio Grande consolidating and provisioning, making ready for a February 17 crossing that would take them to San Patricio and Goliad.

In the Alamo, Jim Bowie had a terrible hangover after a two-week-long drinking binge that resulted from the insult of Travis's being given command of the fort by Neill. Travis had written Governor Smith, stating, "I am unwilling to be responsible for the drunken irregularities of any man." In San Felipe the government was in chaos with Smith impeached but still acting as if he were in power. Lieutenant Governor Robinson was named acting governor, but Smith had the seal.

Sam Houston, the one man who had a realistic viewpoint on the military and political situation, had had enough. Houston knew the Matamoros expedition was extremely reckless, a military disaster in the making. He disliked the strategy of occupying fortresses like Goliad and the Alamo, for it penned up outnumbered Texans behind walls easily smashed by the Mexican army artillery. Or, if Santa Anna wished to ignore the outposts, he could go around them, dealing with them at his leisure. Houston realized that the government had no resources to feed and equip an army. Finally, Houston knew the political wrangling going on in the Grand Council was wasting time and leading nowhere. To Houston, the only chance for Texas was independence won with a mobile citizen army picking its place of battle. But no one else agreed with him, except perhaps Santa Anna. On February 14, 1836, Houston washed his hands of the affair and left to visit the Cherokee in east Texas.

Prior to marching to Refugio as part of the Matamoros expedition, Fannin had spent the month between mid-January and mid-February having his only soldiers with military backgrounds, Chadwick and Brooks, train the men for the expedition. The army waited for ships to carry them to Copano Bay and Refugio as the jumping-off point for Mexico.

The troops boarded the ships at Velasco, sailing for Copano Bay. The geography of the coast of Texas on the Gulf of Mexico is like a fan with the right-hand tip being Port Arthur and the Louisiana border. Starting left from the right-hand tip, an eighth of the way down is Galveston Bay, with Houston fifty miles inward. Velasco is another sixty miles down the coast from Galveston heading southwest. The ships hugged the coast, staying to the shallow waters to avoid the stormy gulf. They passed Port Lavaca, sailing on to Aransas Pass, the entrance to Copana Bay, where they were stopped by winds and constantly shifting sandbars that blocked the entrance to the bay. Copana Bay is two-thirds of the way down the coast from Galveston to Corpus Christie. Along the way Fannin paid for food and transportation with vouchers. He had no cash.

He was also late. Houston had made his partially successful plea to Grant and Johnson's men on January 21 at Refugio and expressed surprise that Fannin and the Georgia battalion were not present. Colonel Johnson wrote a dispatch to the General Council in late January saying he was "quite at a loss" regarding Fannin's location.

By late January, Fannin had decided that Lieutenant Governor Robinson was the main authority and addressed most of his correspondence to Robinson. In reference to the current muddled command structure, Fannin wrote, "With regard to any anticipated difficulties with the general-in-chief, you need have no sort of apprehension; I shall never make any myself." But he does allude to possible difficulties with a Houston command: "should general Houston be ready and willing to take command, and march direct ahead, and execute your orders, and the volunteers are, willing to submit to it, or a reasonable part, of them, I shall not say nay, but will do all in my power to produce harmony and concert of action, and will go forward in any, capacity." Fannin concluded with "But rest assured of one thing, I will go where you have sent me, and will do what you have ordered me, if possible."

Not everyone was convinced of Fannin's willingness to back Houston. George Washington Poe, an artilleryman serving as Houston's acting adjutant general in December 1835, was suspicious. Poe had fought at the first battle of the Alamo and held a series of commissions including captain in the volunteers and third lieutenant of an artillery regiment in the still unformed regular army. Houston referred to him as "major." On February 2, 1836, Poe wrote to Houston after hearing rumors of Colonel Johnson and Fannin replacing Houston. Poe affirmed that he and other members of the staff "do not nor will not know any other General than Sam Houston," stating, "there is no other man in Texas capable of leading an army into the field." Poe was also a Governor Smith man, telling the impeached Smith that he would follow any order from Smith even "if they are to march to the devil." Poe warned Houston, "But beware of Fannin—he is I think aiming at the highest command."

Houston didn't care about Poe's warnings or Fannin's show of support. He was already planning his trip to east Texas and the Cherokees.

Fannin arrived at Refugio, roughly thirty miles inland from Copano Bay, on February 4, 1836. Fannin was convinced he was in command and he wanted to lead the strike against Mexico; however, the command structure was still muddied with the imprecise roles of Colonel Johnson and Dr. Grant.

Adding to Fannin's problems with leading the march to Matamoros was that Johnson and Grant had already set out on their expedition and were now south at San Patricio, where they divided the command.

While Johnson and Grant were on their horse-hunting mission in the south, they left part of the command at San Patricio under Maj. Robert Morris of the New Orleans Greys. Morris received some eye-opening information from Capt. Placido Benavides. Benavides had a good intelligence network of his own and had met with the *alcalde* of Matamoros, who revealed that Santa Anna was leading two armies. The *alcalde* supplied information that the Mexican general wanted to lure the Texans down to Matamoros then skirt them and take San Antonio and Goliad. Benavides caught up with Morris at San Patricio and outlined the scheme. Morris summarized the information in a memo to Fannin dated February 6, then Benavides rode out of San Patricio, rejoining with Dr. Grant. At the battle of Agua Dulce Creek, Grant would direct Benavides to ride through the encircling Mexicans to Goliad to alert Fannin of Urrea's advance.

Benavides himself had been elected *alcalde* of Guadalupe Victoria in 1832 and reelected in 1834, so he was familiar with the politics and politicians of the region. He had sided with the Texans, assisting in training the forces that would take part in the Gonzales "Come and Take It" battle, and later joined the forces of Major Collinsworth in the initial capture of Goliad. Benavides then joined in the fight against Cos at San Antonio.

Though supporting resistance against Santa Anna, Benavides could not support total independence from Mexico. After delivering Grant's message to Fannin, he dropped out of the army and returned to Guadalupe Victoria, where he tried to avoid the war. Even there the war followed him, as he surrendered one of the Goliad survivors, Isaac Hamilton, to the Mexicans. After San Jacinto, he was shunned by the Anglos for his supposed sympathy for the Mexican cause and for turning in Hamilton. Benavides and his family fled for New Orleans, where Placido died in 1837.

For warning Morris and Fannin, Benavides is often referred to as the Paul Revere of Texas.

The message from Morris to Fannin read, "One thousand men are already on the Rio Frio" and "one thousand more on the march near the Rio Grande destined for some point of Texas." The intelligence that Benavides had acquired was extremely accurate, with Morris writing, "It is believed that an attack is intended on Goliad and Bejar simultaneously." Morris credits Benavides, writing, "This information he received from the first *alcalde* of Matamoras. He has been within 20 leagues of the city and corresponded with him." Morris goes on to present Benavides' recommendation that "troops be sent to Bejar as well as others retained in the direction and [Benavides] also assures me that Santa Anna wishes to draw the troops of Texas out to Matamoras in hopes to throw a strong force in their rear while he makes his attack on the upper part of the Colonies." Santa Anna supposedly swore that he would "Take Texas or Lose Mexico."

Fannin did not know whether this was reliable information or not, but a Mexican army on the border prior to spring certainly put a damper on the idea of invading Mexico.

Fannin was doing well in Texas. Less than a year ago he was evading arrest in the United States. Since then he had completed a large land deal, was named a captain, and was hailed as the Hero of Concepion. He had been courted by Austin and Houston and named a colonel. He had not been made a general but in some circles he was considered commander in chief, which was true in fact, if not in the record, as Houston was not on the scene. Finally, he was to command an invasion force that would free Texas and ignite rebellion in Mexico. Pretty heady stuff. Until the dispatch from Morris. If true, he and his men were square in the path of an invading army intent on his destruction. Suddenly things did not look so bright.

Chapter 8

Fortress Goliad

"Fannin was not slow to perceive the feeling coming over the men,
and it caused a corresponding depression of his mind."

The letter from Morris changed everything for Fannin. Texans were always suspicious of Mexican reports but this information looked credible. Fannin took action, dispatching a company of New Orleans Greys under Capt. William Cooke to the aid of Major Morris at San Patricio. In addition, he sent a dispatch to the Grand Council and Lieutenant Governor Robinson summarizing the Morris information.

Fannin had convinced himself that Benavides' intelligence was correct and told the council that "not the least doubt should any longer be entertained, by any friend of Texas, of the design of Santa Anna to overrun the country, and expel or exterminate every white man within its borders." He went on to add, "Apprise all our friends in the United States of our true situation, that a sufficient inducement may be held out to draw them to our standard, in this hour of trial. . . . Evince your determination to live free or perish in the ditch." The reference to the ditch would prove prophetic.

A postscript added to his dispatch noting the possibility of retreat indicated his support for Morris: "I have sent forward a reinforcement to San Patricio, to bring off the artillery and order a concentration of troops at Goliad, and shall make such disposition of my forces as to sustain Bexar and that post."

And he did not neglect politics. "I have barely time to say that an election was holden on yesterday for Colonel and Lieutenant Colonel, and that myself and Major Ward received nearly a unanimous vote."

Some people who should have known better still were not taking the Mexican threat seriously. Colonel Johnson wrote to Fannin and Robinson on February 9 arguing, even at this late date, in favor of the Matamoros campaign and urging them that if "3-4,000 men is set agst [against] Matamoras, Vital Fernandez, who commands with 800 Tamaulipas troops, will immediately join you—And the whole of the frontier Towns will immediately follow. . . Fear nothing for Bexar or Goliad or any point of Texas if an attack is made on Matamoras. . . . the true policy is to unite all your forces here, leaving small garrisons in Bexar & Goliad & proceed without delay into the interior. . . . Felisola [sic] is an old woman—& Santa Anna will not retire unless the Wigwam is in serious uproar," meaning that an attack on Mexico would force Santa Anna to withdraw out of Texas. Johnson was still under the spell of Dr. Grant and the surefire rebellion that would supposedly result in Mexico on account of the expedition. In a separate letter to Lieutenant Governor Robinson, Johnson said his report was "to prevent any undue alarm from an express forwarded to you by Col. Fanning."

Lieutenant Governor Robinson sided with Fannin.

> You will occupy such points as you may in your opinion deem most advantageous it is desirable to maintain the Mission of Refugio . . . Fortify & defend Goliad and Bexar if any opportunity fairly offers, give the enemy battle as he advances, but do not hazard much until you are reinforced as a defeat of your command would prove our ruin—all former orders given by my predecessor, Gen. Houston or myself, are so far countermanded as to render it compatible to now obey any orders you may deem Expedient—.

That seems clear enough, except Robinson added another instruction in a letter the same day that advised Fannin to "always keep in view the original objects of the campaign against the latter place [Matamoros], and dash upon it as soon as it is prudent to do so in your opinion." A set of instructions that would make perfect sense to any politician, corporate or otherwise. Retreat and disregard past orders but go for the original objective when you get the chance.

Fannin should have followed the one order that made sense: Houston's order to destroy the fortress at Goliad and retreat eastward. He did not.

There was a logistical reason for a total withdrawal as well. On February 5 the schooner *Tamaulipas,* carrying two companies of men and the majority of the army's clothing, shoes, and ammunition, smashed into a Brazos River sandbar. Salvage was attempted but much was lost or ruined. Then the *Emeline,* with her cargo of flour and corn, was lost in Matagorda Bay. Another ship with reinforcements was stopped in the Bahamas and seized by the British for piracy. The ship, the *Mattawamkeag,* was eventually released but never reached Texas. Finally, additional provisions could not be sent to Copano Bay because New Orleans insurance underwriters deemed the area, correctly, as too dangerous, insuring only goods landed at ports northeast of Copano near Matagorda. That meant provisions had to be transported overland at distances of sixty-plus miles over bad roads.

Fannin was out of Refugio and in the fortress at Goliad by February 12. A fortress doesn't make sense when the enemy can break down the walls with cannon or simply go around the site. But a fort does offer a sense of security after being out on the prairie or exposed along the coast and having received word that an army is looking for you. And Fannin knew they were out there because as early as February 7 he wrote, "It is useless to controvert the fact that our true strength and geographical situation are well known to Santa Anna." The sense of security found at La Bahia was irresistible to a man with two years of West Point experience who was being hunted by a mobile enemy. The supposed security of the fort also gave the men something to do. Fannin immediately went to work organizing his force and post.

From Refugio, Fannin brought about 250 men to Goliad. Volunteers coming from Kentucky, Alabama, and Tennessee joined him there. On February 28, Fannin reported his strength at 420 men. Upon arrival at Goliad, Fannin started sorting out the command structure, dividing the men into the First Battalion (Georgia) and the Second Battalion (Lafayette), with both together forming a regiment. A unit of Kentucky volunteers under Amon B. King and a company of Montgomery, Alabama Greys commanded by Isaac Ticknor were added to the Georgia battalion. Attached to the Greys was an artillery unit manned by Mexicans under the command of Luis Guerra. Ordered to Goliad, Luis and his men had mixed loyalties, and they quit, with some joining the Mexican army and fighting against the Texans. The Lafayette battalion consisted of the Mobile Greys, the Kentucky Mustangs, a company of the New Orleans Greys—now calling themselves, as veterans, the San Antonio Greys—Captain Shackelford's company of Alabama Red Rovers, a regular army company commanded by Captain Westover, and a company designated as the Louisville Volunteers. Fannin was colonel of the regiment and William Ward was lieutenant colonel.

The New Orleans Greys dispatched to San Patricio to reinforce Morris, Grant, and Johnson were recalled by Fannin after Grant confirmed to Cooke that he intended to continue on the expedition that would cost him his life. The Greys returned to Goliad with the intention of traveling on to the Alamo, but their plan was neglected when Fannin refused them provisions. He told them a shipment was coming in soon and they could leave upon its arrival. Until then the Greys had to stay at Goliad.

The fort then, and now, covers about three and a half acres. It is the size of the Alamo but though in disrepair, it was structurally much better as a fort, with the entire acreage enclosed by walls ranging from eight to ten feet tall and three feet thick. The walls are pierced with embrasures through which defenders could shoot without exposing themselves. Because the fort sits on a hill overlooking the San Antonio River, attackers are at a disadvantage. The main gate is on the south wall with a smaller gate on the north wall. The cathedral runs eighty-five feet along the north wall, near the secondary gate. There is a barracks on the south wall inside the fort as well as one along the east wall. The inside of the fort is mostly parade ground or plaza. There was also a jail. In 1836 additional stone buildings sat outside the walls to accommodate families of the soldiers. The main purpose of the fort was to protect Mission Espiritu Santo, which had been largely abandoned, so the people of Goliad maintained the chapel in the fort, but the fort itself was manned only intermittently and with little upkeep by the Mexicans.

Fannin and his men went to work fortifying La Bahia. But first, Fannin Anglicized the name of the fort. Collinsworth had called the place Fort Goliad and that name stuck with many but Fannin wanting a more militaristic name. Thus they set up a lottery. Fannin drew the name Fort Defiance and the two runner-ups were Fort Independence and Fort Milam, Milam being the dead hero of San Antonio.

Fannin assigned Joseph M. Chadwick, the two-year West Point man, to oversee the restoration of La Bahia. Chadwick was twenty-four years old in 1836. Born in Exeter, New Hampshire, he was admitted into the United States Military Academy on July 1, 1829, but resigned on April 30, 1831. He moved to Illinois for a few years after the academy, leaving for Texas in 1835. He traveled directly to Velasco where he joined the Georgia battalion as sergeant major because of his West Point training. At Goliad he ran for the office of regimental major but lost to Dr. Warren J. Mitchell by a vote of eighty-one to seventy-three. Fannin made him acting adjutant general and Chadwick set about improving the defenses of Fort Defiance.

He began by making a map of the fort. Copies of the map still exist detailing the site and defenses. The map was the basis for the restoration of the fort in 1963-65. Chadwick worked closely with John Sowers Brooks, the marine, in fortifying the position. Brooks and Chadwick cannot be blamed for working on something that was a waste of time. Fannin made the decision to defend Fort Defiance, and the two military men went about their work as best they could.

John Sowers Brooks was even younger than Chadwick, being only twenty-two in 1836. He was from Virginia, had worked for a newspaper, and had served eleven months in the United States Marine Corps before leaving New York for Velasco, arriving in late December 1835. He was made adjutant of the Georgia battalion until February 1835, when he became aide to Fannin, serving as chief of engineer in charge of artillery and ammunition. Brooks is noted to have "designed a half-moon to the fort" and a "machine gun" prototype consisting of sixty-eight old muskets captured by Major Collinsworth. Brooks linked them together so they could be fired all at the same time with a "single match." The device never saw combat.

A more practical addition was the "water gate," located on the north wall of the compound near the chapel. This was the closest point between fort and river. In case of a siege the men would need access to the river for water, so they dug a trench from the gate to a ravine that connected to the river. The trench had a cover for protection and could be defended by cannon fire from the wall of the fort. At each corner of the fortress, there were positions for cannon with the ability to fire to the center, right, and left. The largest of the platforms was that of the northwest corner, directly in front of the chapel. The position pointed toward the river and Mission Santo Espiritu. Fannin reported to Lieutenant Governor Robinson that there would be "nine pieces of Artillery mounted by the Ides of March."

Inside the fort, a trench was dug around the perimeter with the dirt used to thicken and reinforce the walls. Outside the fort, the men burned the *jacales,* huts made of mesquite logs with roofs made of yucca leaves, to open the lines of fire. They burned hedges and cleared undergrowth around Fort Defiance. Finally, a new blockhouse was constructed.

Supplies began to run short. New shipments were sporadic because of ships running aground and the lack of new shipping due to the New Orleans underwriters withdrawing insurance. First the corn ran out and then the salt. The men lived mostly on beef. Clothing became ragged, as most of the men had been in the field for six months, many fighting at San Antonio, without a change. Some had no shoes or boots; most footwear was in disrepair. Fannin described the situation to Robinson: "In relieving guard yesterday, the corporal marched off bare-foot. Many of the men are so naked, that only certain parts of their body are covered."

With all the digging, burning, fixing, and moving of cannon there was little military training or drilling. But there was drinking and many of the men, including officers, patronized a local cantina. The Kentucky Mustangs got their name from the antics of one drunk officer, as described by John Duval, brother of the company commander. Duval wrote:

> Not long after our arrival at Goliad the soubriquet of Mustangs or Wild Horses was acquired by our company from the following incident: M— [J. Q. Merrifield], was a man of great physical powers, but withal one of the most peaceful and most genial men when not under the influence of liquor. But occasionally he would bet on a "spree" and then he was as wild as a "March hare" and perfectly uncontrollable. The Mexicans seemed to know him and fear him, also, and when he was on one of his "benders" they would retreat into their houses as soon as they saw him and shut their doors. This proceeding, of course, was calculated to irritate M—, and he would forthwith kick the door from its hinges. On a certain occasion he battered down the doors of half a dozen houses in one street, and from that time the Mexicans called him the "Mustang," and finally the name was applied to the company.

The local Mexicans soon had enough of the Texans and those who could leave headed south. The locals were mainly soldiers who had completed their tour of duty, descendents of soldiers, or new Anglo colonists. In 1835 the population of Goliad was a little more than seven hundred. When Johnson and Dr. Grant arrived from San Antonio a few months later, the population was down to a handful. Those who remained were primarily Mexicans with but a few Anglo colonists. The majority of Anglos had relocated to east Texas. The Mexicans, while not enthusiastic about Santa Anna, certainly had mixed feelings about the Anglos in their midst. The newest Anglos were not colonists; they were almost entirely adventurers from the southern states. Even Fannin had complained to Robinson, "I doubt if twenty-five citizens of Texas can be mustered in the ranks—nay, I am informed, whilst writing the above, that there is not half that number;—does not this fact bespeak an indifference, and criminal apathy, truly alarming?" The Anglo farmers tried to stay mostly on the sidelines while the Mexicans fled south across the Rio Grande or to ranches in the south and east of Goliad. Some joined Santa Anna. Those who stayed in Goliad were mostly business owners or older citizens without the physical strength to flee.

Not only were there strained relations between the citizens of Goliad and its newly arrived defenders, tensions soon developed in the command structure. Fannin had thrown himself in with Lieutenant Governor Robinson, and his letters were addressed to Robinson or the Grand Council or both. Col. William Ward, the original colonel of the Georgia battalion, was a Governor Smith man, having met Smith upon his arrival with the two quickly becoming friends. This rankled Fannin but he also realized that Ward was a popular and ethical leader of his men. Fannin did not want to alienate Ward as Fannin's dismissal from office could be only another election away.

Governor Smith and William Ward communicated frequently through letters, at least one of which was delivered to Ward by Fannin. Ward showed Fannin one of the letters from Smith. The letter contained references to the political hot water that Smith was encountering. After Smith was impeached, Fannin shared some of the issues in the correspondence with Smith's political enemies. The Grand Council demanded to see the Smith letter or a copy and on February 20 Ward responded in a forthright and strong refusal, writing,

> You call upon me to furnish you with the copy of a letter written by the said Smith to me some time during the last month, extracts from which have been furnished you by Col. J.W. Fannin, Jr. I feel myself compelled to decline compliance with your request, and a sense of self-respect and courtesy to your body prompts me to explain to you frankly the reasons which prompt me to adopt this course . . . in yielding it [the letter] to the possession of enemies, would I not act the part of a traitorous and faithless friend?
> . . . Col. Fannin was himself the bearer of the letter from Gov. Smith to me. . . . I submitted the paper to his inspection. He made several applications to me for the purpose of obtaining a copy and the liberty of using the privilege with which I

had confidentially intrusted him, to all of which I gave an unqualified and prompt denial, judge of my surprise and astonishment then, when your letter informed me that I thought appertained to a character with which Col. Fannin acknowledge no affinity, he had used me and my confidence to feed the flame of discontent and hatred against the Governor, in which it seems he is ambitions to act a conspicuous part. . . .

[Ward concluded], In the character of an informer, he should give a false coloring to the document.

"He made several applications to me" meant that Fannin pressured Ward to hand over the letter. The phrase "the liberty of using the privilege with which I had confidentially intrusted him" claimed that Fannin had betrayed a confidence. Ward's words "he had used me and my confidence to feed the flame of discontent and hatred" and his final characterization of Fannin with the claim that "In the character of an informer, he should give a false coloring to the document" labeled Fannin a cheat and a liar. Duels have been fought over less. However, in five weeks when the end came for both, the two would die bravely within minutes of each other.

There was discontent among the men as well. These were primarily young adventurers who had come to Texas for fame and glory, not to dig ditches. They didn't like being boxed up in a fort. Many thought of themselves as veterans, bloodied by the street fighting at San Antonio where they whipped five Mexicans for every one of them. If they didn't like something, they called for a vote, which rankled Fannin with his West Point upbringing. Dr. J. H. Barnard, a recent arrival from Chicago and private in the Red Rovers, recorded the mood in his journal: "The signs of coming danger began to produce a feeling of anxiety, which was further increased by many vague and groundless rumors that circulated among the men." He also noted the lack of enthusiasm for staying in the fort, writing, "The confinement in the garrison became irksome. Our provisions, of which we had at first an abundant supply were becoming short. The restraints of discipline, now more necessary than ever in their enforcement, produced discontent and

murmurs, and a loss of confidence in their commander."
Finally, Dr. Barnard noted that Fannin was aware of his wan-
ing popularity with the men: "The practicality of maintaining
such forts, as it was in the wilderness, were fully discussed.
Fannin was not slow to perceive the feeling coming over the
men, and it caused a corresponding depression of his mind."

In a letter to Robinson dated February 22, Fannin is
extremely forthright and honest. He admits that he is ready to
throw in the towel. After describing the lottery to rename the
fort, he goes into the dilemma of his command. "I am critical-
ly situated. General Houston is absent on furlough, and neither myself nor army have received any orders as to who
should assume the command. It is my right; and, in many
respects, I have done so, where I was convinced the public
weal required it." With Houston out of the picture, Fannin
assumes the command is his right. Nevertheless, he tries to rid
himself of it, noting with a bit of paranoia that other men are
jealous of him or wish him no good. He claims he never wanted that command or any other, contradicting earlier correspondence where he asked to be promoted to a general.

> I well know that many men of influence view me with an
> envious eye, and either desire my station, or my disgrace.
> The first, they are welcome to and many thanks for taking it
> off my hands. The second will be harder to effect. Will you
> allow me to say to you, and my friends of the old or new
> Convention, that I am not desirous of retaining the present,
> or receiving any other appointment in the army? I did not
> seek in any manner, the one I hold, and, you well know, had
> resolved not to accept and but for Colonel Barnet and
> Clements, and Kerr, would have declined.

Then Fannin offers a blunt self-appraisal: "I am a better
judge of my military abilities than others, and if I am qualified
to command an army, I have not found it out." This is the
quote found in most histories. It is very revealing, but so is the
rest of the paragraph, where he notes that while he may not be
a great officer, there is no one better in Texas. He continues,
"I well know I am a better company officer than most men

now in Texas, and might I do with Regulars &-c for a Regiment. But this does not constitute me a commander. I also conscientiously believe that we have none fit for it now in the country; at least their talents have not been developed."

He then lectures the government on how to recruit commanders and leaders:

> With such as have been in the field since October, I do not fear comparison. But this is not the thing. I think you can get several first-rate officers from the United States. Do not cherish the hope of getting an officer now in service there with subaltern appointments. If you make offers of any such, give the field-offices at once, no matter who is left out. In organizing the army, do not say that the Major General shall be Commander-in-Chief. It may be necessary to appoint some such man as Carrol or Ripley, and no Major-General in Texas ought to complain of having such men raised over him. Leave room that it can be done, if an opportunity offer, and necessity requires it.

After a recommendation on governmental bureaucracy and a few pointers on a constitution—"I would recommend a War Bureau, and an experienced, energetic man at the head of it. Guard well the Constitution, and avoid such parts of that of the United States as have caused so much contention, and given rise to such various constructions"—finally, he asks for some time off to see his wife and children after his eighteen-month absence.

The request would not be granted, for three days later James Bonham rode into Fort Defiance. He carried a message dated February 23, 1836, and addressed directly to J. W. Fannin, Jr. from Travis and Bowie that would change everything for Fannin and Texas.

> We have removed all our men into the Alamo, where we will make such resistance as is due to our honour, and that of the country, until we can get assistance from you, which we expect you to forward immediately. In this extremity, we hope you will send us all the men you can spare promptly. We have one hundred and forty-six men, who are determined never to retreat. We have but little provisions, but enough to

serve us till you and your men arrive. We deem it unnecessary to repeat to a brave officer, who knows his duty, that we call on him for assistance. . . . W. Barret Travis James Bowie

The news raced through the fort. Fannin was no coward and he did not hesitate to answer the call from Travis and Bowie. He ordered Captain Westover and his company of regulars to remain and garrison Fort Defiance. Everyone else was ordered to be ready to march to San Antonio, one hundred miles away, in the morning. He informed Lieutenant Governor Robinson:

> I am well aware that my present movement toward Bexar is any thing but a military one. The appeal of Cols. Travis & Bowie cannot however pass unnoticed—particularly by troops now on the field Sanguine, chivalrous Volunteers— Much must be risked to relieve the besieged—If however I hear of the fall of Bexar before I reach them, I shall retire on this place & complete the fortification now in state of forwardness & prepare for a vigorous defence, waiting anxiously in any event for the arrival of reinforcements from the Interior. I leave from 80 to 100 men for the present defence of this place with the expectation of a speedy reinforcement from Matagorda &c J. W. Fannin Jr.

The first sentence is revealing. Fannin realized that trying to relieve the Alamo with little more than four hundred men was not a sound military move. But he had to make an attempt.

The troops were ready for a fight and ready to go to the aid of the Alamo. Herman Ehrenberg, described in some histories as a "German Jew," wrote in his memoirs: "Elated by this decision, we packed our things, left the fort and made camp on the other side of the river, taking it for granted that next day we should be on our way to the scene of our first triumphs."

Ehrenberg had fought at San Antonio as a member of the Greys and was eager to return. He and the others advanced to the other side of the San Antonio River but didn't get much farther. Unfettered oxen had wandered off during the night, wagons broke down, and there was no food because they could not find the oxen to pull the supply wagons.

Dr. Barnard realized the futility of the mission. He explained,

> A further consideration of the enterprise served to display it in its true light. With but three or four hundred men, mostly on foot, with but a limited supply of provisions, to march a distance of nearly one hundred miles through an uninhabited country, for the purpose of relieving a fortress beleaguered by five thousand men, was madness.

Then he did the numbers.

> Many Americans believed themselves able to cope with five times their number, and events had in many instances justified the idea, but the disparity here was out of all reason. Besides, the Mexican army was well appointed with cavalry and artillery and their scouts would give them the earliest intelligence and they could select any advantageous position on the route and cut us off. [And that could very well have been the case.] Indeed it has been subsequently found out that they were appraised of Fannin's movements, and had made their plan to attack us in the road. More than that, was there the least chance of relieving the Alamo, and successfully maintaining it?

Finally, there was Urrea to consider. The doctor writes, "Yet this measure was actually abandoning Goliad to Urea [*sic*], without a blow. There was not a hundred men left there, and Urea would have nothing to do but march in and quietly take possession."

Fannin met with his officers and took a vote. According to Barnard, "After full deliberation, Fannin and his officers abandoned the expedition as impracticable and useless, we therefore returned to the fort and resumed our old quarters."

The decision caused rumblings in the ranks, especially among the veteran Greys. Ehrenberg noted,

> Great therefore, was our surprise when a new command directed us to return to our quarters in the fort. The only explanation offered us for this sudden overthrow of our new hopes was that most of the volunteers in our group were against the march to San Antonio and preferred to stay in

Goliad. How Fannin obtained this information is a mystery to us, since he never gave the troops a chance to express their opinion about this unexpected reversal of his plans.

The Greys had no recourse save bitter regret over this desertion of their old comrades at such a critical moment; for we were helpless without Fannin's support, and as long as we could not induce him to go to the rescue of the Alamo, we were compelled to share his inaction and isolation.

The Greys were not happy with Fannin, who was caught between the hard facts as presented by Dr. Barnard and the romanticism and naiveté of the volunteers. It was not a comfortable position, as Fannin explained to Robinson in a letter dated February 26.

Yesterday (Feb. 25) after making all the preparations possible, we took up our line of march (about three hundred strong, and four pieces of artillery) toward Bexar, to the relief of those brave men now shut up on command of this post. Within two hundred yards of town (Goliad), one of the wagons broke down, and it was necessary to double teams in order to draw the artillery across the river, each piece having but one yoke of oxen. Not a particle of bread-stuff, with the exception of half a tierce of rice, with us no beef with the exception of a small portion that had been dried and, not a head of cattle, except those used to draw the artillery, the ammunition, etc., and it was impossible to obtain any until we should arrive at Seguin's Rancho, seventy miles from this place.

Fannin then states that the volunteers approached him for a council of war: "This morning whilst here I received a note from the officer commanding the volunteers requesting, in the name of the officers of his command, a Council of War, on the subject of the expedition to Bexar, which, of course, was granted." Fannin attributes the decision to halt the expedition to the commissioned officers, saying, "it was by them unanimously determined" that going forward was dangerous, and the expedition returned to Fort Defiance.

The Council of War consisted of all the commissioned officers of the command and it was by them unanimously determined, that, inasmuch as a proper supply of provisions and means of transportation could not be had; and, as it was impossible, with our present means, to carry the artillery with us, and as by leaving Fort Defiance without a proper garrison, it might fall into the hands of the enemy, with the provisions, etc., now at Matagorda, Dimmitt's Landing and Cox's Point and on the way to meet us; and, as by report of our spies (sent out by Col. Bowers) we may expect an attack upon this place, it was deemed expedient to return to this post and complete the fortifications, etc., etc. . . . I sent an express to Gonzales to apprize the committee there of our return. J. W. Fannin.

The officers may have presented the proposal to go back (we only have Fannin's account of the council of war), but the men and some officers were increasingly uncomfortable with Fannin and the conduct of the campaign. "Col. Fannin was truly a brave and good soldier but too free and good natured for a commander," wrote Capt. Benjamin H. Hughes of the Georgia battalion. He complained that the men were "a general confused mob" with Fannin lacking "the necessary austerity for a commander to enforce disiplin [*sic*]."

The officers were becoming very aware of the forces coming their direction. They were also very realistic about the behavior of the advancing Mexican army. John Brooks wrote his sister about the probable fate of the Johnson/Grant party and his possible fate as well.

Up to this time, they have uniformly killed all the Americans they take, and it is reasonable therefore to infer that not one of that ill fated party survived.

We will probably be attacked before I can write you again. The advance of the enemy is within 25 miles of us. If we are defeated, it will be after a hard fight. Tell everyone of the family to write to me, and mail their letters different days.

Events are thickening upon us. I will write to you again, the first opportunity that occurs. In the mean time write to me by several different mails; and if I die, reflect that it will be in a good cause.

Your affectionate brother,
John Sowers Brooks

Brooks adds a postscript to his note.

> I am nearly naked, almost barefooted, and without a cent
> of money. We have had nothing but beef for several days. We
> suffer much and labor hard in repairing the fort.
> Brooks

At Washington-on-the-Brazos, the Convention of 1836 met
and on March 2, 1836, voted unanimously for a declaration
of independence. The declaration was signed by fifty-six delegates, including Sam Houston. The news reached Fort
Defiance on March 5 and was greeted with much enthusiasm.
The garrison raised the flag of the Georgia volunteers over
the fortress but when lowered at sunset, the flag became
entangled in the ropes and shredded.

Chapter 9

Split Command: The Refugio Battle

"There were two dirty Mexicans wiping the blood off their swords
and the poor boy was breathing his last; she said, 'My poor boy,'
and one of them replied; 'Here you got no boy.'"

Even with the siege of the Alamo, it was politics as usual in
Washington-on-the-Brazos. Governor Smith, Lieutenant
Governor Robinson, and the Grand Council were still feud-
ing and ignoring the crisis in the field. Responding to
Fannin's request for aid, a furlough, and the acknowledgment
of his inadequacies as a commander, Robinson essentially
told Fannin he was on his own: "In answer permit us to say
that unfortunately we are too much divided for the benefit of
our country and promotion of the true interest to render you
that effectual aid you so much need."

This is a very clear-cut answer to Fannin's request. The
next response is a bit in code: "Party spirit lays hold with her
infernal fangs, upon everything that might be of any service
to our country in their deadly struggle for her rights. The
spirit of party rages to an unprecedented height, & its better
rancor is truly alarming & heartrending to any true friend to
the country." In other words, politics (party spirit) is the
major obstacle in the way of any real action.

Robinson also complains of spying by his opponents,
whom he claims are intercepting Fannin's correspondence,
"and in fact the very letters addressed to us by you are seized
by others and Read and commented upon before we are permitted to see them." Despite the political instability and
intrigue, he still believes he is in power: "Not withstanding
this we feel that we are still legally in office & will continue
to act until superceded by some future government."

Though he states that he holds the power of his office,
again Robinson makes it clear that Fannin is on his own, "In
accordance with our official duty & our oaths we have to say
& instruct you to use your own discretion to remain where

you are or to retreat as you may think best for the safety of the brave Volunteers Under your command, & the Regulars & Militia, and the interest of our beloved country requires."

And then Robinson drops the bombshell, telling Fannin that Houston is his commander and "has been by this new convention confirmed & appointed commander in chief of the Army of Texas Militia & volunteers; as well as regulars." Houston is back. He signed the declaration of independence and is in command of everything, with Robinson making that clear in his final statement.

With no aid, no furlough, and a new boss in Houston, Fannin went back to his work on the fortress. On March 1, he felt that Fort Defiance could withstand a siege though short on food and ammunition. Fannin dispatched troops to the coast to bring in supplies, but the bad roads and lack of adequate transport made this resupply effort difficult and time-consuming, with the companies not returning until ten days later.

At Washington-on-the-Brazos on March 6 the convention received Travis's last appeal, written March 3, the same date as Robinson's letter to Fannin. The Alamo fell that day, but the delegates were unaware of the defeat. Houston ordered Fannin and Neill at Gonzales to go to the aid of the Alamo. Fannin received the order on March 12 and readied three hundred men for the march to join Houston at Gonzales and then on to San Antonio. But something got in the way, again.

Fannin has come down through history as a man of indecision unable to move in a crisis. In reality, he was more of a crowd pleaser reacting to the next plea for help but not delivering. Earlier, he had started out to join the Matamoros expedition but withdrew with the arrival of Urrea. Fannin reacted immediately to Travis and his call for help, but logistical problems and the reluctance of his officers, according to Fannin's written account, forced him to abandon Travis. Now he was ready and willing to join Houston in breaking the siege at the Alamo. He would have, except for the intervention of Lewis Ayers.

Lewis Ayers was an Anglo colonist from New Jersey who

settled in San Patricio in 1834. He became active in politics, siding not surprisingly with the Texans and attended first the Consultation at San Felipe and then the General Council as an elected delegate. He returned home to San Patricio on January 1, 1836, promptly moving his family to Refugio to avoid the oncoming Mexican army. David Moses, one of the few survivors of the skirmish at Agua Dulce Creek, fled to Refugio after the fight. He and Ayers met, and Ayers joined Moses in riding to Goliad.

On March 3, Ayers appealed to Fannin for help in moving his and other colonists' families to safety, out of the way of Mexican and Karankawa marauders. The colonists needed wagons and troops for protection, but there weren't any wagons, as they had been sent to the coast to pick up supplies. Fannin, again a man of action, assigned Capt. Amon King and his Paducah Volunteer Light Company of twenty-eight men to escort the wagons to Refugio to bring the colonists into Fort Defiance—only they had to wait for the wagons, which did not arrive back at Fort Defiance until March 10. A week was wasted. Amon King and his men started for Refugio at nine in the morning on the eleventh of March, arriving there late in the evening.

Escort duty did not appeal to these men. Upon arrival they camped with the families around the town church. A colonist, widow Sabina Brown, noted the men's mood:

> When at supper time they heard that there was a band of the enemy on a ranch ten or twelve miles below the Mission, they said to one another "Jolly, now for a fight; maybe they will come tonight," but morning came and no Mexicans, much to the disappointment of the Texans who were starving for a fight. And then they began clamoring "If they can't come we can go there"; and away they went.

The Texans went to the ranch of Estaban Lopez, two miles out of town, to collect the Ayers family and a Mrs. Hill and her children. Six Mexican riders arrived and the Anglo colonists told King that at least five of them were looters of abandoned ranches in the area. One of the riders,

Encarnacio Vasquez, was a judge in Goliad. King detained him for associating with the others.

King was told by the colonists that there were more looters at another Lopez location eight miles away. King was twenty-nine years old and had been marshal of Paducah, Kentucky, prior to organizing his men and going to Texas. With his law enforcement instincts taking over, he and sixteen men marched to the lower ranch. Whatever his motives, he was clearly disobeying orders to evacuate the colonists.

The other members of the company remained in Refugio to make the necessary arrangements for evacuation while King marched on the lower Lopez ranch location. King and his men marched into a trap, as the marauders had been tipped off. When King and his men arrived at the ranch, gunfire opened up on them from both sides of the road. The Mexican force was Capt. Carlos de la Garza's Victoriana Guardes serving as Urrea's advance scouts and cavalry.

Somehow the Texans avoided any casualties, and King and his men retreated back to the upper ranch. They rapidly loaded the wagons with furniture, household goods, women, and children and started for the mission at Refugio. The rancheros caught up with the caravan as the wagons were fording a stream. The Mexican force opened fire, hitting one woman and breaking her leg. King and his men took cover in the riverbank, holding off the attackers while the wagons made it across the stream and gained the safety of the mission walls. King and his men then withdrew as well to the mission with no additional casualties.

The mission was soon surrounded by more than two hundred Mexican troops. The Mexican force consisted of Captain de la Garza and his men, more rancheros under Capt. Guadalupe de los Santos, and perhaps forty Karankawas. Urrea sent additional regulars under Capt. Rafael Pretalia. A Mexican courier named Rios raced by the mission on horseback and a Texan shot his horse out from under him. Rio hid behind the dead horse, raised his head, and was promptly shot dead. There were no other casualties although gunfire continued throughout the day. A local Irish boy escaped in the evening and made it to Goliad by one o'clock on the morning of the thirteenth of March.

Hearing the boy's report, Fannin went into action, making another mistake. He split his command, sending Colonel Ward and 120 men to help King out of the trap of his own making. Ward and his men arrived at the mission on the evening of the thirteenth and quickly dispersed the Mexicans. The widow Sabina Brown described the action.

> Colonel Ward left the old fort [La Bahia] with one hundred men, and arriving at the Mission between sundown and dark. At the head of a little gully that puts out from the river above the church the Mexicans had a camp, and Ward and his men, who were called the Georgia Rattler, ran into this camp, unexpectedly, and then the row began. They drove the Mexicans back to the river in a panic, and a horse with a saddle on ran very nearly into the church and disturbed the families who were cooking their supper.

Ward and King should have set out immediately on the thirty-mile trip back to Goliad, but they did not. Ward allowed his men to rest for the evening with the intention of heading back to Goliad first thing in the morning.

King and his men, even after fighting most of the day, somehow still had enough energy and stupidity to want more action. A newspaper article printed in 1840 and written by Lewis M. H. Washington, assistant adjutant general to Fannin, recorded the bizarre night of the thirteenth:

> A little before midnight a strange fire was seen about a mile down the river in the direction of a rancho, and the boys always ready for a lark, cried out for a little Indian play. Capt. King immediately called for volunteers, and in five minutes he had thirty men under arms. They sallied out silently and crept along the edge of the wood until they were opposite the fire which stood in the prairie about 150 yards from the timber. They then filed out into the open ground until they were within 40 yards of the enemy. The extreme darkness of the night favored them, and they took ground without being discovered. The party consisted of seven or eight Mexican officers and

three Indians. Their leader was instantly recognized; he was a Mexican Lieutenant named Blanco who had joined Colonel Fannin at Velasco, as a friend to the Constitution of 1824. He had accompanied the army to Copano Bay, from thence to the Mission, and even to Goliad, where he remained some time.

Fannin had generously permitted him to leave the encampment, nominally to return to New Orleans.

He journeyed west and was then with Urrea, though his extreme temerity had led him to venture without the lines for the night. As soon as he was known, his treachery was apparent to every man of the party, and at a given signal thirty rifle bullets laid himself and his comrades "dead in their tracks." The single volley sufficed as a death warrant for the whole party. There were found on them 510 duboons [doubloons], firearms, etc.; and on the person of the Lieutenant were found letters and papers which proved beyond a doubt that he had been in correspondence with the enemy while enjoying the hospitality and protection of Col. Fannin. Our little party of thirty made good their retreat to the church, and great was the exultation over their success.

The Mexican population was not so thrilled, viewing the event as cold-blooded murder. Regardless, this event and Ward's decision to not immediately return to Fort Defiance would lead to more trouble.

While all this was taking place, Urrea and his army, now in excess of one thousand men, were moving toward Refugio. Urrea was receiving reinforcements from Santa Anna now that the fighting at the Alamo was over, and he knew from his scouts that King and Ward were still in the mission. Urrea went forward with a force of 180 infantry, one cannon, and 100 cavalry, leaving Col. Francisco Garay in command of the main unit.

Ward's command awoke in Refugio on the morning of March 14 with the intention of leaving immediately for Goliad, colonists in tow. A sentry heard a bugle call, and Ward sent Maj. Warren J. Mitchell and a scouting party out to investigate. Mitchell, for some reason, decided to destroy a nearby ranch during his exploration. In addition, Amon King could not contain himself and he and twenty-eight of his men went back to the Lopez ranch. Finding nothing, they stopped at a few more deserted ranches before heading back to the mission at Refugio. Arriving outside Refugio, King found the tables turned. Ward had been surprised by Urrea's force and was now fighting from inside the mission. King retreated.

Gen. Vicente Filisola, the Italian-born general, and second in command to Santa Anna, described the battle: "The enemy in number a hundred men, were occupying the church, the only defensible point in this miserable village. Over on his left, and at a distance of an eighth of a league [600-700 yards], he had, in ambush another fifty men. This force remained there, cut off by the cavalry of Guanajuato, which had anticipated by some moments the arrival of the division."

Ward attacked the cavalry but retreated into the mission when the main Mexican force arrived. Filisola went on, "Although, in the beginning, only three parties were detached to attack the enemy, the rest of our infantry became engaged, soon after the enemy was shut up in the church, and even part of the cavalry of Cuautla attacked, dismounted. All, however, was in vain."

Urrea was losing his patience. He had ordered two infantry charges, both of which were repulsed, and so directed the infantry back to a house and corral twenty paces from the mission. Then he commanded his seasoned cavalry to dismount and attack. The cavalry were supposed to inspire the infantry, but their attack failed as well. Urrea ordered the cavalry to withdraw.

Ward's men were confident, taunting the Mexicans. "Strong in their position, by reason of our little caution, they mocked us with impunity, and made us pay dearly for our temerity, since there was on our part thirteen killed and forty-three wounded, among them four officers, without their having more than one wounded on theirs."

Urrea called for reinforcements, and Filisola explained, "In this situation the General ordered Colonel Francisco Garay, who was coming up with the force from the Aransas, to leave behind everything which might impede his march and hurry forward with all the force at his disposal; which the said officer obeyed without loss of time, and so arrived in camp about five o'clock in the afternoon, and was told by the General what had occurred in the morning."

Urrea briefed Garay on the situation and then switched his attention to King and his men. Garay "was shown the wood in which the enemy were posted; and prepared to take measures to dislodge them from it. His dispositions were completed satisfactorily before nightfall, causing the enemy a loss of five killed and two prisoners; the said gentlemen having a loss on his part of three killed and ten wounded."

While Garay's troop placements, as described by Filisola were correct, King and his men were not dislodged. But they were running out of ammunition and King ordered his men to cease fire and lie down out of sight. Waiting for dark, King and his command were able to make their escape during the night. But not for long.

On the inside of the mission, Ward told his men to hold their fire until the enemy was well within rifle range to conserve ammunition and make each shot count. Ward's command only had three wounded. One was Lewis Ayers' brother-in-law, who was hit in the chest by a musket ball. William Shelton, fifteen, was wounded in the leg when he foolishly left the cover of the mission to get a better shot at the Mexicans. Christopher Winters was seriously wounded and not expected to survive. One report put Mexican losses at four to five hundred dead.

The mission itself was a natural fortress. On three sides of the church there was nothing to provide cover for the attacking force. The entire three sides were a killing zone for the Texans with their long rifles. On the fourth side of the mission was the "church-yard," the church cemetery, which was about fifty yards in length and walled. The ground sloped away from the wall but once the wall was scaled the tombstones could provide cover. Ward knew his weak point. The first two charges were frontal assaults with devastating results for the Mexicans. As one Texan noted, "At the first discharge of rifles from the building, as many Mexicans bit the dust. This produced some confusion in the Mexican ranks, and one or two parties retreated, but others recovered and made a rush towards the building. A second discharge from within, not less fatal than the first, cut down the foremost ranks and put the survivors to flight."

The Mexican emphasis shifted to the cemetery. During the frontal assaults, a column of Mexican soldiers had advanced on the wall around the cemetery. They had progressed to within one hundred yards of the cemetery when a "little band" of Texans concealed behind the wall rose up and fired into the advancing soldiers. The fire was deadly. "Several of the ranks fell, almost in a body, as many, perhaps, by the panic as by the bullets; the remaining ranks fell back a few yards, but a further retreat was stopped by the efforts of a few brave officers."

The "few brave officers" continued to lead attacks throughout the day but with no success. The Texans held off each attack with the Mexicans suffering heavy casualties.

Inside the mission, even conserving ammunition, Ward was running low. He ordered two riders to attempt a breakout and ride to Fort Defiance for relief. Neither courier made it, both being captured almost immediately upon leaving the mission.

At Fort Defiance, Fannin was frantic over the whereabouts of Ward and King. He sent his own couriers out looking. They carried orders to Ward and King to return to the fort immediately. One courier was killed and the other, Edward Perry, a citizen of Refugio, was captured by Garay's men. General Filisola documents his capture and Garay's ruse:

> [The colonel discovered the man was] but a courier from La Bahía who was trying to introduce himself into the church. This having been learned from questioning him, he produced a letter directed by Colonel Fannin to the so-called Colonel Ward, commanding him, the moment he should receive it, to prepare to evacuate the position which he then held, regardless of sacrifices he might be compelled to make and the difficulties to be overcome, directing himself without delay to Fort Defiance (so he called La Bahía) where he could expect him without fail on the following day.

Colonel Garay then tried his trick. Garay wanted Ward and his men out in the open so he could destroy them with cavalry and overwhelming manpower. Filisola described the deception, writing, "Col. Garay, considering it advisable that Ward should receive this communication, permitted the prisoner to deliver it without letting him know that he understood its contents."

Garay believed Ward would drop everything and return to Fort Defiance on receipt of the order. If Ward attempted to break toward Goliad, it would be easy to catch him out in the open. Perry, the courier, recognized Garay' tactic and told Ward so when he gained entry to the mission. Ward assumed correctly that the Mexicans would patrol the direct route to Goliad, the La Bahia road, whereas they probably would not control or patrol the way to Copano Bay. Ward and his men escaped from the church during the night along this route, making their way through woods and swamps to avoid the Mexican cavalry.

Joseph W. Andrews, a member of Ward's command, described the escape. It began with Ward holding a "consultation" wherein it was decided to "force a retreat." It was now after dark and rain was falling. The men formed in single file, creeping out the mission through a window. They then "marched in silence between two of the fires unmolested by the foe; meeting with Centinel [sentinel]."

Ward had made a hard decision—he left the women, children, and wounded behind. Andrews counted six or seven women in the mission and five or six children. Ward had not taken any chances, telling his men to be quiet so the women and children would not awaken and "commence screaming." One Texan, Woods, refused to leave the mission, preferring to take his chances with the Mexicans. Woods made the wrong decision. He and the wounded—Anderson, Ray, and Ayers' brother-in-law—were later "put to death."

The morning after the soldiers' silent escape, widow Sabina Brown awoke to find the men gone. At first nothing happened and "all was quiet until morning when the Mexicans came running in." Sabina attempted to help one of the young wounded men, hoping "to save the poor wounded boy by telling them that he was my boy and not a soldier, and the first that came passed him by and repassed him for nearly an hour." She left the boy's side briefly to make him a cup of tea, and when she returned, "there were two dirty Mexicans wiping the blood off their swords and the poor boy was breathing his last; she said, 'My poor boy,' and one of them replied; 'Here you got no boy.'"

The Mexicans looted the mission, robbing the women of "everything of value." They then collected their dead, "which made a pile as big as twenty cords of wood." One resident of the town had "fenced in his town lot with a ditch four feet deep and four feet wide, they began to drag their dead into it and throw them in and filled it to the top then they raked the dirt in on it and this caused his lot to be marked with a ridge, and thus ended King and Ward at the old Mission of Refugio."

Having made their escape, Ward and his men marched away from Goliad eastward toward Victoria to avoid the Mexican army and scouts. On the third day out of the mission, Ward and his men crossed the San Antonio River, the same river that runs in front of Fort Defiance, on their way to Victoria.

On March 21, Ward and his men had been on the run for a week. Ward knew that Fannin might make a break from Goliad and if so he, like all of Texas, would fall back to the east. Ward continued northeastward toward Victoria, crossing the Guadalupe River. It was an unpleasant surprise to Ward and his men when they found the town occupied by Mexican troops. On the plains outside the town, they were discovered by the Mexican cavalry but managed to escape into the timber.

Ward and his men made their way to Dimmitt's Landing on the Lavaca River near Matagorda Bay. Upon their approach to the settlement, Ward sent scouts into town who were immediately captured by Urrea's men. The scouts were forced to lead the Mexicans to Ward, and the Texans were surrounded, again. From the lines of their captors, the scouts yelled to Ward telling him the size of the Mexican force and suggesting he ask Urrea for terms of surrender. Ward, Major Mitchell, and Capt. Isaac Ticknor met with General Urrea. When the officers returned to the men, Ward explained the terms offered by Urrea: surrender and they would be considered prisoners of war. They would then either march to Copano Bay to be put on ships for New Orleans or exchanged at some later date.

Ward smelled a rat. He opposed surrendering. He argued that this was the same enemy they had beaten at Refugio, they had escaped then and the odds were good they could do it again by waiting for nightfall, and he believed they would be slaughtered if they surrendered. However, the men knew they were low on ammunition and the possibility of a boat ride to New Orleans looked pretty good to them. Ward put it to a vote and the surrender option won. Ward was prophetic, telling his men that he would go along with the vote, "but if you are destroyed, do not blame me." Ward, accompanied again by Mitchell and Ticknor, met with General Urrea and agreed to the terms. The Texans came out of the timber, their ammunition was taken, and their guns were disabled.

General Urrea, in his diary, confirms most of the details:

> On March 22. I marched, with two hundred foot and fifty horse, to a mountain pass called Las Juntas. Here I met with four men from Ward's company, who were in search of provisions, and from them I learned that the whole band was in ambush in a neighboring wood. I immediately surrounded it, and sent in one of the prisoners to announce to his leader and companions, that unless they surrendered at discretion, they would be cut to pieces. Mr. Ward, known under the title of their colonel, desired to speak with me; and after a few minutes' conversation, he with his troop of one hundred men surrendered at discretion.

Urrea does not mention any boats to New Orleans, prisoner of war status, or exchanges.

Amon King and his men were not so lucky. As noted, after his rescue by Ward on March 13, King showed his gratitude by arguing with the colonel about pursuing some local marauders. Ward, unbelievably, didn't have a problem with King's request but wanted one of his officers, Mitchell, to lead the patrol. King disagreed, leaving with his men to revisit the lower Lopez ranch. On the fourteenth, King started back to the mission but found his way blocked by the Mexicans. He took up a defensive position on the banks of the Mission River, where he was attacked by the cavalry of Col. Gabriel Nunez and the infantry of Garay. The Texans suffered one dead and four wounded, including King, whose arm was shattered by a musket shot.

Lewis Ayers, the colonist, later recorded the fight.

The moment we saw the enemy, we were discovered by them, and a party of Horsemen amounting to upwards of 100 men galloped to cut off our retreat to a piece of woods to which we hasted about 600 yards when we reached there we found our number reduced to 22 men by the desertion of 6. We had time before attacked to choose a good fighting position, and for each man to have his station assigned to him, which was maintained by all throughout an engagement of about one half hour, when the enemy retreated with about 20 killed and a large number wounded. After an interval of about one hour we were again attacked by about 200 of the enemy in two parties opening a cross fire upon us, we still maintained our ground and after an hour of hard fighting we compelled them to retreat. One of our party was killed within 3 feet of me, and four were wounded, the number of the enemy killed and wounded was very large, but I have not been able to learn the number. Towards night we were attacked a third time from the opposite side of the river, Capt. King then directed us to lie close, protecting ourselves as much as possible by the woods, and not to fire again, holding ourselves in readiness for an expected attack on our side of the river, which however did not take place, the enemy after wasting as I suppose all their powder and ball and without doing us any personal injury, retired. I was saved from death in the second engagement by a ball glancing from one of a pair of pistols which I wore in front, they were given me by Capt. King. When night came on it was very dark, not a star to be seen, we crossed the river at the battle ground, where it was not considered fordable, the water reached my chin, there was a ford just above and one just below us but we expected the enemy would guard them, the banks were so steep that we had to assist each other in the ascent, the wounded accompanied us with much pain.

While the Texans were crossing the river, the water up to their chins, their powder got wet. King and his men were defenseless. They managed to make it to the ranch of John Malone, but on March 15 they were captured there by Colonel de la Garza, the colonel who ambushed them at the Lopez ranch a few days earlier. The men were tied together with a single rope and marched to Refugio, eight miles away.

Upon reaching the mission, King and his men were led out to be executed. The processional was halted when Col. Juan Jose Holzinger overheard several of the men speaking in German. Holzinger, a German engineer and house designer (he built Santa Anna's villa), ordered the prisoners back to the mission. Holzinger released two Germans and six colonists, including Lewis Ayers.

Ayers described his situation:

> Our treatment during the next 24 hours was most brutal and barbarous. I had not asked for neither did I expect any mercy at the hands of the enemy. My wife however with four children presented herself to Gen. Urrea and excited his sympathy by their tears, she was aided by some Mexican officers who were opposed to the barbarous course pursued of murdering prisoners, and the General agreed to save my life, which was done, and I was given in some degree my liberty, after receiving a severe lecture on account of my hostility to Mexico and charging me to behave myself better in the future and let politics alone—I merely bowed and said nothing.

The next day the remaining prisoners, now down to twenty-five, were marched one mile north of the mission, positioned on a draw, and shot. Their bodies lay unburied.

After the battle of San Jacinto and the return of the colonists, the bones were collected and buried. The burial spot was lost until 1934 when sixteen sets of bones were found in a mass grave in the Mount Calvary Catholic Cemetery near Refugio and identified as members of King's command. The remains of the others have not been found but legend maintains they are in another nearby cemetery.

At Fort Defiance, Fannin waited for the men to return. He had orders to march to Houston at Gonzales and on to San Antonio to save the Alamo. But the Alamo had fallen.

Chapter 10

Fannin at Goliad
Houston at Gonzales

"Col. Fanning seemed to have his mind unsettled about it."
"General Houston understood the situation—he was a born leader of men."

The second week of March saw a lot of activity. King and his men rode out of Fort Defiance on March 11, ignorant of the fact that the Alamo had fallen on March 6. Also on March 11, Fannin received the order to bring his force to Gonzales and join Houston. That same day Houston arrived at Gonzales to learn the Alamo had fallen. He dispatched Capt. Francis J. Dusanque from Gonzales to Fort Defiance. Two days later, on the thirteenth, Fannin dispatched Ward to bring back King from Refugio so they could all leave for Gonzales.

Despite previous messages to the contrary, Dusanque carried orders from Houston to Fannin requesting that he not come to Gonzales. Instead, Fannin was ordered to retreat to Guadalupe Victoria "as soon as practicable." Any artillery that could not easily make the trip was to be dumped in the river. Fort Defiance was to be blown up, and Fannin was to defend Victoria if possible, or evacuate if necessary. One-third of his command was to be sent to Houston at Gonzales. Houston urged Fannin to act: "The immediate advance of the enemy may be confidently expected as well as rise of water. Prompt movements are highly important."

The timing could not have been worse for Fannin's reputation. Accounts differ, with Fannin receiving Houston's retreat order either on March 12, 13, or 14. Most likely he received it on the thirteenth. Due to his delay in responding to the order, Fannin is thought by some historians to have willfully disobeyed Houston. One account has Fannin telling the couriers, "No, Tell him I will not give up Fort Defiance." That is probably not the case. Fannin most likely ignored the call for "prompt movements" and latched on to "as soon as practicable," assuming Ward and King would be returning soon.

169

He waited for the men to return so the consolidated force could proceed to Victoria after demolishing the fort. Again, his decision was probably not willful disobedience but merely hoping for the best and getting the worst.

Houston did not have a great deal of confidence in Fannin, as he admitted in a note to James Collinsworth attached to a copy of his order to Fannin. Collinsworth was now chairman of the Convention of 1836 military committee. Houston noted the fall of the Alamo, included his order to Fannin, and then added,

> The enclosed statement [the fall of the Alamo], which came here a few moments after my arrival, has induced me to adopt a course very different from that which I intended before the information was received. The enclosed order to Colonel Fannin will indicate my convictions that, with our small unorganized force, we cannot maintain sieges in fortresses, in the country of the enemy. Troops pent up in forts are rendered useless; nor is it possible that we can ever maintain our cause by such policy. The want of supplies and men, will insure the success of our enemies.

This was not new thinking on the part of Houston. He had argued against occupying the Alamo and ordered Bowie and Travis to destroy it. Both disobeyed Houston's direct order. Now, Houston was not surprised at the outcome in San Antonio. He continued, commenting on Fannin:

> On seeing the various communications of Colonel Fannin on this point, I could not rely on any co-operation from him. I am using all my endeavors to get a company to send in view of the Alamo; and if possible, arrive at the certainty of what all believe—it's fall.

He concluded the letter to Collinsworth saying he believed Goliad to already be under siege.

Houston was trying to get a handle on the events at San Antonio. Where was Santa Anna? What was he doing? When was he marching? Houston did not have enough horses to send a company to scout the Alamo; instead he sent for Erastus "Deaf" Smith and Henry Wax Karnes. Karnes was the originator of the crowbar attack at the first battle of San Antonio against Cos. Though Smith was forty-nine and Karnes only twenty-four, they had formed a close bond and friendship scouting and fighting together. When hostilities first broke out, Smith was suspect because he was married to a Mexican widow, but any suspicion was forgotten because of his service at the battles of Concepion and San Antonio. Smith was deaf as a result of a childhood disease, but he could speak, although in a squeaky voice, and Houston determined that Smith's disability heightened his other senses. The scout could detect movement before others and his eyesight was extremely good. At San Jacinto, Houston would rely on Smith to gain the ultimate victory.

Houston needed confirmation of the fall of the Alamo and the whereabouts of Santa Anna. He asked if Smith and Karnes needed more men, but Smith said only the two were needed and they would go alone. They expected to be gone three days, enough time to scout the Alamo and return. Houston provided them with the best horses in the camp.

It didn't take Smith and Karnes three days. They were back with all they needed to know the same day. Twenty miles out of Gonzales, Smith and Karnes found Susannah Dickinson, widow of Almeron Dickinson, riding a horse and carrying Angelina, her fifteen-month-old daughter. Dickinson was escorted by former slaves Ben and Joe. Joe had been Travis's slave and Ben had been on the household staff of Santa Anna.

At the start of the attack on the Alamo, Susannah and Angelina had been hidden in a small room in the chapel with two Mexican women. As the fighting died down, a Mexican officer approached, calling out for her by name. She was escorted to Santa Anna, who took a liking to Angelina. Putting her upon his knee, Santa Anna proposed adopting Angelina and raising her in Mexico, but Susannah declined the offer. After telling Susannah that he had just seen the bodies of Crockett, Bowie, and Travis, Santa Anna appointed Ben to be her escort to Gonzales. Ben was the orderly to Col. Juan Nepomuceno Almonte, aide to Santa Anna. Santa Anna gave Ben a proclamation granting pardon to all Texans who ceased fighting and gave up their arms. The implied threat was that those who continued the fight would die like the defenders of the Alamo.

Susannah, Angelina, and Ben left San Antonio on March 11. They were joined on the road by Joe, Travis's slave. Joe had left San Antonio a few days earlier, not wanting to stay with the Mexicans, and hid until he saw Susannah and Ben. Smith and Karnes rode upon them on the thirteenth. After hearing Susannah's story, Smith dispatched Karnes to ride back and report to Houston.

Joe would give his account of the fall of the Alamo to the Texas cabinet on March 20. The cabinet was impressed with the clarity of the account and Joe's calm demeanor. Sent back to the Travis estate at Columbia, Texas, he escaped from slavery the next year. A reward of fifty dollars was offered, but Joe was never captured. He was reported to have been seen in Austin as late as 1875. Little, if anything, is known about the life or fate of Ben.

After giving her version of the fall of the Alamo to Houston, Susannah was besieged by the widows of the Gonzales men killed at the Alamo. They clamored for any keepsakes or mentions of their dead husbands. Soon, with the fall of the Texas forts and Santa Anna's unopposed march east, Susannah and Angelina would join in the Runaway Scrape— the period of panicked flight among the Anglo colonists— leaving Gonzales by oxcart and not stopping till they reached the Sabine River. After San Jacinto, she appealed to the young republic for aid but the republic pleaded limited resources and her appeal was denied. In 1837 she remarried, but the marriage lasted only a year, with the divorce petition citing wife and child neglect and beating.

Susannah is said to have then moved into the Mansion House, a "rowdy" restaurant and hotel, with "rowdy" being code for house of prostitution. The establishment was owned by Pamela Mann, famous for loaning the Texan army the oxen that pulled the "Twin Sister" cannon of San Jacinto fame. She didn't let the oxen go to battle, however, confronting Houston before the battle and taking the oxen away. She had thought the army was going to Nacogdoches, not San Jacinto. In later years she was sentenced to death for forgery but pardoned by Gov. Mirabeau Lamar. Susannah entered into another marriage in 1838 that ended shortly thereafter when the husband died of either fever or drink or both. Susannah then married Peter Bellows in 1847 with the marriage ending in 1857. The divorce petition cited Susannah for adultery, abandonment, and living in a "house of ill fame." Susannah did not appear in court to deny the charges.

Susannah and Angelina moved to Lockhart, twenty-five miles south of Austin and set up a boarding house. She finally found marital happiness when she married Joseph W. Hannig, a German immigrant and woodworker. Hannig was impressed with her cooking. The newlyweds sold the league of land that was passed down from her first husband and established Joseph in a shop in Austin where he expanded into furniture making, milling, and undertaking. Susannah embraced religion and became a local celebrity for the events at the Alamo. She told her story to numerous audiences including courtroom juries and judges, as she was often called as an expert witness in matters relating to the appeals of descendents of the Alamo dead. Susannah died in October 1883 in Austin. Joseph Hannig died in 1890.

Angelina Dickinson never found peace like her mother. Angelina was only fifteen months old at the time of the Alamo, becoming famous as "the Babe of the Alamo." Angelina would marry twice, the first marriage reportedly arranged by Susannah. Both marriages ended in divorce, producing four children whom Angelina abandoned. Angelina drifted from town to town though she spent some time in Galveston nursing plague victims. One Galveston newspaper report called her a "courtesan." She died of a ruptured uterus at the age of thirty-seven, never having received any aid or recognition from the state of Texas.

After coming upon the few survivors of the Alamo making their way east, Henry Karnes reported the fall of the fort to

Houston. More importantly, he also reported that Santa Anna was advancing on Gonzales, due east and only seventy miles from San Antonio. Another scout told Houston that Santa Anna could be in Gonzales by Monday, the next day. Finally, Urrea was only ninety miles due south of Gonzales, near Goliad, and on the march. He could lay siege to Fort Defiance or merely go around it and advance on Gonzales or points farther east.

Houston had no real army and he knew it. Finally confirmed as commander in chief of all military units in Texas, Houston arrived in Gonzales to find an "army" of 374 men commanded by Col. Edward Burleson. Burleson did something that others had not. He immediately placed himself subservient to Houston based on the orders of the Convention of 1836. The men in the army may have preferred Burleson, but Houston was commander. Houston also knew this army was like all other Texan armies: underfed, many of the men without adequate clothing, and more importantly, many without arms.

Houston went to work. The men held their customary election with Burleson elected as colonel. Houston read the Texas Declaration of Independence and his appointment as commander along with his orders to go to the aid of the Alamo, though that order had obviously changed.

Houston was finally in total control with no competing commanders in chief. The convention had confirmed it. Burleson went along with it. Fannin, a one-time competitor, was bottled up in Goliad. Dr. Grant was dead. Colonel Johnson had had enough of revolution after his narrow escape from the Matamoros expedition. If Bowie or Travis or even Crockett had any aspirations for command, it was too late. They were all dead.

The bravery of the men at the Alamo cannot be denied, but it was not the kind of war Houston wanted to fight. Houston was convinced that his men with their rifles and mobility could defeat the larger, more ponderous Mexican army made up largely of poorly trained conscripts. Santa Anna wanted to fight Waterloo while Houston wanted to use the technology of the day, the rifle, against masses of men. The siege at the Alamo gained thirteen days. There is no doubt of that, but there is no doubt as well the thirteen days were squandered playing politics rather than raising or training an army. With the fall of the Alamo and the ascension of Houston, petty politics were over for the time being. A declaration of independence was signed, and there was no more time wasted over whether Texas should somehow remain a state of Mexico. An independent Texas was born.

That independent Texas was to shrink rapidly because Houston's plan was to retreat. With the report given by Susannah, Houston decided to break camp. At 8:30 that same evening he ordered his men to be ready to march out of Gonzales by 11:30. The plan was simple: draw Santa Anna farther into the interior, string out his army, and then attack and destroy part of that strung-out army when the Texan army was larger and better provisioned. Or, just keep moving to the Sabine and end up in, or near, the United States. There his army would swell with the volunteers streaming out of Louisiana into Texas. Settlers were joining the army out of desperation, but the real growth came from the adventurers on their way west. The possibility that Santa Anna would invade Louisiana was remote. He did not want war with the United States, he only wanted Anglo settlers out of Mexican territory, or dead.

Finally, Santa Anna had no intention of staying to see the end of the campaign. He felt his work was done in that remote region. Santa Anna had marched his armies more than a thousand miles to kill 189 rebels at the Alamo and bottle Fannin up at Goliad. The longer he was away from the center of power in Mexico City, the more time elapsed for internal dissension and rebellion. Rebellion had already broken out again in Mexico proper, and he needed to squash it. The general made arrangements for a naval ship to take him home. He would leave Matagorda on or around April 1, sailing to Veracruz for a few days of rest prior to putting down the next rebellion.

Santa Anna placed Gen. Vicente Filisola in overall command of the army. Filisola was forty-seven at the time, born in Italy but his family had moved to Spain when he was young. He joined the Spanish army at the age of fifteen and made lieutenant by twenty-one. He arrived in Mexico in 1811, serving as a captain of the artillery and then captain of grenadiers, but he joined the rebels of Iturbide when Iturbide offered to make him a general. Filisola, like Santa Anna, was good at putting down rebellions, specializing in those in the south of Mexico.

With the expected arrival of the naval ship at Matagorda, Santa Anna developed his battle plan for mopping up Texas. First, Santa Anna believed that with the fall of the Alamo and the pending resolution of the Goliad garrison, the military campaign was nearly over. All that was left was to fully terrorize the settlers so that no Anglo would ever want to set foot in Texas again. He fully intended that his army would enforce the law that anyone caught with arms was a pirate and would be executed, legally, as such. All land was to be confiscated, with Mexican settlers replacing the Anglo colonists.

Santa Anna ordered the army to split into three groups, something Houston was banking on. Urrea, already coming up northeast along the coast, would deal with Goliad, take Victoria, and continue to hug the coast. Gen. Antonio Gaona, who had arrived after the fall of the Alamo, would lead his seven hundred men out of San Antonio taking a northern route through Bastrop, Washington-on-the-Brazos, and present-day Huntsville with Nacogdoches, near the Louisiana border, as the target. Gen. Joaquin Ramirez y Sesma was ordered to Gonzales in pursuit of the rebel army, then on to San Felipe, ending his journey at Lynch's Ferry on the San Jacinto River. The focus of the three smaller eastward-marching armies was to push the settlers out. The Texas army was an afterthought that Sesma would destroy at Gonzales.

Houston didn't know the extent of the plan, but he knew he had to withdraw. He could not fight any of the armies with less than four hundred men. He had to buy time. A few minutes past midnight on the evening of March 13, 1836, the small army marched out of Gonzales. Panicked settlers—men, women, and children—joined the exodus. Though not all the civilians wanting to flee had yet made it to Gonzales and the protection of the army, Houston could not, and would not, risk losing his army. He left a mounted company commanded by Juan Sequin behind to organize the settlers who arrived late and to scout for the oncoming Mexicans.

In preparation for the retreat, Houston had had two cumbersome brass cannons tossed in the river. The army's one wagon was loaded with ammunition and provisions. Women, children, and the elderly were loaded on any available civilian wagons. By dawn the caravan had gone ten miles and was camped in the woods near Peach Creek. The rear guard burned the town. Gunpowder barrels, some said whiskey barrels as well, exploded, awakening the soldiers and civilians sleeping on the creek.

The guard under Seguin rejoined the army late that morning along with the newly arrived civilians. Sequin was given the job of foraging off the land, bringing in free range cattle to feed the army and civilians. In the meantime the soldiers and civilians made do with hardtack, flour and water cooked over a fire. It would have to do until Sequin and his men could bring in something better.

A member of the army, J. H. Kuykendall, described the events leading up to the evacuation of Gonzalez.

> On the evening of the 13th, Mrs. Dickinson and Travis' negro man arrived at Gonzales with the astounding intelligence that the Alamo had been assaulted and taken on the morning of the 6th and all of its defenders slain. Superadded to this news, a rumor became rife that two thousand of the enemy—the advance division of the Mexican army—might be hourly expected at Gonzales. As may reasonably be supposed this news produced intense excitement in our camp. In the little village of Gonzales the distress of the families was extreme. Some of them had lost friends and near and dear relations in the Alamo and now the ruthless foe was at hand, and they unprepared to fly. To facilitate their exit, Gen'l. Houston caused some of our baggage wagons to be given up to them; but the teams, which were grazing in the prairie, were yet to be found, and night had already set in. In the meantime, orders were

issued to the army to prepare as fast as possible to retreat. As most of the companies [all infantry] had been deprived of the means of transportation, all our baggage and provisions, except what we were able to pack ourselves, were thrown into our campfires. Tents, clothing, coffee, meal and bacon were alike consigned to the devouring element. Tall spires of flame shot up in every direction, illuminating prairie and woodland.

Houston needed to travel as fast as he could, and that meant traveling light. But Houston wanted his retreat to be strategic, not a rout.

About ten o'clock one of the captains marched his company to Gen'l. Houston's tent and said: "General, my company is ready to march." The general, in a voice loud enough to be heard throughout the camp, replied: "In the name of God, sir, don't be in haste—wait till all are ready and let us retreat in good order."

Another soldier described Houston as both agitated at times and cool at times:

Some have remarked that our Commander was unduly excited on this occasion, but I observed the General several times that evening and night, and he appeared and acted as a cool and collected man, although he exhibited much anxiety, and at times became irritated because of his difficulty in controlling the troops, also in allaying, as far as possible, the high excitement of the citizens.

Houston's anxiety is understandable, but anxious or not, he didn't slow down. He organized and moved.

In contrast, many citizens did panic, some thinking they were being left behind. The troops did not help the situation, as described by Kuykendall:

We were formed four deep and at the command: "Forward March!" commenced this memorable retreat. (Mar. 13, 1836.) The night was warm, but so dark as to constrain the army to move at a very moderate pace. Silent and indeed, solemn was the march. As we passed through the streets of

Gonzales, we noticed great lights in the houses and the people packing up their household effects in all possible haste. A man came out on the piazza and said (addressing the army): "In the name of God, gentlemen, I hope you are not going to leave the families behind!" Some one in our ranks answered: "Oh yes, we are looking out for number one."

In the face of such danger, many family relations became strained, with Stephen S. Sparks, soon to be a San Jacinto veteran, noting the friction between a cowardly husband and his ready-to-fight wife:

> It was a complete panic. One man, living a few miles from Washington, together with his wife and three or four little children started. They had ten or twelve head of cattle, and a pony; they were driving the cattle, and his wife was riding the pony, with the youngest child on behind her. Before they got to Washington some people passed them, and told them to go as fast as they could, for the Mexicans were close behind. This was more than the heroic man could stand. He told his wife that it would be better for one of them to escape, than for all to be killed; then he took her and the child off the horse, left them in the road, and came on and crossed the river. But his wife and children drove the cows, and in an hour or so they crossed the river, too, and found him sitting by a tree. She went to him and said, "Now you get behind this breast-work of cotton bales and fight." But he said it was not worth while, for they would kill everybody that stayed and fought them. She said, "Well, I will. If I can get a gun, I'll be durned if I don't go behind that breast-work and fight with those men." We had an old musket with us, and my mess-mate, Howard Bailey, said, "Madam, here is a gun." She took the gun and remained over half the night behind the breast-works.

Finally, one soldier, reflecting years later, summed up the situation and the commander: "General Houston understood the situation—he was a born leader of men. He recognized the helplessness of making a stand at or anywhere near Gonzales, and his only object, his only hope, was to hold these excited men together while falling back, and while doing so to form them into some semblance of a real army."

There was the key. Houston was a realist. In retrospect, his actions seem perfectly logical; anyone could see that a small, ill-equipped army could not hold off Santa Anna. But in 1836 Texas, Houston was the only one to see it. Travis didn't. Bowie didn't. Crockett didn't. Grant and Johnson didn't. Fannin didn't. Only Houston took the time to develop a plan and execute it.

In addition, he communicated the plan to his men in detail, as described by soldier Creed Taylor.

> He went among the men, talked, reasoned, and harangued them in groups and companies, explained the situation, denounced idle rumors, and appealed to their patriotism. He pointed out the necessity of retreat to the Colorado, the Brazos, or beyond, if need be. He explained that Fannin, with 400 men, and a fine park of artillery, had been ordered to evacuate that outpost and join the regular army, and with this addition of men and arms, augmented with constant recruits from the settlements, and from the states, his army would be increased to such proportions as to enable him to meet and defeat any force Santa Anna could bring into the field; and there could be no question as to the ultimate triumph of Texas—if they only remained firm in duty and loyalty to authority. The butchery of the Alamo men, he said, would fill the hearts of all Texans with fiery indignation; the people of the United States would take up the cry for vengeance, and the call to arms would resound in every hamlet and village, volunteers would rush forward to the seat of war, and Texas would be free. Such, in substance, was the General's appeal to the insubordinate factions in his command.

That was Houston's strategy. With the fall of the Alamo and the advance of the Mexican army, Houston:
- struck his camp and was on the road within three hours,
- took what panicked civilians he could with him and left a guard to gather and protect the civilians that followed,
- burned the provisions he couldn't carry,
- burned the town so it would be of no use to the enemy,
- grew his army as he retreated by pressing men, horses, oxen, and wagons into service as he came upon them.

Finally he ignored the heavy rain that began falling. Nothing would stop him from heading east.

By March 17, Houston's army had swelled to over six hundred men and had crossed the Colorado River at Burnham's Ferry. On March 19, he headed south to Beason's Ferry, still on the Colorado, where he rested his army. Houston, in six days, had moved his army and his civilians seventy miles from Gonzales, putting a rain-swollen river between him and Santa Anna's armies.

Compare this to Fannin. On March 11, Fannin sent Amon King and his company south to escort colonists to safety. On the thirteenth Fannin sent Ward and the Georgia battalion to rescue King. Fannin then received Houston's order to abandon and destroy Fort Defiance, retreat to the defense of Victoria, and send one-third of his force to Gonzales. No order could be more explicit, but Fannin chose to wait, waiting for King and Ward to return.

Fannin would be accused of disobedience, but Dr. Barnard considers the actions of Fannin a sin of omission, not a sin of commission. "About this time, certainly before to-day came in the order from Gen. Houston to Col. Fannin, to retreat to Victoria. This was the first and only communication had from Gen. Houston, while he was at Goliad. In fact, it was the first intimation we had of his whereabouts." The doctor is wrong here, as Houston had earlier directed Fannin to join him at Gonzales to march to the relief of the Alamo, but the doctor soon gets to the crux of the problem, explaining, "The necessity of a retreat was now palpable to all. So far from Col. Fannin wishing to disobey the order, I know from his own lips that he intended to conform to it, *as soon as the Georgia Battalion should return* [emphasis added]; and I heard him before this express a wish that Gen. Houston would come on and take command of the troops." How Houston "would come on and take command of the troops" is inexplicable given the fact that he was retreating and counting on Fannin to do so as well. Dr. Barnard concludes, "The alleged disobedience of Col. Fannin to Gen. Houston's order is an undeserved censure on a gallant soldier, and that he wrote back a refusal I know to be false. Circumstances enabled me to possess a positive knowledge on these points, and justice to both the dead and the living require me thus to state it."

Jack Shackelford backs up Dr. Barnard, noting,

> It was not until the evening of the 18th that we received any intelligence from Ward, and that not of a satisfactory character. I have mentioned this circumstance, if possible, to dissipate an unworthy prejudice which has been created in the minds of many, that Fannin wished to forestall Houston in the command of the army, and therefore disobeyed his orders. I have said, that he committed an error in separating his forces. Had he not done this, we should have been prepared to fall back on Victoria, as ordered, with a force sufficient to contend with every Mexican we might have encountered. Fannin's great anxiety alone, for the fate of Ward and King, and their little band, delayed our march. This delay, I feel assured, was not the result of any wish to disobey orders.

A litany of "ifs" and "buts."

The harsh reality is that by Wednesday, the sixteenth, nothing had been done about retreating from Fort Defiance except sending out couriers looking for Ward and King. A Captain Fraser volunteered to ride to Refugio and return within twenty-four hours provided he did not get killed or captured. Fraser left and the fort went back to waiting. Fraser returned around four o'clock on March 17 with the news that King and his men had been caught and executed. He had no news of Ward and the Georgia battalion.

Fannin met with his officers and it was agreed to retreat the next day. Then another distraction. Col. A. C. Horton and his men had been out on patrol and returned to the fort reporting that an additional force of fifteen hundred Mexicans under Colonel Morales were uniting with Urrea's army just south of Refugio. The commanding officers met again and reconfirmed a retreat for the eighteenth. Then additional scouts came in with news that a large enemy force was near the fort.

Fannin backtracked. He earlier had ordered the cannon

buried and now had the men dig them up and remount them. The fort was made ready for attack, with Fannin ordering what remained of the town of La Bahia burned and any remaining obstructions outside the fort leveled to provide a clean line of fire. There was no attack on the seventeenth.

Early on the morning of the eighteenth, a Mexican cavalry patrol was spotted outside the fort. Colonel Horton and a few of his men mounted up and rode off on the offensive. Horton put the Mexicans on the run—right into a larger party of Mexican cavalry who turned the tables and chased Horton and his men back to the fort. Seeing Horton coming, all the available horses were mounted and the Texans rode out of Fort Defiance to chase the Mexicans across the river. Horton and his men changed direction, again pursuing the Mexicans. Horton then again ran right into a larger force of Mexicans who soon trapped him in the Mission Espirit Santo, where he had been compelled to seek refuge from their numbers. Dr. Shackelford and the Red Rovers crossed the river and advanced on the mission.

All of this was observed from the fort with the men manning the walls cheering on the Texans. Dr. Barnard and a few men climbed the bell tower to watch the action. The Mexicans finally had enough and withdrew. Horton and his men, along with the Red Rovers, returned to the fort.

The cavalry that had done all the chasing back and forth was not the main force of the Mexicans. Urrea had learned from his local intelligence network that Fannin planned on retreating to Victoria. To Urrea it made sense to retreat with a force of little more than three hundred men in front of an army of over one thousand now being reinforced, but what Fannin decided really did not matter to Urrea. If Fannin stayed in the fort, Urrea could besiege it. If Fannin retreated, Urrea could catch the army in the field. Too, Urrea could just ignore Fort Defiance and go around it or employ a combination of these tactics. Urrea held all the cards because Fannin had not acted decisively. Fannin would continue to vacillate.

The activities of Horton and Shackelford had taken up most of the day, breaking the monotony of burying and then digging up cannon. The men cheered from the walls of the fort, abandoning their work duties. The oxen that had been made ready for the soldiers' withdrawal were left untended and unwatered. Wagons were left partially loaded. Fannin, expecting an attack, had shifted his priorities and reinforced the guard rather than preparing to abandon his fort.

He walked the walls that night with Captain Westover checking the men and defenses. He stopped at one station to talk to Abel Morgan, a forty-four-year-old former member of the North Carolina legislature who left for Texas to get away from a violent wife. Fannin asked Morgan for his opinion about leaving the fort and retreating. Morgan felt the time for escape had passed. Noting the fort had six weeks of provisions and 360 men, Morgan argued for staying and defending Fort Defiance. Westover, according to Morgan, agreed and noted they should have left three or four days before but now they were no doubt surrounded. Morgan, who also went by the name Smith, was a member of Westover's regulars. Morgan wrote, "Col. Fanning seemed to have his mind unsettled about it." The two officers left Morgan, warning him that an attack could come at his position, as he was overlooking a gully running from the river to the fort. Morgan assured the two officers that if he were attacked, he would fire his cannon as a signal.

Urrea did not attack. He had no intention of doing so. Rather he was beginning to think that Fannin would not, or could not, retreat now. Urrea began planning for a long siege, but Fannin would surprise him.

Chapter 11

The Battle of Coleto

"We whipped them off yesterday and we can do so again today."

Saturday, March 19, 1836, dawned cold, wet, and foggy at
Fort Defiance. The Texans did not get an early start, taking
until eight or nine to get breakfast and finish destroying provisions that could not be taken. Fire marks from this destruction can still be seen on the front wall of the chapel. Finally,
nine cannon, along with wagons of ammunition and supplies,
were ready for departure. Some accounts say they left the
fort at nine o'clock, but others put the time later in the
morning due to the destruction. One thing is known for sure:
no food was packed for the trip.

The San Antonio River was the first obstacle on the road to
Victoria. The high banks of the river made the crossing, even
at the ford, difficult. Wagons were unloaded and then
reloaded. The oxen teams were already exhausted, as they
had been fettered and unattended during the night. The cannon, which Houston had ordered dumped in the river if
unable to be moved, were the worst to handle. Obviously they
were heavy and cumbersome. The steep bank of the river
made the task even more difficult. Shackelford wrote, "much
time was consumed in consequence of the inability of the
team to draw our cannon up the bank. I waded into the river
myself, with several of my company, assisting the artillerists
by putting our shoulders to the wheels, and forcing the guns
forward. We then moved on briskly and in good order."

Captain Shackelford's Red Rovers led the expedition followed by Duval's company with Colonel Horton's company
scouting in front. Horton's company of thirty men rode horses, the rest of the men walked. Finally leaving the river
behind, the troops marched six miles, crossing Manahuilla
Creek, with Horton's scouts still reporting the way ahead as

clear. Horton did report that the enemy army was four or five miles away but apparently not in pursuit.

Just as the Texans were making some progress in their escape, Fannin ordered a halt to rest and to allow the oxen to graze. Shackelford could not believe it, noting the need to reach the protection of the timber lining Coleto Creek, for they had stopped in the middle of a wide-open plain known as the nine-mile prairie. The captain confronted Fannin. "I remonstrated warmly against this measure, and urged the necessity of first reaching the Coleta, then about five miles distant. In this matter I was overruled, and from the ardent manner in which I urged the necessity of getting under the protection of timber, I found the smiles of many, indicated a belief that at least I thought it prudent to take care of number one." Shackelford felt his objections were considered cowardly by the other officers, who, along with Fannin, were not taking the threat seriously. He later defended his stance: "Here let me state one thing, lest I may be misunderstood: Col. Fannin and many others could not be made to believe that the Mexicans would dare follow us. He had too much contempt for their prowess, and too much confidence in the ability of his own little force."

How could Fannin, at this late date and knowing he was being chased by at least one thousand Mexican soldiers, show "too much contempt for their prowess"? Fannin still believed one Texan could best five Mexicans.

Then Shackelford provides a description of Fannin: "That he was deficient in that caution which a prudent officer should always evince, must be admitted; but that he was a brave, gallant, and intrepid officer, none who knew him can doubt." Shackelford sums up Fannin, the enigma. Though Fannin was not a very smart officer, he was "brave, gallant, and intrepid." Since Shackelford would lose his son and two nephews in the massacre, a more damning indictment of the man commanding the army might be expected from him.

John C. Duval, the twenty-year-old son of the governor of Florida and brother of Burr Duval, captain of the Kentucky

Mustangs, was thinking along the same lines as Shackelford. He recorded,

> We entered the large prairie extending to the timber on the Coletto, a distance of eight or nine miles. When we had approached within two and a half or three miles of the point where the road we were traveling entered the timber (though it was somewhat nearer to the left) a halt was ordered and the oxen were unyoked from guns and wagons, and turned out to graze. What induced Col. Fannin to halt at this place in the open prairie, I cannot say, for by going two and a half miles further, we would have reached the Coletto creek, where there was an abundance of water and where we would have had the protection of timber in the event of being attacked.

Duval had a different read from Shackelford on the reaction of the other officers. Duval believed most deplored the halt, explaining, "I understood at the time that several of Col. Fannin's officers urged him strongly to continue the march until we reached the creek, as it was certain that a large body of Mexican troops were somewhere in the vicinity; but however this may be, Col. Fannin was not to be turned from his purpose, and the halt was made."

Duval comes to the same conclusion as Shackelford regarding Fannin's opinion of the Mexican forces: "Possibly he may have thought that two hundred and fifty well armed Americans under any circumstances would be able to defend themselves against any force the Mexicans had within striking distance, but as the sequel will show the halt at this place was a most fatal one for us."

While everyone took a rest break lasting an hour, Horton and his scouts went forward to check Coleto Creek for a place to ford. He and his men would never make it back to the group. By the time they scouted the woods, the Mexicans had surrounded the wagon train. Horton would later incur a great deal of criticism for not going to the aid of the men in the square but Shackelford exonerates Horton, writing later that one of Horton's officers, a Lieutenant Moore, thought the idea of going back would mean certain death and most of the men agreed.

Instead the scouts rode for Victoria hoping to bring back Texan forces, only to find Victoria occupied by the Mexican army.

Even with the misdirected criticism for his actions at Coleto, Horton was popular enough after the war to be elected to the First and Second Congresses of the Texas Republic. When Texas entered statehood, Horton was elected the first lieutenant governor of the state in 1846. He was not reelected, returning to his plantation near Matagorda. He managed the plantation successfully and was a member of the board of trustees that founded Baylor University. At the beginning of the Civil War, Horton was regarded as one of the wealthiest men in Texas, but he lost most of his fortune during the war. Horton died in September 1865 in Matagorda.

Back on the prairie around Goliad, Abel Morgan was facing the unnerving appearance of the Mexican army. He describes, "by the time that we got about one mile into the prairie the whole Western border of the prairie was lined with Mexicans, and by the time that we got half a mile further they broke in a cloud as it were ahead of us to the East."

Herman Ehrenberg was part of the rear guard and waxed poetic on the pastoral scene that would soon turn ugly.

> Our route led us through one of those charming landscapes where little prairies alternate with thin forests of oak without any undergrowth. Frequently we saw herds of cattle grazing on the luxuriant grass; and immense herds of deer looked with amazement at the little army wending its way through the stillness of the west. And the noble Andalusian horses, that had their beginning here with the horrible conquest of Mexico by Cortez, stamped away in close formation over the undulating prairie, and long after they had disappeared one could still hear the rumble of their fleeing hoofs. Eight miles from Goliad begins a considerable treeless prairie, known as the nine-mile prairie. It was in this prairie that the army had warily advanced from four to five miles by three o'clock in the afternoon.

Herman and his friends were about two miles behind the main army when they were first provided hints concerning the approaching force.

Since not the least trace of an enemy had shown itself so far we rode carelessly along until we accidentally turned around [and] noticed at a distance of about four miles a figure in the part of the forest through which we had just come that looked like a rider on horse back. Since, however, it did not move, we came to the conclusion that it was a tree or some other lifeless object.

Still unconcerned about their surroundings, the group grew tired and "decided to halt a little while to graze and rest our horses." In some accounts the young men are reported to have fallen asleep. If they were, they awoke to see:

behind us near the edge of the forest a long black streak on the plain. It was impossible for us to tell what it was. A few thought possibly that they were large herds of cattle that the settlers were driving eastward out of reach of the Mexicans. But this seemed improbable . . . as we looked more intently and observed the disturbing object more closely, we noticed a moving and twisting in the dark mass that grew larger and larger and in proportion to the distance ever plainer. We could no longer doubt that it was the Mexican cavalry that was following us in full gallop.

The young men were now wide awake. "Hastily we mounted our horses and dashed off at full speed to our comrades to prepare them for the reception of the enemy. The news was received with a hurrah. Everything was at once prepared for battle. A hollow square was formed, and in this way, of course very slowly we continued our march."

Ehrenberg describes Fannin and his actions upon receiving the news of the approaching Mexican army using almost the same wording as Shackelford: "Fannin, our commander, was a gallant and spirited warrior, but for the commanding officer, where he should act with independence, understanding, and decision, he was totally unfit. Instead of trying to reach the forest one mile away for the sake of our safety, where the Americans and the Texans are invincible, he decided to offer battle on an unfavorable, open terrain."

Herman Ehrenberg returned to the main force. His three comrades did not. Dr. Barnard wrote,

> It appears that four horsemen had been left in the rear and that they, instead of keeping a lookout, had, under a false sense of security, laid down, and were only aroused by the approach of the Mexicans. They now came at full speed, one of them, and one only (a German by the name of Ehrenburg) joined us. The other three, in the greatest apparent terror, passed about a hundred yards on our right, without even stopping to look at us, and under the strongest appliance of whip and spur, followed by the hearty curses of our men.

Fannin ordered the army forward toward the cover of the woods but at a deliberate pace. He told the men the enemy in sight was only going to skirmish and not engage in a full-scale battle. The column had gone about one mile when disaster struck.

A half-mile from the timberline upon entering a piece of low ground, the ammunition wagon broke down and "we were compelled to take our position in a valley, six or seven feet below the mean base, of about one fourth of a mile in area." The Mexicans caught up quickly with a company of cavalry taking position on the right flank of the Texans and another on the left. Mexican infantry came upon the rear. Additional cavalry moved around to block the front, or east, of the Texans and put themselves between the Texans and the tree line. Fannin had two choices: take as much ammunition as they could carry and charge the cavalry or fight in a depression in the open valley. Fannin chose to fight in the open.

Urrea began the day believing that Fannin had abandoned his planned retreat, and Fort Defiance would fall only after a prolonged siege. No one in the Mexican army was even aware of Fannin's departure until an hour after the Texans had left, when scouts discovered the empty fort. Urrea dispatched his cavalry in pursuit. He then started marching his men after the Texans. Urrea ordered Colonel Garay to send the slower-moving artillery and additional ammunition after the cavalry and infantry and then occupy the presidio with his remaining men.

greetings to advantage. The moment arrived, our ranks opened, and the artillery hurled death and destruction among the enemy. Their horses, to which the confusion of battle was a terror, reared up wildly. The effect of our fire was frightful. Herds of horses were running without rider, while others were wallowing in blood and kicking furiously. The resulting confusion to some extent retarded the attack of the enemy, and consequently we began to move forward again. But we could do this undisturbed only for a short time as we were soon threatened with a new attack.

The Greys wanted to make for the safety of the tree line, but Fannin called for another halt. On the verge of mutiny they went to Fannin. They "saw themselves obliged to indicate to him that they would march off alone. But it was now too late. The enemy had already appeared on the elevation ahead of us, and there was nothing for us to do except either to fight our way through or to offer battle in the unfavorable position in which we then were." The officers met, but "before the captains, who had assembled for consultation could reach a definite conclusion, the countless bugles of the Mexicans from all directions sounded for the attack. The cavalry itself rapidly advanced from all sides at once, not in closed ranks but in broken formation and with yelling and constant firing."

The Mexican infantry advanced and the cavalry pulled back. Cavalry was not cannon fodder; infantry was. This cannon fodder was, however, not the conscripted Indians who made up much of the Mexican army. The square was charged by the Tampico regiment that Santa Anna had called "the best troops in the world." Shackelford described the attack.

When at a convenient distance, they gave us a volley and charged bayonet. So soon as the smoke cleared away, they were received by a piece of artillery, Duval's riflemen, and some other troops, which mowed them down with tremendous slaughter. Their career being thus promptly stopped, they contented themselves with falling down in the grass and occasionally raising up to fire; but whenever they showed their heads, they were taken down by the riflemen.

Attacks now came from all sides.

The engagement now became general; and a body of cavalry, from two to three hundred strong, made a demonstration on our rear. They came up in full tilt, with gleaming lances, shouting like Indians. When about sixty yards distant, the whole of the rear division of our little command, together with a piece or two of artillery, loaded with double canister filled with musket-balls, opened a tremendous fire upon them, which brought them to a full halt and swept them down by scores. The rest immediately retreated, and chose to fight on foot the balance of the day. Our guns had now become hot—we had no water to sponge them—many of our artillerists had been wounded, and we had to rely alone on our small-arms. These were industriously handled, as all our men were kept busy during the balance of the day.

The day was ending, and Urrea had achieved his purpose. Fannin was surrounded on the prairie with no water and no food. Urrea ordered individual snipers up into the tall grass surrounding the Texans. Their sniper fire was accurate, killing four men and wounding fifty in all. The Texas force of 250 was taking heavy casualties. With darkness the sniper fire ceased, as the gun flashes gave away the sniper positions. Then Urrea withdrew his men into the woods.

The number of troops available to Urrea has always been in dispute, but one thing is not. He was bringing up reinforcements by the hour with infantry and artillery coming to join the battle. Urrea divided his command into three units. One guarded the road to Goliad, the second blocked the way to Victoria, with the third ready to go either way in case the Texans attempted a breakout. Urrea also conducted a bit of psychological warfare, having his buglers do calls throughout the night.

The Texans went to work to improve their position by digging a ditch around the perimeter and using the dirt to reinforce the wagons and baggage. The Texan cannon were fouled and therefore useless due to the lack of water to cool the cannon barrels and clean the bores. The artillerymen had also taken heavy casualties as targets of the snipers. The lack of water affected the men and animals as well as the cannon. The Texans were miserable with many wounded, no food, and no water. It was a cold March night, so few got any sleep. Dr. Barnard described that wakeful night in the square.

> Wearied and supperless I lay down on the bare earth, without any cover, in order to obtain some repose, but the coolness of the ground soon benumbed my limbs and roused me from an unsatisfactory slumber, to seek for warmth in some exercise. This was supplied us by an order to make an intrenchment. . . . We went to work with our spades and dug a ditch, two or three feet in depth. . . . I worked with the spade until fatigued, then lay down for a little troubled sleep, until the chilliness of my limbs forced me to seek for warmth by using the spade again; and in such alterations, the dismal night wore away, and day at last dawned up on us.

With the dawn came the one thing a military square could not withstand—artillery. Urrea had received five hundred additional troops, a fresh supply of ammunition (he had used most of his in the previous day's battle), and the artillery. Urrea started the morning with several cannon shots into the square.

The Texan officers had been busy during the night planning for the next day. They fell into three camps. One group wanted to make a dash for the timber. Another group wanted to fight where they were and one group considered surrender. All were concerned for the wounded that would be left behind if a move were made for the trees.

With the crash of the cannon, everyone, except Fannin, realized the futility of staying in the square. The Mexicans had an elevated position and could lob shell and grapeshot into the square or blow the wagons to bits, spraying splinters of wood as additional missiles. Fannin called a quick council of his officers, presenting the alternatives to the men. Fannin's position was clear, as reported by Shackelford: "When the matter was first proposed to Colonel Fannin, he was for holding out longer, saying, 'We whipped them off yesterday and we can do so again today.' But the necessity of the measure soon became obvious." The plight of the wounded was the overriding factor. After a brief discussion, it was decided to pursue the possibility of an honorable surrender. The massacre at the Alamo was forgotten. A white flag was hoisted over the square.

Urrea tells his side of the story in his diary.

At half past six in the morning the ammunition arrived which, as stated before, had been lost the day before; and although more had been ordered from Col. Garay, this had not arrived up to this time. One hundred infantry, two four pounders (not a twelve-pounder), and a howitzer were added to my force. I placed these as a battery about 160 paces from the enemy protected by the rifle companies. I ordered the rest of the infantry to form a column that was to advance along the left of our battery when it opened fire. As soon as we did this and began our movement as planned, the enemy, without answering our fire, raised a white flag. I immediately ordered my battery to cease firing and instructed Lieut. Col. Morales, Colonel Juan Jose Holzinger, and my aide, José de la Luz González to approach the enemy and ascertain their purpose. The first of these returned soon after, stating that they wished to capitulate. My reply restricted itself to stating that I could not accept any terms except an unconditional surrender. Messrs. Morales and Salas proceeded to tell this to the commissioners of the enemy who had already come out from their trenches. Several communications passed between us; and, desirous of putting an end to the negotiations, I went over to the enemy's camp and explained to their leader the impossibility in which I found myself of granting other terms than an unconditional surrender as proposed, in view of which fact I refused to subscribe to the capitulation submitted consisting of three articles.

Addressing myself to Fannin and his companions in the presence of Messrs. Morales, Salas, Holzinger and others I said conclusively, "If you gentlemen wish to surrender at discretion, the matter is ended, otherwise I shall return to my camp and renew the attack."

In spite of the regret I felt in making such a reply, and in spite of my great desire of offering them guarantees as humanity dictated, this was beyond my authority. Had I been in a position to do so, I would have at least guaranteed them their life. Fannin was a gentleman, a man of courage, a quality which makes us soldiers esteem each other mutually. His manners captivated my affection, and if it had been in my hand to save him, together with his companions, I would have gladly done so. All I could do was to offer him to use my influence with the general-in-chief, which I did from the Guadalupe.

Urrea knew Santa Anna's order; he had had King's men executed at Refugio. He had also, on at least two occasions, "expelled" prisoners to Mexico rather than execute them. Urrea would prefer not to execute almost three hundred men in cold blood if he could avoid it, but he was aware that execution may be necessary, so the best he could offer the Texans was "surrender at discretion."

Dr. Shackelford saw it differently, recording that after corresponding with the enemy, Major Wallace and two other representatives "reported that the Mexican General could capitulate with the commanding officer only. Col. Fannin, although quite lame, then went out with the flag."

Shackelford had a word with Fannin before he left the lines. He wanted to make sure that Fannin received surrender terms ensuring they would not be slaughtered. If that was not certain, Shackelford preferred to go down fighting.

> When he was about to leave our lines, the emotions of my mind were intense, and I felt some anxiety to hear the determination of the men. I remarked to him, that I would not oppose a surrender, provided we could obtain an honourable capitulation; one, on which he could rely: that if he could not obtain such—come back—our graves are already dug—let us all be buried together. To these remarks the men responded in a firm and determined manner; and the Colonel assured us, that he never would surrender on any other terms.

Fannin returned with a document written in both English and Spanish. The surrender terms were agreed on and then, according to Shackelford, "signed and interchanged in the most formal and solemn manner." The terms were as follows:

> 1st. That we should be received and treated as prisoners of war according to the usages of the most civilized nations.
>
> 2d. That private property should be respected and restored: that the side arms of the officers should be given up.
>
> 3d. That the men should be sent to Copano, and thence to the United States in eight days, or so soon thereafter as vessels could be procured to take them.
>
> 4th. That the officers should be paroled and return to the United States in like manner.

Shackelford was convinced this was an honorable surrender, one they would all survive, and that without such terms, the men would never have surrendered.

There is no known existing English copy of the surrender document. Urrea wrote his version of the surrender document in his memoir.

> Art. 1. The Mexican troops having placed their battery at a distance of one hundred and seventy paces from us and the fire having been renewed, we raised a white flag. Colonels Juan Morales, Colonel Mariano Salas and Lieutenant Colonel Juan Jose Holzinger, a German and an engineer came immediately. We proposed to them to surrender at discretion and they agreed.
>
> Art. 2. The commandant Fannin and the wounded shall be treated with all possible consideration upon the surrender of all their arms.
>
> Art. 3. The whole detachment shall be treated as prisoners of war and shall be subject to the disposition of the Supreme Government.
>
> Camp on the Coleto between Guadalupe and La Bahia, March 20, 1836. B. C. Wallace, commandant, J. M. Chadwick, Aide.—Approved, James W. Fannin.

There is no mention of the terms included in Shackelford's account.

Years later, Shackelford would comment on Urrea's

description of the surrender. "Here let me remark that I have read General Urrea's pamphlet. . . . On this point, as well as his denial of any capitulation, I never read a more villainous falsehood from the pen of any man who aspired to the rank of general."

Whatever the truth of the terms, the Texans surrendered. Dr. Barnard recalled that the Mexicans immediately took possession of their surrendered munitions, even those of the officers. The men were assured that all such arms and ammunition would be "safely returned to us on our release, which they flattered us would shortly take place." Abel Morgan was allowed to keep his knife, or dirk, for use in eating due to his lack of teeth. Those able to walk began the march back to Goliad. The wounded waited for transportation.

Not all the men wanted to surrender, especially the young hotheads of the New Orleans Greys and the Red Rovers. Ehrenberg said that one Grey, Johnson, was so outraged by the surrender that he threw a lighted cigar into the ammunition wagon and was killed in the explosion along with several Mexicans. Abel Morgan disputes that account, saying it was the Mexicans and "their segars" that caused a fire and resulting explosion.

The truth of the conditions of the surrender surely lies somewhere in between what the Texans recalled and what Urrea recalled. Urrea wanted the battle over. He probably made the conditions seem as good as he could. Certainly at the disadvantage, the Texans put the best light on any terms. What they did not realize was that Urrea was not the decision maker.

Chapter 12

The Massacre and Escape

"... but with a "The Republic of Texas Forever!"
I threw myself into the rescuing floods.

Holzinger's prediction appeared to be coming true.

After the surrender, Col. Juan Jose Holzinger, born Johann Josef Holzinger in Mainz, Germany, had comforted the surrendering Texans by telling them, "Well, gentlemen, in eight days, liberty and home." Holzinger was the only Mexican officer who spoke English and not very well at that. The surrender negotiations had been done in three languages: English, Spanish, and German. Holzinger negotiated the fine points of the surrender with German-born Texans who translated back into English for the non-German speaking Texans while Holzinger translated back into Spanish for his Mexican colleagues.

Holzinger was not a soldier of fortune. He left Germany for Mexico in 1825 as an employee of an English mining company, Real del Monte. Holzinger became well known for his engineering skills and Santa Anna hired him to build the house on the dictator's estate, Manga de Clavo. When Santa Anna led the revolt against the Centralist government of Anastacio Bustamante, he made Holzinger captain of his engineers and then a colonel of artillery when he invaded Texas. Holzinger was protective of prisoners, especially those of German origin, as shown when he spared members of King's company from execution.

Even Holzinger's timing seemed right. With the Texans back at the Goliad fortress on Saturday night, March 26, 1836, the night before Palm Sunday and seven days after the surrender, the Mexicans passed the word that a ship had been found at Copano Bay to take the prisoners to New Orleans and freedom. The prisoners packed their few remaining possessions and made ready to leave in the morning. They spent the night singing songs including "Home,

Sweet Home" accompanied by a prisoner who had somehow shielded his flute from his captors.

Colonel Fannin, having returned from a trip to Copano that day with Holzinger, spent the evening in a small ante-room off the chapel at Fort Defiance with his adjutant Chadwick, Dr. Barnard, and the other doctors. Though wounded three times at Coleto and traveling the past two days, Fannin was in good spirits as Dr. Barnard dressed his wounds. Fannin spoke of soon seeing his wife, Minerva, and his daughters. Dr. Barnard ended the evening with his "spirits raised."

In reality, the rumor spread by the Mexicans was a ruse to keep the Texans unsuspecting while the fort commandant, Col. Jose Nicolas de la Portilla, worked out the mechanics of killing almost four hundred prisoners. He also had to resolve a moral dilemma. Early in the evening of the twenty-sixth, Portilla received a copy of a directive from General Santa Anna to General Urrea. Santa Anna was irritated that the Goliad prisoners were still alive. He stated, "As the supreme government has ordered that all foreigners taken with arms in their hands, making war upon the nation, shall be treated as pirates, I have been surprised that the circular of the said supreme government has not been fully complied with in the particular. I therefore order that you should give immediate effect to the said ordinance in respect to all those foreigners."

The punishment for piracy was death and perfectly legal under Mexican law. Portilla sent a courier to Santa Anna's headquarters in San Antonio with the message that the prisoners would be executed at four in the morning on the next day. At eight o'clock that same evening Portilla received a communiqué by messenger from his direct commander, General Urrea, who was chasing rebels toward Victoria, with the orders to "Treat the prisoners well, especially Fannin. Keep them busy rebuilding the town and erecting a fort. Feed them with cattle you will receive from Refugio."

Portilla was caught between a direct order from the commander of the army and the president of Mexico and his immediate commanding officer, General Urrea. Portilla struggled with the conflicting orders—"What a cruel contrast in these opposite instructions"—but eventually took the pragmatic approach and put in motion the events for the morning. He added that there was a "great struggle of feeling among the officers and soldiers—a profound silence. Sad at heart, I wrote to General Urrea, expressing my regret at having been concerned in so painful an event." Touching, but his next line shows his pragmatic nature: "I also sent an official account of what I had done, to the general-in-chief."

Portilla knew executing close to four hundred prisoners was no easy task. Firing squads would not work, as the prisoners would revolt when the process started. Also, he could not simply command his men to start shooting as, again, the prisoners would revolt and his eight hundred men might be overwhelmed. A divided group of prisoners believing they were on the verge of being released was the only way to keep them complacent until their deaths.

Portilla's plan was effective in the short run. Less than thirty of the rebels would survive Palm Sunday. But the long-term impact was threefold. First, with the death of Fannin, all leadership opposition to Sam Houston was eliminated. Bowie, Travis, and Crockett were dead at the Alamo, Grant had been captured and killed, and Johnson was only too glad to have escaped San Patricio. Sam Houston was the last man standing and became commander in chief in reality, not just in name. Second, the bickering, the uncoordinated expeditions into the heart of Mexico, and the lack of centralized planning was over. After Goliad, Houston was able to concentrate his army and lure Santa Anna and his forces off the plains and into the swamps of coastal Texas and destroy it. Third and most important, the Texans realized this was total war. The Alamo, while a tragedy, held the romanticism of heroes going down fighting against overwhelming odds. The actions at Goliad, legal or not under Mexican law, were murder in the minds of Texans and they would fight at San Jacinto knowing there was only victory or death. Portilla's obedience to Santa Anna's decree guaranteed the birth of an independent Texas.

Working late into the night, Portilla put his plan into action. The rumor about Copano Bay was floated and Portilla gave his captains their orders for the next day. The prisoners were to be divided into three groups, marched out of the presidio with one group taking the San Antonio road, one group down the Victoria road, and the final group on the road to San Patricio. Portilla's adjutant, Augustin Alcerrica, would command one group while the others were commanded by Capt. Luis Balderas and Capt. Antonio Ramirez.

After a careful reading of Santa Anna's decree, Portilla decided to spare the eighty or so men of Maj. William C. Miller's command. This group had traveled overland from Nashville to New Orleans and then by ship, the *William and Frances*, to Copano Bay, landing on March 17. Disembarking, they were immediately surrounded by the Mexican army, even before they could unload their weapons. This saved their lives. The decree stated that "all foreigners taken with arms in their hands, making war upon the nation, shall be treated as pirates" and executed. To Portilla, surrendering with no "arms in their hands" made them exempt from the decree. They arrived in the fort on March 24 and were given white armbands to identify them as noncombatants and differentiate them from the other prisoners.

The execution did not take place at four o'clock in the morning as Portilla had said in his message to Santa Anna. It was closer to eight o'clock when the prisoners were finally divided into the three groups. One group was told to collect their belongings, as they were leaving immediately for Copano Bay and freedom. The other two groups were told they would depart later; they were needed now to collect firewood and herd cattle. None of the Texans paid attention to the fact that four Mexican cannon previously pointed out of the fort had been turned inward during the night, or that many of the Mexican soldiers had changed into parade uniform.

The three groups filed out the front gate of the presidio, marching between a contingent of approximately seven hundred Mexican soldiers placed on each side of the prisoners' column. The group, made up largely of the New Orleans

Greys, split and headed northeast toward the San Antonio River. They were to ford the river and then take the road eastward to Victoria. The group of prisoners that included Captain Shackelford's Red Rovers, named because they wore red denim pants, started southward toward the Refugio road. The final group headed for the road to San Antonio.

There were warning signs, but they were largely ignored by the prisoners. John Duval, the twenty-year-old son of the Florida governor and brother of the captain of the Kentucky Mustangs, had studied Spanish at a "Catholic institution in Kentucky" (St. Joseph's College) and overheard Mexican women muttering *pobrecitos* (poor fellows) but the "incident at the time made but little impression on my mind." As the group split into three columns, Duval wondered about the separation as his group headed toward the San Antonio road, "but still I had no suspicion of the foul play intended for us."

The terrain that met the eyes of the prisoners as they left the presidio was open field for several hundred yards before a heavy tree line along both banks of the San Antonio River. The river runs atop the north side of the presidio and then curls gently right to left in front of the fort on its way to the Gulf of Mexico. The river is barely forty feet across but its banks are steep and heavily forested in oak, elm, and thick underbrush. The river would be the savior of the few survivors of the massacre.

Herman Ehrenberg, eighteen, had emigrated from Germany to New York in 1835 and then on to New Orleans, where he attended a recruiting meeting for volunteers to go to Texas and fight for independence. Caught up in the enthusiasm, he volunteered and became the youngest member of the New Orleans Greys. He had assisted Colonel Holzinger as an interpreter at Fannin's surrender at Coleto. At eight o'clock on Palm Sunday he marched out the front gate with the Greys and split off on the road to Victoria, not the way to Copano Bay. The prisoners finally started getting nervous and "the intolerable silence of the usually talkative Mexicans and the sultry heat increased the nervous expectations that were now lying in the breasts of all of us. . . . I glanced over at the escort and now first I noticed their festal uniforms and the absence of camping equipment. Bloody pictures rose up in my mind, among others those of Tampico, San Patricio, and the Alamo."

Dillard Cooper, a member of Captain Shackelford's Alabama Red Rovers noticed contradictions in the Mexicans' story. "We had been given to understand that we were to be marched to Capono [sic], and from there shipped to New Orleans." But this morning they were told they were to hunt for cattle, "though I thought at the time that it could not be so, as it was but a poor way, to hunt cattle on foot."

Cooper and the Red Rovers marched southwest from the fort and were ordered to stop about a half-mile from the presidio. Each prisoner was guarded by two soldiers. They were positioned in front of "a brush fence, built by the Mexicans" and were ordered to form up single file with the fence eight feet behind them and the Mexican soldiers facing them eight feet away in the other direction. The commanding officer asked if any of the prisoners spoke Spanish. No one answered. The officer then ordered the prisoners to turn their backs to the guards. No one complied and the officer came forward, grabbed the prisoner at the end of the line by the shoulders, and turned him around.

By now even the dimmest prisoner realized what was going on and several began begging for mercy. Cooper remembered "one, a young man, who had been noted for his piety, but who had afterwards become somewhat demoralized by bad company, falling on his knees, crying aloud to God for mercy, and foregiveness [sic]." But the soldiers were impassive and "no gleam of piety was seen for defenseless men who stood before them." Not all begged for mercy, some became defiant. On Cooper's left was Robert Fenner, who "while some of them were rending the air with their cries of agonized despair, Fenner called out to them saying: 'Don't take on so, boys; if we have to die, let's die like brave men.'" Not only was Fenner brave, he would save Cooper's life.

Duval and the Mustangs, marching on the road to San

Antonio, were also becoming suspicious. This was not the route to Copano Bay. After about a mile, the column was halted and the guards on the river side of the column filed around to join their comrades. Duval's group was in the same position as Cooper's—a barrier behind them and Mexicans with muskets in front of them. Any mystery vanished as "hardly had this maneuver been executed, when I heard a heavy firing of musketry in the directions taken by the other two divisions. A prisoner yelled out, 'Boys, they are going to shoot us!' and at the same instant I heard the clicking of musket locks all along the Mexican line. I turned to look."

Herman Ehrenberg of the Greys was getting increasingly nervous as the column marched on the road to Victoria, and he started preparing an escape attempt. He began dropping his meager belongings and his "few remaining articles rolled through lines of the Mexicans out on the fresh green prairie so that I would not be hindered in my movements in case of need." A quarter of an hour had passed and "and not a word had passed over our lips nor over those of the enemy. Every one seemed to have dropped into deep reflections." The commanding Mexican officer ordered the prisoners off the road and to the left, toward the river. As the prisoners did not understand the command, the officer led the way off the road. Ehrenberg describes the scene:

> My companions in misfortune still carelessly followed the leader. To our left a little five or six feet high mesquite hedge extended straight to the roaring San Antonio River about a thousand yards away, whose clear waves here at right angles with the hedge pushed their way through bluffs between thirty to forty feet high, which rise perpendicularly from the water level on the side. Our feet were directed down the hedge and towards the river.

As with Cooper's and Duval's group, the Mexican column on the left halted and then filed around to form a double line of soldiers. Mounted lancers also joined the guards. At that moment there came the "ruffled rolling of the musket volley in the distance." The Mexican soldiers, only three steps away, leveled their muskets. The officer gestured with his sword and commanded the prisoners to kneel down. The prisoners heard a second volley of musket fire and then cries of the wounded. The cries "startled our comrades out of their stark astonishment which had lasted from five to six seconds. New life animated them, their eyes flashed and they cried out: 'Comrades! Listen to that crying, it means our brothers, hear their cry! It is their last one! Here is no more hope—the last hour of the Grays has come! Therefore—Comrades!'"

They got no further.

The gunfire Ehrenberg heard was directed at Dillard Cooper and the Red Rovers. With his back to the Mexicans and Fenner exhorting the others to die like brave men, Cooper looked over his shoulder and saw the flash of a musket. He fell immediately to the ground and Fenner, mortally wounded, landed on him just as he started to rise. Because Fenner knocked him down, another prisoner named Simpson "got the start of me" and ran through an opening in the brush fence followed closely by Cooper. A Mexican officer tried to block the opening after Simpson got through and thrust his sword at Cooper, who was wearing a cloak that fastened with a clasp at the throat. The officer's sword tangled in the cloak and Cooper tore at the clasp, escaping as the cloak fell to the ground.

Through the gap Cooper entered into open prairie two miles wide with the closest tree line to the southwest. He saw Simpson heading for the trees chased by three Mexicans. Cooper had outrun the Mexicans pursuing him but wanted to avoid those chasing Simpson. To regain his breath he stopped running and started walking toward the tree line. Two points of the tree line poked into the prairie and Cooper started walking toward the one farthest away to avoid Simpson and his pursuers. Simpson made the tree line and the Mexicans halted. Turning, they saw Cooper and started between the points to cut off his access to the woods. Cooper walked slowly toward the Mexicans. The Mexicans stopped, thinking Cooper was coming to them to surrender. When he was sixty yards from the three Mexicans, he wheeled and ran as fast as he could for the point where Simpson had entered the tree line. The Mexicans, worn out from chasing Simpson, did not run after Cooper but fired a volley after him. "The bullets whistling over my head caused me to draw my head down as I ran."

Cooper made it into the woods, found Simpson, and ran for the river. As they were running along the river, they heard noises and jumped in the water. The noises came from two other escapees, Zachariah Brooks and Isaac Hamilton. Hamilton was badly wounded, having been shot and bayoneted once in each thigh. Brooks was wounded as well but could walk. The group swam down the river and hid in underbrush on the shore waiting for night.

At 10 o'clock that night they left the river with Simpson and Cooper carrying Hamilton. They were northwest of the presidio and wanted to get east. They came close to the fort and "could not at first account for the numerous fires we saw blazing. We were not long in doubt, for the sickening smell that was borne towards us by the south wind, informed us too well that they were burning the bodies of our companions. And, here, I will state that Mrs. Cash, who was kept a prisoner, stated afterwards that some of our men were thrown into the flames and burned alive." They bypassed the fort and reached a spring. After refreshing themselves, they set out again but kept losing their way and came back to the spring three separate times. They finally gave up and rested throughout the next day, knowing that travel during daylight would be too dangerous. After dark they set out again.

They came across an abandoned colonist's house and found eggs, corn, and some chickens. They tried to get a fire going but failing that decided to eat the eggs raw. Simpson was in the act of putting his shoes back on and remarked, "Boys, we would be in a tight place if the Mexicans were to come upon us now." Looking out a window, Simpson then saw the Mexican army with a group of cavalry heading directly toward the house. Simpson, with one shoe on and one shoe off, and Cooper grabbed Hamilton, and the group ran for the brush.

They hid and somehow eluded the Mexican search. The Mexicans withdrew and after a period of waiting, Cooper and Simpson returned to the house to get the lost shoe and some food. They returned to their hiding place and then Brooks convinced Simpson to go back again in search of a chicken. Stepping out of the brush, they saw the Mexican soldiers before the soldiers saw them. The Mexicans searched the area all day but found no one. At nightfall the Mexicans left a patrol guarding the road, the only way out for the Texans.

Knowing the Mexicans would surely find them the next day, the prisoners came up with a plan to crawl across the prairie, through the woods, and across the guarded road. Cooper went first, having told his companions "to remove every leaf and stick in the path, and to hold their feet up, only crawling on their hands and knees, as the least noise would betray us to the enemy." It took them two hours to crawl two hundred yards, but they eluded the guards and were finally able to walk, though Hamilton had to be carried. They reached a pond—and relative safety—and collapsed.

Hamilton's wounds were now "irritated and inflamed" so much that even being carried was close to intolerable. Brooks had been lobbying Simpson and Cooper to leave Hamilton behind. Simpson finally agreed but Cooper did not until Hamilton, having overheard Brooks, said, "Boys, Brooks has told you the truth; I can not travel any further, and if you stay with me, all will be killed. Go and leave me, boys; if I have rest I may recover, and if I ever should get off safe, you shall hear from me again." Hamilton gave Brooks, a fellow Alabaman, his gold watch and forty dollars in gold, telling him to give it to his mother. Simpson and Brooks left, but Cooper changed his mind and decided to stay with Hamilton. Only another talk by Hamilton convinced him to go and Cooper soon caught up with the other two. They skirted numerous Mexican patrols and traveled around the army, finally swimming the Colorado River and entering Texan territory. They "procured horses, with the intention of joining Houston's army; but before we reached there, San Jacinto had been fought and won."

Hamilton didn't die. He stayed by the pond for nine days, soaking his wounds until he had recovered enough to walk. He found a skiff on the San Antonio River and rowed it down to Dimmitt's Landing, where he saw an old friend, Don Placido Benavides, working in a field. Benavides, the Paul Revere of Texas, had been a soldier in the Texas army but quit over divided loyalties. Nonetheless, Hamilton thought him a friend and took him up on his offer of help. Loading Hamilton into the back of a wagon, Benavides headed toward town. There he betrayed Hamilton, turning him over to the Mexican army.

Awaiting execution, Hamilton was put to work hauling water for the troops. Not moving fast enough because of his wounds, he was beaten and clubbed nearly to death. His beating was interrupted by a woman who berated an officer for letting his soldiers attack a defenseless man. The beating stopped and the woman gathered Hamilton up and took him to her tent where she bandaged his wounds. Early the next morning, she awakened Hamilton and brought a horse to the tent. She pointed Hamilton in the right direction and he rode off to be found three hours later by a Texas patrol. Hamilton returned to Alabama to recover but soon came back to Texas. He was granted a league of land near present-day Beaumont in 1858 but he died, never fully recovering from his wounds, in 1859. The woman who saved Hamilton was Francita Alavez, the "Angel of Goliad."

Duval's experience on the San Antonio road mirrored that of Dillard Cooper. Just as one prisoner yelled out, "Boys! They are going to shoot us!" Duval heard the clicking of the Mexicans' musket locks and turned to look as the Mexicans opened fire, "killing probably one hundred out of the one hundred and fifty men in the division. We were in double file and I was in the rear rank." The prisoner in front of Duval was killed and knocked Duval to the ground as he fell. Duval stayed on the ground for a minute and finally rising found the Mexicans had charged past him, chasing other prisoners running for the trees and river five hundred yards away. Duval was in the uncomfortable position of having the

Mexicans between him and safety, but it was the only route open because everything else was open prairie. Duval would have to catch up and run through the Mexican line to reach the river.

As Duval made his decision, a Mexican surprised him and made ready to run him through with his bayonet. Just as the soldier lunged, another escaping prisoner ran between them, and the bayonet was "driven through his body. The blow was given with such force, that in falling, the man probably wrenched or twisted the bayonet in such a way as to prevent the Mexican from withdrawing it immediately. I saw him put his foot upon the man, and make an ineffectual attempt to extricate the bayonet from his body, but one look satisfied me, as I was somewhat in a hurry just then."

Back with the Greys, the alert Ehrenberg was ready to run as soon as the firing started. Herman made use of the smoke from the muskets to cover his escape. Smokeless powder was fifty years in the future and prior to that battlefields were shrouded in smoke once the first rounds were fired. He was knocked down with the first volley but not hit.

[I] jumped up quickly, and concealed by the black smoke of the powder . . . rushed down the hedge to the river. I heard nothing more and saw nothing. Only the rushing of the water was my guide. Then suddenly a powerful sabre [sic] smashed me over the head. Before me the little figure of a Mexican lieutenant appeared out of the dense smoke, and a second blow from him fell on my left arm with which I parried it. I had nothing to risk, but only to win. Determinedly I rushed upon him. Forward I must go, and the coward took flight in characteristic Mexican gallantry. Now the path was open, near was the point of my escape. Another few moments had passed. The smoke rolled like a black thundercloud over to the other side, and I stood with rapidly beating heart on the rocks and back of me the hangmen were pursuing.

With prose worthy of a dime novel, Ehrenberg continued his tale of escape: "like a corps from hell they set in after me, but with a 'The Republic of Texas Forever!' I threw myself into the rescuing floods. Swimming slowly toward the opposite bank and prodded from time to time with the poorly aimed bullets that the enemy sent after me, I swam through the current of my savior."

The company mascot was not so lucky:

> Another victim was to fall through the Mexican barbarity, namely, our faithful dog that accompanied the company from the beginning to the end and that now sprang into the water after me to share my pleasures and sufferings with me in my flight through the unknown prairie. He had already reached the center of the stream when the Mexicans made a target of him; and although they seldom hit, the faithful friend, wounded, disappeared under the waves.

Ehrenberg scrambled up the bank, avoided the mounted lancers, and started across the prairie. He wandered for seven days, finding food in several abandoned farmhouses. Finally he had enough and coming across the main camp of General Urrea decided on a bold plan. He entered the camp posing as a lost, unarmed German traveler. His first encounter was with Colonel Holzinger, who supposedly did not recognize him. Either Ehrenberg was extremely lucky or Holzinger went along with the young man's story, as it is hard to believe that Holzinger did not recognize the youth who helped negotiate the surrender at Coleto. General Urrea was suspicious and confronted Ehrenberg with other Texan prisoners. Warned off by a wink from Ehrenberg, the prisoners said they had never seen him before. The ruse worked.

Shortly after Ehrenberg's arrival, Urrea took his force to chase Houston, leaving Colonel Holzinger, four hundred soldiers, and the prisoners at Matagorda with orders to build a fort. Holzinger, in addition, ordered the Texans to build a boat, more like a raft, twenty feet in length. On April 24, 1836, news came of San Jacinto and Santa Anna's defeat. Holzinger ordered his four hundred soldiers to march back to Mexico while he, Ehrenberg, eight Mexicans, and five Texans took the boat and a scow they found and sailed for Mexico.

The party camped on the shore each evening and after a few days the Mexicans became careless. Escaping one night, the Texans made it back to Matagorda, now in the hands of the Texas army. With the return of the former prisoners and their news of their captors' location, a patrol went out and captured Holzinger and his men, bringing them to Matagorda. A mob threatened to lynch Holzinger, but Ehrenberg and another prisoner defended the German and he suffered no harm. When it became known that Holzinger had actually saved some Texans from execution, he was released with the thanks of the Texas government and allowed to board a ship for New Orleans. He eventually returned to Mexico where he became a large landowner, dying in 1864. He is buried in Mexico City.

Ehrenberg received an honorable discharge on June 2, 1836, from Secretary of War Mirabeau B. Lamar. He was granted a large parcel of land but never claimed it. His heirs emigrated from Bohemia in 1880 and were awarded the land. After his discharge, Ehrenberg went back to Germany to study mining at Freiburg University. He returned to America and went on a fur-trapping expedition to Oregon, traveled to Hawaii and became a government surveyor, journeyed to California for the gold rush of 1848, and made his way back to Texas to survey the Gadsden Purchase. He incorporated a mining company in Arizona and surveyed and incorporated the town of Colorado City in addition to being an Indian agent for the Mojaves. Ehrenberg was killed by robbers near present-day Palm Springs, California, in 1866. There is an Ehrenberg Peak in Grand Canyon National Park and the town of Ehrenberg in Arizona is named in his honor. Ehrenberg wrote and published *Texas und Seine Revolution,* his history of the Texas Revolution, in Germany. The book was not translated into English until 1925.

One Mustang survived by not running simply because he couldn't. William Hunter was hit by a musket shot. The majority of the Mexican soldiers were armed with British war surplus muskets called the Brown Bess, most of which were initially issued to the armed forces of the East India Company. Known as the India Pattern musket, they were inferior in quality to those carried by the regular British infantry. Inferior or not, the shot was deadly at ten yards, ineffective at a hundred yards. The musket ball was almost three-quarters of an inch in diameter and if it hit anything solid such as bones or organs at ten yards, the victim had almost no chance of survival. Hunter was "pierced" by a ball and fell. A soldier, seeing him wounded but not dead, cut his throat with a butcher knife but not deeply enough to sever the jugular vein. The Mexican stabbed Hunter with his bayonet, bashed him over the head with the musket, and stripped him, leaving him for dead. Hunter, thankfully unconscious, lay in the open field until night when "the cool air and dew revived him, and by degrees he regained his senses." Hunter was weak and thirsty from lack of water and loss of blood but dragged himself from the open field to the river, where he drank and then bound his wounds with his only remaining clothes, his shirt. He fell asleep in the brush.

In the morning he had recovered enough to swim the river. He headed toward a Mexican ranch where he knew the owners with the intention of throwing himself on their mercy, as his wounds made it impossible for him to travel alone through the wilderness. Before he got to the ranch he was discovered by a Mexican woman. She warned him he would be killed at the ranch and told him to hide in the undergrowth. She would bring him food and clothing after dark. Hunter felt she would betray him but in his condition he had no choice but to trust her. To his surprise, the woman returned after dark with food, water, and a "suit of Mexican clothes." The woman returned every night for a week, dressed his wounds, and brought him food and supplies, including a flint and steel for making fire.

Hunter regained his strength and set out eastward, taking his "course through the wilderness, and having a pretty good idea of the 'lay of the land,' after many narrow escapes eventually made his way to the Texan army under General Houston." Hunter returned to Goliad and was elected chief justice of Refugio County and then served three terms in the Republic of Texas House and one term as senator. He married and lived in Goliad the remainder of his life, dying in 1886 at the age of seventy-seven.

After his narrow miss with the Mexican bayonet, John Duval made ready for his dash through the Mexican lines. Duval snuck up slowly behind the Mexicans, accelerated through their line heading directly and as fast as he could for the river. That he outdistanced the Mexicans is not surprising, as they had run a good distance already, were in full uniform with shakos, and carried muskets six feet in length with bayonet and weighing almost eleven pounds.

At a run Duval plunged into the river and swiftly swam across untouched by the bullets hitting the water around him. The bank on the other side proving too steep and slippery, Duval went back in the river, swimming downstream. He grabbed a vine hanging near the surface of the water and started climbing it "hand over hand, sailor fashion, when a Mexican on the opposite bank fired at me with his *escopeta,* and with so true an aim, that he cut the vine in two just above my head, and down I went into the water again." Duval floated farther down the river, finally finding a spot where the bank was not so steep and climbed out. Now on the side of the river away from the Mexicans, Duval thought himself safe and started to exit the tree line, heading into open prairie. Spotting a group of mounted lancers, however, he retreated into the trees before they saw him. He saw a messmate name Holliday running through the trees headed straight for the prairie and the lancers. Duval called out "as loudly as I dared, and fortunately, being on the 'qui vive' he heard me, and stopped far enough within the timber to prevent the lancers from discovering him." Soon they were joined by another escapee, Samuel T. Brown from Georgia.

Brown was overwrought from the ordeal and having "lost to some extent his presence of mind" suggested taking their chances on the prairie with the lancers since "the Mexicans are crossing the river behind us, and will soon be here." Duval reasoned that may be the case "but they are not here yet, and in the mean time something may turn up to favor our escape." Something did. Another group of escaped prisoners exited the woods and the lancers pounced, killing and robbing the group. Duval saw his chance and his group darted across the prairie. They had run less than two hundred yards when the lancers returned and took up their original position, but "strange to say, however, they never observed us, although we were in plain view of them for more than a quarter of a mile, without a single brush or tree to screen us."

The group wandered for three days, avoiding Mexican patrols and heading for, they thought, Victoria. Finally, believing they were near the rebel-held town, they started using the roads because they no longer feared being discovered by Mexicans. Cresting a ridge, they panicked. Half a mile away sat Fort Defiance, the presidio. They had walked in a circle for three days. They ran west till they collapsed.

After two days circling back east, they swam the Guadalupe River and again thinking they were near Victoria, they relaxed, only to be discovered by a patrol of five Mexican soldiers. The soldiers fired and the Texans ran in three different directions. Duval never saw the others again. He hid for a day in shrubs and then came upon a house abandoned by fleeing Texan colonists. There he found cornmeal, bacon, sugar, coffee, potatoes, and pumpkins. He stayed and rested for a week and finally started east again, eventually being discovered fifteen miles north of Victoria by a patrol of Texas scouts.

Duval was sick of the fighting and went back east to study engineering at the University of Virginia. But Texas had a hold on him and he returned in 1840 to become a surveyor and member of the Texas Rangers. Duval was against Texas secession but joined the Confederate army at the age of forty-two as a private, returning home a captain. He wrote and published his memoirs and several books of western fiction. John

C. Duval died in Fort Worth, Texas, in 1897 at the age of seventy-seven.

Between twenty and thirty prisoners escaped and lived. But more than 350 men lay dead on the fields around the fortress. Soon there would be more.

Chapter 13

Murder in the Chapel

"Oh, why did I not know you had a son there?
I would have saved him at all hazards."

Forty or so wounded Texans were hospitalized either in the stone chapel or in a small tent in the square and had not taken part in the so-called prisoner release of their Goliad comrades. Our Lady of Loreto chapel is located in the northwest corner of the presidio and is small, seating perhaps 150 in a long, narrow sanctuary. The building has a bell tower on one corner and double doors. A small attached side building, also stone, housed Fannin and his lieutenants. Today, the chapel is beautiful with dark wooden pews, white and pink painted walls, and a mural of Jesus and Mary on the wall facing the parishioners. The fresco was painted in 1946 by Antonio Garcia, the "Michelangelo of South Texas." Located in a niche over the chapel entrance is the statue of Our Lady of Loreto done by Lincoln Borglum, the sculptor of Mount Rushmore.

In March 1836 the chapel was filthy, having housed all the prisoners immediately after the surrender. The building was so crowded that most of the prisoners had to stand up during their ordeal, with only the smallest being able to slide to the floor. After several days of little food and water, the healthy prisoners were released to the square but the wounded remained.

On Sunday, March 27, after those prisoners able to walk had left the fort, the Mexicans turned to the execution of the wounded. Soldiers entered the chapel ordering the prisoners who were able to stand and walk to find a companion. They were told the same thing as the healthy prisoners: they were going to Copano Bay and freedom. They gathered whatever belongings they had left and waited.

An officer came into the hospital tent and ordered those able to walk to go outside. The order was translated into English by Andrew Boyle. Boyle, born O'Boyle, emigrated from

Ireland to New York and then to Texas in 1834, where his family, less his father who had abandoned them, helped found the town of San Patricio. It was there that a simple act of kindness would now save Boyle's life. At the start of Santa Anna's invasion of Texas and with part of the army camped at San Patricio, a local woman invited Col. Francisco Garay to dinner in her home. The woman charmed the colonel, sometimes identified as Greek rather than Mexican, and during dinner told him she had a brother, Andrew, serving with Fannin. She asked Garay to look for Andrew and treat him with kindness if they ever met. The colonel promised he would.

In the square of the fort, an officer yelled out Boyle's name. Boyle, who was in line to be executed, raised his hand. The officer approached and ordered Boyle to the officer's hospital, where his wound was attended to and he was ordered to lie down. Boyle lay in a bunk next to Capt. John Sowers Brooks, Fannin's aide, who shattered a hip during the battle of Coleto and had experienced premonitions of death for many months. Boyle found Brooks totally oblivious of events and filled him in on the executions taking place outside. Brooks replied, "I suppose it will be our turn next." Four soldiers entered the hospital, took Brooks out on his cot into the street "not fifteen feet from the door," and shot him. The soldiers took his gold watch, stripped the body, and threw it in a ditch by the side of the street.

At the chapel, the wounded were led out by twos into the small courtyard in front of the chapel doors, blindfolded, and ordered to sit down on their blankets with their backs to their captors. The Mexicans formed three-man firing squads with two of the soldiers firing their muskets point-blank at the sitting Texans. The third member would check to see if the two prisoners were dead and if they were not, he would fire his weapon to finish the job. Often both prisoners would still be alive and they were clubbed to death with muskets. Either because they were secluded in the chapel or in denial, the prisoners only realized their fate when they entered the courtyard. Some protested or struggled, but "the greater part of them sat down calmly on their blankets, resolutely awaiting their miserable fate; some turned pale, but not one displayed the least fear or quivering." Some shouted, "Remember the Alamo!" and "Freedom and justice forever," but within an hour all the wounded were dead. The soldiers and camp followers stripped the bodies in their search for valuables.

While the killing was taking place, Colonel Garay engaged in more acts of mercy. Earlier in the morning, Garay had approached Dr. Shackelford and Dr. Barnard in their quarters telling them to exit the fort and go to his headquarters, located in a peach orchard about three hundred yards away. Entering Garay's tent, the doctors saw two men lying on the ground covered by blankets. The doctors thought they were called to treat the men, but before they had a chance to examine them, a "lad came in, and addressed us in English; we chatted with him some time, he told his name was Martinez, and that he had been educated at Bardstown in Kentucky." The doctors became somewhat impatient and made a move to return to the fort, but Martinez told them his orders were explicit and they were to stay in the tent. A volley of musket fire was explained away by Martinez as "soldiers discharging their muskets for the purpose of cleaning them."

Running from the tent, the doctors heard men screaming. Colonel Garay "now appeared, and with the utmost distress depicted in his countenance said to us, 'Keep still gentlemen you are safe; this is not from my orders, nor do I execute them.' He then informed us that an order arrived the preceding evening to shoot all the prisoners, but he had assumed the responsibility of saving the surgeons and about a dozen others under the plea that they had been taken without arms." Saving Boyle's life was an act of gratitude but saving the surgeons' lives was an act of pragmatism, as the Mexican army had no doctors and little medicine. Garay wasn't finished. The two men under the blankets were carpenters named White and Rosenbury. They had done some work for Garay, and he was so impressed that he had sent for them during the night and sheltered them throughout the massacre.

After the massacre, Shackelford and Barnard were sent to San Antonio to treat the Mexicans wounded at the battle of the Alamo. The first Texans to visit the site after the battle, they treated hundreds of wounded, many of whom died. Based on the number of wounded and firsthand accounts of the battle, Shackelford estimated the Mexican dead at the Alamo between four and six hundred men. Shackelford also toured the Alamo, including the room where Bowie was killed, noting Bowie's splattered brains staining the wall.

The doctors remained at the Alamo until May 6, 1836, when they noted "great excitement" in the fort. The army was in an uproar, with couriers arriving and officers huddling in small groups. Runaway slaves told the doctors of rumors of Santa Anna's defeat at San Jacinto. The rumors were confirmed the next day when the army started its retreat into Mexico. Shackelford and Barnard walked away from the Alamo and into San Antonio as free men. They traveled east to Velasco, the seat of the Texas government, where they confronted the imprisoned Santa Anna. Disgusted by the benign treatment of the dictator, Shackelford requested a discharge from military service and returned to Courtland, Alabama. He returned to face the family members of the men he had recruited and to learn of a memorial service they held for the dead, including himself. Shackelford died in Alabama in 1857 at the age of sixty-seven. Barnard stayed in Texas and was elected to the House of the Eighth Congress in 1843. He resided in Goliad and died during a visit to Canada in 1861.

The young woman Francita Alavez was also busy that Palm Sunday morning hiding and saving as many of the prisoners as she could. Early in the morning, she approached Colonel Portilla to plead for the lives of Major Miller's men. They had been captured as they landed at Copano Bay but were not carrying their weapons so were technically not bearing arms against Mexico and thus not pirates subject to death. Portilla had already decided to spare the eighty-five men. She then woke certain prisoners, hiding them in the belfry of the church and her tent. As the prisoners were being marched out of the presidio, supposedly on their way to Copano Bay and freedom, she spotted a fifteen-year-old drummer boy and pleaded with Colonel Holzinger to release the boy, Franklin Hughes of Kentucky, to her custody. Holzinger agreed and Hughes escaped the firing squad. A few days after the massacre, Francita met Dr. Shackelford and learned that his son had been among those killed. She burst out, "Oh, why did I not know you had a son there? I would have saved him at all hazards." In addition to his son, Shackelford lost two nephews.

Little is known of Francita except that she was in her early twenties, beautiful, originally thought to be the wife of Capt. Telesforo Alavez, and known throughout history varyingly as Alavez, Alvarez, or Alevesco. Her first name is alternately given as Panchita, Francisca, or Pancheta. Research in 1935 determined that Captain Alavez was already married before Francita appeared with the Mexican army, though he had abandoned his wife in Mexico City in 1834. Regardless of marital status, Francita came to Texas with the captain by ship from Matamoros to Copano Bay. After the Texan victory at San Jacinto, the Mexican army retreated back to Mexico and Francita retreated along with Captain Alavez. At Matamoros she aided Texan prisoners before traveling on to Mexico City where Captain Alavez, repeating his previous behavior, abandoned her. She returned to Matamoros penniless and then moved on to Texas, where she was befriended for her efforts during the war. It is believed she found work on the King Ranch, married, and had children whose descendents continued to work the ranch. One descendent went on to be chancellor of Texas Tech University and secretary of education in the Reagan administration. Descendents of Francita Alavez still live in and around Goliad. For saving over one hundred men, she is known in history as the Angel of Goliad.

The rescuing, meager as it was, was over. The wounded prisoners were executed and only Ward and Fannin remained. Col. William Ward, Fannin's second in command, was captured at Victoria after the battle of Refugio. His force of one hundred men had been traveling and fighting on and off for days with little or no ammunition or food remaining. Surrounded in Victoria, Ward argued with his men to keep fighting, as he felt they could expect no mercy. But his men voted to surrender, with Ward insisting they could not blame him if they were all slaughtered. In the end, Ward was right. His men were killed in the massacre and his time had come. Ward was led into the courtyard. An eyewitness, Sabina Brown, wrote that a member of the firing squad told Ward to kneel, "which he refused to do. He was told that if he would kneel, his life might be spared. Standing straight he replied that they had killed his men in cold blood, and that he had no desire to live; death would be welcome." The soldiers fired and Ward was dead.

Joseph Spohn, an eyewitness and participant in the execution of Col. James Walker Fannin, Jr., would survive the war and relate Fannin's execution in an article printed in the *New York Star* in the summer of 1836. Spohn, a "young, attractive Creole from Louisiana," wrote the article in the third person. Early in the morning of Palm Sunday, Spohn was pulled from the line of departing prisoners because he spoke Spanish and was needed as an interpreter. He was ordered to tell the wounded prisoners that they were being taken to Copano Bay though they were really being led out the chapel doors to be executed. Spohn still considered himself to be in the group to be executed and was merely waiting his turn when approached by a wounded Mexican soldier who urged Spohn to ask Portilla to spare his life. At that moment, Fannin "came out of the church for a particular purpose." Fannin appeared calm and unaware of what was happening, though this seems impossible given the noise, yelling, and killing. However, it could be plausible given that Fannin had been in his own room off the chapel, which had thick stone walls and no windows. The door he exited to the interior of the fort is bricked up today, but the outline can be seen upon careful inspection.

As Spohn was speaking with the wounded Mexican soldier, a captain and six soldiers of the Tres Villas battalion approached. The captain asked Spohn to "call" Fannin and pointed to a certain part of the courtyard to which he wanted Fannin brought. Spohn asked the captain if they were going to shoot Fannin and the captain "cooly replied, 'Yes.'"

Spohn approached Fannin and "the Colonel asked what was that firing, and when he told him the facts he made no observation, but appeared resolute and firm, no visible impression on Colonel Fannin, who firmly walked to the place pointed out by the Mexican captain, placing his arm upon the shoulder of Spohn for support, being wounded in the right thigh, from which he was very lame."

Fannin hobbled to the northwest corner of the small courtyard in front of the chapel doors. The Mexican captain conferred with Spohn and ordered him to translate so Fannin would understand "that for having come with an armed band to commit depredations and revolutionize Texas, the Mexican Government were about to chastise him." Fannin listened and then asked to see the commandant. The captain refused, asking why Fannin wanted the commandant. Fannin replied that he wished a remembrance be entrusted to the commandant for delivery to his wife and he "pulled forth a valuable gold watch." The captain reiterated that Fannin could not see the commandant, but if Fannin gave him, the captain, the watch he would thank him. According to Spohn, the captain "repeated in broken English, 'tank you—me tank you.'" Fannin continued to negotiate even though, of course, he had little strength for negotiating. Fannin struggled on, telling the captain, through Spohn, that he could have the watch if he would bury Fannin after his execution. The captain smiled and bowed and promised that this would be done—"*con todas. Las formalidades necessarias*" (with all necessary formalities). Fannin handed over the watch.

Fannin then pulled out of his right pocket "a small bead purse containing doubloons, the clasp of which was bent, he gave this to the officer, at the same time saying that it had saved his life." The musket ball that caused Fannin's thigh wound had hit the clasp of this purse, bent it, and lost part of its force before entering him, carrying the clasp and a silk handkerchief into the wound along with the ball. Fannin recalled pulling on the end of the handkerchief extending from the wound, bringing out the clasp, handkerchief, and musket ball, which fell to his feet. He then reached into the pocket of his overcoat, made of India rubber, and withdrew a piece of canvas containing a "double handful of dollars, which he also gave to the officer."

The captain was now impatient to complete the affair and ordered Spohn to blindfold Fannin. Fannin handed Spohn his handkerchief. Spohn was too nervous to fold the material properly and the captain ripped the handkerchief from his hands. The captain folded the handkerchief but could not place it as Fannin was substantially taller than the Mexican captain. The captain ordered Fannin to sit in a nearby chair and "stepping behind him bandaged his eyes, saying to Col. Fannin, in English, 'good, good'—meaning if his eyes were properly bound—to which Fannin replied 'yes, yes.' The captain then came in front and ordered his men to unfix their bayonets and approach Col. Fannin; he hearing them near him, told Spohn to tell them not to place their muskets so near as to scorch his face with the powder."

The officer ignored Fannin and brought the muskets of the firing squad within two feet of Fannin's face, drew out his handkerchief, and dropped it as a signal to fire. Fannin fell dead on the right side of the chair with most of his head blown away and "thence rolled into a dry ditch, about three feet deep, close by the wall." All that Fannin asked for—his watch to be given to his wife, not to be shot in the face, and to buried—were denied.

General Urrea made Spohn a coachman and after San Jacinto took him to Matamoros, where Spohn, with Urrea's permission, joined the Mexican merchant marine, eventually making his way back to the United States.

The massacre was finally over. A campaign that began with overconfident Texans, adventurers both naive and calculating coming across borders in search of land and adventure, thinking that any one of them could beat five Mexicans, ended its second round in tragedy just as it had the first round at the Alamo. With too many commanders and too many independent commands, the Texans were easy prey for Santa Anna, and they paid for their recklessness.

Did the hopeless defense of the Alamo and the surrender

and massacre at Goliad do any good, add anything to the fight for Texas independence? In the glory days after the war, and perpetuated by the Fess Parker and John Wayne films in the 1950s and '60s, the thirteen days at the Alamo were portrayed as delaying Santa Anna long enough for Houston to gather his army and defeat the Mexican army. In revisionist history, the Alamo is a minor speed bump and Goliad receives little recognition, as surrenders and massacres are not the stuff of legends. But Goliad had more impact on Texas independence than the fall of the Alamo. It eliminated the final threat to Houston's authority with the death of Fannin, but more importantly it stripped any glory or romanticism from the conflict. Houston and his army now knew they were in total war—win or die. They would yell "Remember the Alamo" at San Jacinto but Goliad was their motivator. There would be as little mercy at San Jacinto as there was at Goliad, maybe less.

Chapter 14

The Runaway Scrape
and the Battle of San Jacinto

"Me no Alamo! Me no Goliad!"

The fall of the Alamo followed by the massacre at Goliad panicked the Texan colonists and set off what would later be nicknamed the Runaway Scrape by irreverent Texans. Farms and towns were abandoned as the occupants fled eastward toward the Sabine River, the Louisiana border, and safety.

With most of the men in the army, the women took charge and loaded carts and wagons with furniture and belongings that soon were thrown to the side of the overcrowded roads as horses and oxen became exhausted. These women were also angry, which did not bode well for the Mexican army, as one settler remembered years later that "if mother shed a tear, I never knew it, though there was an unusual huskiness in her voice that day. Mother was brave and resolute, and I heard her say to a lady while crossing the Brazos, under great difficulties, that she was going to teach her boys never to let up on the Mexicans until they got full revenge for all this trouble." Adding to the misery were the spring rains that poured down on the columns of women, children, and old men—"but in proportion the men were few, and so the women and children were forced to perform most of the labor. Thus these half-clad, mud-besmeared fugitives, looking like veritable savages, trudged along." The scrape was on.

Learning of the tragedies at the Alamo and Goliad, Houston set to restructuring his army. With the deaths at the two forts, the number of men in the rebel army dwindled to between six hundred and eight hundred with less than four hundred in Gonzales with Houston, two hundred on the coast, and the rest sprinkled throughout east Texas. Houston's falling back and retreating out of the plains of central Texas toward the swamps and forests of east Texas was not a complete rout, for on the way Houston worked on his organization, forming the "1st Texas Volunteer regiment" with Col. Edward Burleson commanding and Lt. Col. Sidney Sherman as second in command. Houston put all his scouts under Erastus "Deaf" Smith. They scoured the countryside for Mexican forces and spread the word for civilians to flee. The scouts burned Gonzales to the ground.

While the settlers, and the Texas government, did flee pretty much in panic, the army retreated in order with Smith and his scouts continuously patrolling and shadowing the Mexican army, keeping Houston aware of movements and avoiding potential surprises. However, the Mexicans weren't concerned. Santa Anna had become overly confident as a result of the battle of the Alamo and the surrender and massacre at Goliad. He envisioned a routine mopping-up of the few remaining Texan soldiers, the execution of a few politicians, and the revolt would be finished, allowing his army to return to the interior. The Anglo scourge would be obliterated and no settlers would be allowed back into Mexican territory. Santa Anna became so overconfident he planned a ship voyage to Vera Cruz and then on to Mexico City before the end of the campaign. He was talked out of the trip by his generals and decided to stay and enjoy his victory before returning in triumph to Mexico.

Santa Anna led his army out of San Antonio toward Gonzales after directing General Urrea to move eastward up the coast. A third column under Gen. Antonio Gaona was directed north from San Antonio and then eastward toward the Brazos River. The plan was to concentrate all three forces in about a month at the Brazos and march to the border on the Sabine River, forcing the settlers out of Mexican territory and demonstrating to the United States that Santa Anna and Mexico were capable of defending the border.

As Santa Anna split his command, Houston was bringing his together with the plan of hitting Santa Anna before the three Mexican columns reunited. He needed a month to retreat, train his army of raw recruits into something resembling a military force, and extend the supply lines of the

Mexican army. "By falling back," Houston said, "Texas can rally, and defeat any force that can come against her." The strategy made sense, as it had the additional advantage of getting the battle out of the plains where the Mexican cavalry could attack at will. The battle would take place in the crowded and contained forests and swamps of southeast Texas.

The plan was not popular with the army, which wanted a fight and wanted it now. The rebel army now was made up of adventurers and settlers in almost equal numbers. They were volunteers and as such felt they could come and go as they pleased. They owed their allegiance to their immediate commanders, not to Sam Houston, as their officers were mostly elected, the time-honored tradition of Southern militias. Plus, to the settlers, a family in need outweighed any military obligation. But for all that, they were also brave, young, and ready for a fight.

Even with the comings and goings, the army was growing, fed by more volunteers from the United States and settlers who returned to the ranks when their families reached safety. The Mexican army numbered between five and seven thousand but it was split into the three columns, overextended, and overconfident. Nevertheless, rumors running through east Texas had the enemy army numbering as many as thirty thousand men.

Houston was not concerned about the numbers. He was concerned about strategy, writing, "We can raise three thousand men in Texas, and fifteen hundred can defeat all that Santa Anna can send to the Colorado. We would then fight on our own ground, and the enemy would lose all confidence from our annoyance." At the same time, early April, Santa Anna continued to exude confidence, summing up the situation: "The capture of the Alamo, in spite of its attendant disasters, and the quick and successful operations of General Urrea give us a prodigious moral prestige. . . . Our name terrified the enemy, and our approach to their camps was not awaited. They fled disconcerted to hide beyond the Trinity and the Sabine. . . . The attainment of our goals was now almost certain."

Besides destroying the rebel army Santa Anna wanted to capture the Texan government that had fled Washington-on-the-Brazos and was making its way to southeast Texas and escape by sea. Santa Anna wanted the ringleaders but, in his desire, he made a fatal mistake. To speed the chase, he divided the army again. On April 14, Santa Anna and 750 cavalry and infantrymen split off from the main army and headed toward Harrisburg.

In the rebel camp, pressure was building on Houston to fight. His untrained army wanted blood and the fleeing government wanted a battle before being pushed out of Texas. The president of Texas, David Burnet, asked Secretary of War Thomas Rusk why Houston was retreating ahead of "a contemptible Mexican force." Burnet was not afraid to put the question directly, which he did in a letter to Houston saying, "Sir: The enemy are laughing you to scorn. You must fight them. You must retreat no further. The country expects you to fight. The salvation of the country depends on you doing so."

Houston ignored the politicians and continued his withdrawal. He didn't like the landscape and his army was too small and untrained. However, he faced internal dissent when two of his commanders, Wiley Martin and Mosley Baker, refused Houston's orders to abandon San Felipe and retreat east of the Brazos. Mosley and Baker wanted to stand and fight and threatened to do so. Pragmatically, Houston took the offensive and ordered them to fight, with Martin guarding the crossing at Fort Bend and Baker defending the crossing at San Felipe. Houston took the remaining five hundred men eastward to drill and train. The lessons of the Alamo and Goliad were lost on Martin and Baker and even Burnet. Rumors and discontent were so rampant in the army that Houston "caused notices to be written and stuck on trees with wooden pegs, to the effect that the first man who should beat for volunteers should be courtmartialed and shot." The orders to Martin and Baker and the notice nailed to trees bought Houston a bit more time, but the army could not be contained much longer.

Santa Anna made his dash to the coast in one day but

arrived just as a boat carrying most of the Texas politicians, including President Burnet, set off from shore headed for Galveston Island. Santa Anna missed catching the politicians but they were at least technically offshore. He turned his attention to Houston, whom he assumed was still retreating, bogged down by refugees, toward the Sabine.

But events had changed, finally, in Houston's favor and Houston knew it because he had reports from Deaf Smith with the location of Santa Anna and the smaller force. Houston now had to weigh the odds and the facts: his men were impatient and near mutiny at not being able to fight, they were better trained and there was little that could be done to train them further, their number had grown to near-ly eight hundred, and, most importantly, Santa Anna had reduced his army to seven hundred and fifty men. For the first time since the invasion, the Texans outnumbered the Mexicans. The rebel army also had some firepower. The City of Cincinnati donated two cannon, nicknamed the "Twin Sisters," which arrived at Houston's camp via New Orleans and Galveston. Houston now had something stronger to fire at the Mexicans than muskets and rifles. Finally, Santa Anna was exposed and ahead of his main body of troops. By going southeast toward Galveston, Santa Anna put Houston and Houston's army in between himself and the bulk of his army.

Houston came to the decision to fight by not acting. The rebel army was marching eastward and came to a split in the road at the Roberts' farm. The road that split left went to the Trinity River and retreat, and everyone in the army knew it. The road to the right led to Harrisburg and Santa Anna. All eyes were on Houston. Farmer Roberts stood in his field and seeing Houston, pointed his finger to the right and yelled out to the general, "That right hand road will carry you to Harrisburg just as straight as a compass." The men began yelling, "To the right, to the right" as they marched. Houston did not move or speak as his rebel army took the road to the right.

They marched on and crossed Buffalo Bayou. Their goal was Santa Anna and his army camped at the juncture of the San Jacinto River and Buffalo Bayou. The rebels marched until midnight and slept by the side of the road for a few hours until Houston ordered them awakened and on the march again, reaching Santa Anna's camp near noon.

The battlefield is small, covering less than three square miles, and appears very much the same today as it was in 1836 except for the oil refineries that surround the site, the battlefield memorial, and the presence in the bayou, now ship channel, of the U.S.S. *Texas,* the last surviving dreadnought-class battleship. The field is a triangle facing south with Buffalo Bayou at the top, a tree line skirting the bayou. An open field borders the San Jacinto River on one side and trees bound the other side of the triangle. At the southern point of the triangle there is a small lake with swamp and trees. The rebel army was at the top of the triangle, safely in the trees with their backs to Buffalo Bayou. The Mexican army was at the southern end. Between the two armies was open field with a small rise in the middle.

The bizarre events of this brief but brutal battle started to play out. As the rebels crossed Buffalo Bayou, Santa Anna's scouts reported their arrival. Santa Anna was ecstatic and jumped on his horse, riding through his men shouting, "The enemy are coming! The enemy are coming!", which was exciting to Santa Anna but terrified his soldiers, who realized their small number. Santa Anna formed a column and advanced across the field around two o'clock in the afternoon. The Texans stayed in the safety of the trees, the Twin Sisters trading cannon shots with their Mexican counterparts. The only casualties were the wounding of the Mexican captain Urriz, who had fought at the Alamo, and James Neill, who had been commander of the Alamo before Travis.

Houston would not emerge from the safety of the tree line. In the rebel camp many of the officers seethed at Houston for not attacking. Sidney Sherman, second in command of the First Texas Volunteers, argued that a good cavalry charge would rout the Mexicans. Houston knew the Texans were not true cavalrymen and doubted their worth against Santa Anna's cavalry with their renowned horsemanship and long lances. Sherman ignored Houston and gathered sixty riders.

Houston could not stop them but ordered Sherman to only scout and not to engage the enemy.

Sherman ignored Houston's order and charged the first Mexicans he saw. Dismounting to reload their weapons, the sixty were surrounded by Santa Anna's cavalry with Sherman waving his arms, trying to get Houston's attention and help. Houston ignored Sherman, as he had no intention of risking his army to save sixty men. A company of volunteers rushed to the rescue. One private of the company, Mirabeau Lamar, saved two men (one was Secretary of War Rusk, who had gotten caught up in Sherman's enthusiasm) with equestrian skills so extraordinary the Mexican lancers broke out in applause. Houston was infuriated with Sherman but promoted Lamar to colonel in command of the rebel cavalry. Lamar would go on to succeed Houston as the second president of the Texas Republic. He started the Texas public education system and founded Austin, the state capital and home of the University of Texas.

After his rescue Sherman got into a shouting match with Houston, accusing Houston of cowardice. Houston ignored him. He knew his army was safe in the trees and the skirmish with the Mexican regulars again raised doubts in his mind about his soldiers' ability to stand up to the Mexicans in an open-field battle. Houston retired that evening undecided about events for the coming day. Before falling to sleep, he read from Jonathan Swift's *Gulliver's Travels* and Caesar's *The Gallic War*. When he awoke on the morning of April 21, 1836, Houston found himself outnumbered again.

General Cos, Santa Anna's brother-in-law, loser of the first battle of the Alamo and parole violator, arrived with five hundred men early in the morning. Houston's detractors couldn't believe the bad news and viewed the previous day as a lost opportunity. In reality, Santa Anna dressed down his brother-in-law for bringing a bunch of worthless conscripts rather than more elite members of the army. In addition, the soldiers were exhausted after marching all night and needed food and water. By the time the newly arrived soldiers had all entered camp and found shelter it was early afternoon of April 21, 1836.

In the Texas camp, Houston still waited, convinced that his tree line was the best defense. He waited for Santa Anna to attack. The attack didn't come and the Texans grumbled. Gen. John Wharton, a War Dog, went through the camp proclaiming, "Boys, there is no other word today but fight, fight! Now is the time!" The camp responded with shouts and cheers until Houston finally declared, "Fight, and be damned." He could not contain his men forever. At three o'clock he gave the order to assemble the army at the tree line. An hour earlier, he had ordered Deaf Smith and six men to ride to Vince's Bridge and destroy it and in doing so block any further reinforcements from reaching Santa Anna. The destruction also cut off the escape routes of both armies. The battle would be to the death.

Santa Anna did everything possible to make the attack easy for Houston. He assumed that any rebel offensive would come in the morning, not late in the afternoon, so he posted no sentries or pickets in front of his camp. There was a hastily thrown together defensive line made up of packs, sacks of food, branches, dirt, and one cannon but it was basically unmanned. The camp itself was indefensible, with Peggy Lake in the rear and no room to maneuver. Colonel Delgado complained, "The camping ground of His Excellency's selection was, in all respects, against military rules. Any youngster would have done better." Santa Anna didn't care and ordered the siesta. He retired to his tent and was asleep at three-thirty.

The rebel army was assembled in two thin lines stretching less than one thousand yards with on the left Sidney Sherman's Second Texas of 260 men, Burleson's First Texas Regiment of 220 men, and the Twin Sisters manned by the Cincinnati Battery with 31 artillerymen. The right was anchored by Lt. Col. Henry Millard, in command of the 240 men of the Texas Regular Battalion. Finally, on the far right were 50 cavalrymen commanded by the ex-private, now colonel, Mirabeau Lamar. Most accounts have the army led by a drummer, black in some accounts, and at least one fifer. The musicians knew only one number, the risqué ballad

"Come to the Bower," with the following refrain:

> Will you come to the bow'r I have shaded for you?
> Our bed shall be roses all spangled with dew.
> There under the bow'r on roses you'll lie
> With a blush on your cheek but a smile in your eye!

The rebel flag that day was a bare-breasted Lady Liberty swinging a sword with a banner reading "Liberty or Death" hanging from the tip. The men were armed with rifles or muskets with most carrying two or three pistols, swords, and Bowie knives. Houston, mounted on a large white stallion named Saracen, rode in front of the two lines of rebels waving his sword and at three-thirty in the afternoon, he ordered them forward out of the woods.

The lines advanced undetected to within five hundred yards of the Mexican camp. A Mexican bugler finally sounded the alarm and the single Mexican cannon fired high and no Texans were hit. The Twin Sisters were turned and fired shot made up of old nails and horseshoes from a range of two hundred yards. The infantry charged on the run toward the Mexicans and the Twin Sisters were moved to within seventy yards of the Mexicans' improvised line, blowing holes in the packs, bags, and men. Some Mexicans did return fire and Saracen was hit and fell dead. Houston grabbed another mount and rode forward. This time both he and the horse were hit, the horse fatally and Houston with a grapeshot wound to his right ankle. Hobbling, Houston found another horse and mounted, throwing his wounded leg around the pommel. The Second Regiment hit the barricade first, pushing through the thin line of the Matamoros Battalion on the left, and then came the First Regiment, hitting the center. The single Mexican cannon was silenced after firing only five rounds. Lamar's small band of cavalry attacked on the Mexicans' left, cutting and slashing their way through the panicked Mexican soldiers.

Mexican officers tried to rally their troops, but there was nothing they could do to stop the panic. Gen. Fernandez Castrillon was in his tent shaving when the attack came. He ran out to the barricade to organize his men but they ran like a river around him. Trapped by the Texans, his men urged him to flee, but he shouted back, "I have been in forty battles and never once showed my back. I'm too old to do it now!" The brave but corrupt general stood with arms folded as Secretary of War Rusk ran up and tried to save the old warrior, knocking aside gun barrels as he approached. But it was too late; the Texans shot down the general where he stood. The massacre was on with the rebels yelling, "Remember the Alamo! Remember Goliad! Remember La Bahia!"

Resistance crumbled and the mob retreated. One Mexican colonel observed after the battle, "Mexican soldiers, once demoralized, cannot be controlled." The average Mexican soldier had great reason to be demoralized. While the officers ate fine meals and lived in fine tents, the average soldier survived on beans and a few tortillas a day and marched, never rode, in or out of battle. They would be the ones who paid most heavily for Santa Anna's atrocities.

The Mexican soldiers fled, running into the swamps, the San Jacinto River, and Peggy Lake, chased by the rebels who cut down the stragglers with musket, sword, and knife. With the enemy trapped in the river and lake, the Texans shot, reloaded, and shot again. There was no chance of missing. Mexicans pleaded for their lives, saying, "Me no Alamo! Me no Goliad!" but their pleas had as much impact as those of the Texans at Goliad and the Alamo. Some rebel officers tried to stop the killing. Colonel Wharton, the War Dog, soon tired of the slaughter but was warned by one Texan, "Colonel Wharton, if Jesus Christ were to come down from heaven and order me to quit shooting Santanistas, I wouldn't do it, sir!" He then cocked and pointed his weapon at Wharton's chest. Wharton rode away. Some were more successful in saving officers, but even Houston could not stop the killing. He ordered his drummer to beat a retreat but it was ignored. He yelled, "Parade, men, parade!" but none paid attention. Finally, he got some attention shouting, "Gentlemen! Gentlemen! Gentlemen!" and with the quiet, he told them, "Gentlemen, I applaud your bravery, but damn your manners" and rode off knowing there was nothing he could do to stop the killing. Many of the Texans had relatives killed at the Alamo and Goliad. Houston read them correctly: no mercy at Goliad meant no mercy at San Jacinto.

The Mexicans in the rebel army joined in as well, as told by Nicholas Labadie:

> [I] pursued a fresh trail into the marsh, and came upon Col. Bertrand, who had bogged, and on his knees he begged for his life. Supposing myself alone, I extended my left hand to raise him up, but was surprised to hear a voice behind me saying, "Oh, I know him; he is Colonel Bertrand of San Antonio de Bexar. General Teran made him a colonel." This was said by one Sanchez, a Mexican, in Capt. Seguin's company, composed of some thirty Mexicans (Tejanos) fighting on our side. He had scarcely done speaking when I observed three others coming up with leveled guns. I cried out to them: "Don't shoot, don't shoot; I have taken him prisoner." These words were hardly spoken, when bang goes a gun, the ball entering the forehead of poor Bertrand, and my hand and clothes are spattered with his brains, as he falls dead at my feet.

Robert Hunter recalled one officer's reaction to the call to stop the killing and take prisoners. "Capt. Easlen said, 'Boys, take prisoners—know how to take prisoners. Take them with the butt of your guns, club guns,' and said, 'Remember the Alamo, remember La Bahia (Goliad), and club guns, right and left, and knock their brains out.'"

Between six hundred and seven hundred Mexicans were killed and over seven hundred captured. The rebels suffered two killed outright. Six more would die of their wounds and eighteen would recover, including Houston. The entire battle took eighteen minutes. The Texans took the camp and four stands of colors, the cannon, six hundred muskets, two hundred pistols, three hundred swords, and enough gold to give each victor eleven dollars' worth.

Less than one hundred Mexicans escaped the massacre. Santa Anna was one of them. Jarred awake by the rebel attack, he left his tent and was "running about in the utmost excitement, wringing his hands and unable to give an order." Santa Anna calmed down enough to assess the situation, see that it was hopeless, grab a saddled horse from an aide, and flee. He raced toward Vince's Bridge. Unable to cross the bayou because of the burned bridge, he slipped into the pines to the deserted home of a colonist. There he spent the night and changed from his general's uniform into white pants and a blue jacket. The next day he started out across the plains but was soon scooped up by a Texas mounted patrol.

The Texans didn't know who they had captured, but a few things made Santa Anna stand out. He was commonly dressed and said he was a cavalryman but the scouts noted his red worsted slippers and a silk shirt buttoned with diamond studs. He also did not exhibit the stamina of a common soldier. Prodded forward by lance point, he walked only two miles before protesting he could go no farther. One scout suggested shooting the prisoner, but Joel Robinson, a Spanish speaker, pulled Santa Anna up behind him on his horse. The two chatted, with Santa Anna naturally concerned about the treatment of prisoners and asking about the size of the rebel army. He expressed disbelief when told the army was less than eight hundred men. Robinson may have had his doubts about the identity of his prisoner but any doubt evaporated upon entering camp. Upon Santa Anna's entrance, the Mexican officers rose up and the troops rushed forward yelling, "El Presidente, El Presidente."

Most Texans naturally wanted to execute Santa Anna, but the two principals, Houston and Santa Anna, sat down to serious negotiations. Santa Anna was negotiating for his life, Houston was negotiating for Texas. Houston knew an army of at least twenty-five hundred men was within a day's march and could smash his small command. A surprise victory like San Jacinto could not be repeated, so the Mexican army had to be made to withdraw or the rebels would be crushed. Santa Anna knew he had to make this happen or he was worthless to the rebels and would be executed before any future battle.

Santa Anna was told to order General Filisola, general of

the closest army, to surrender. Santa Anna replied, "He will not do it. He will not do it. You have whipped me. I am your prisoner. But Filisola is not whipped. He will not surrender as a prisoner of war. You must whip him first. But if I give him orders to leave the limits of Texas, he will do it." The deal was on the table and Houston took it. Santa Anna wrote letters to Filisola, Urrea, and Gaona ordering them to withdraw, and quickly. In a separate letter to Filisola, he wrote, "I recommend to you that as soon as possible you carry out my order concerning the withdrawal of the troops since this is conducive to the safety of the prisoners, and in particular that of your most affectionate friend and companion who sends you his deepest regards. Antonio Lopez de Santa Anna."

Filisola, Urrea, and Gaona commiserated and grumbled but reluctantly agreed. The Mexican army exited and Texas was a republic. Urrea would lead two rebellions, end up in prison, fight the United States in 1846 and die in 1849. General Cos was captured at San Jacinto and released. He returned to Mexico, stayed in the army, fought against the United States in 1846, and died in 1854.

Houston would be elected president of the Republic twice, oversee annexation and statehood, be elected to the United States Senate, and then serve as governor of the new state. He would be ousted from office when he opposed secession in 1861 and die at the age of seventy. He is the Father of Texas. Santa Anna would continue to talk his way out of trouble (he was almost lynched boarding a boat to New Orleans) and serve as president of Mexico five times. He lost a leg during the Pastry War with France and thus endeared himself to the population, for a while. Exiled on Staten Island in 1855, he helped found a United States institution when his secretary, James Adams, noticed Santa Anna chewing chicle. Adams added sugar and invented Chiclets. The box carries Adams' name to this day. After the United States, Santa Anna lived in exile in Cuba, the Dominican Republic, and the Bahamas. He was finally allowed back into Mexico, where he died in 1876 at the age of eighty-two.

The battle for Texas after San Jacinto was over, but tensions between the former territory and Mexico never would go away. They exist still today. The martyrs of the Alamo had inspired the rebels to fight. On the fields around the presidio the charred bones of Fannin and his men had terrified them. Goliad convinced the rebels that "Victory or Death" was not a slogan, but a reality, and from this reality was born the Republic of Texas.

Bibliography

Publications

Brands, H. W. *Lone Star Nation.* New York: Doubleday, 2004.

Brown, Gary. *Hesitant Martyr in the Texas Revolution: James Walker Fannin.* Plano, TX: Republic of Texas Press, 2000.

Campbell, Randolph B. *Gone to Texas: A History of the Lone Star State.* New York: Oxford University Press, 2003.

De Bruhl, Marshall. *Sword of San Jacinto: A Life of Sam Houston.* New York: Random House, 1993.

Derr, Mark. *The Frontiersman: The Real Life and Many Legends of Davy Crockett.* New York: William Morrow and Company, Inc., 1993.

Fehrenbach, T. R. *Lone Star: A History of Texas and the Texans.* New York: Macmillan Publishing Co., Inc., 1968.

Haley, James L. *Sam Houston.* Norman, OK: University of Oklahoma Press, 2002.

Hopewell, Clifford. *Remember Goliad—Their Silent Tents.* Austin, TX: Eakin Press, 1998.

Houston, Sam. *The Writings of Sam Houston Volume 1 1813-1865.* Edited by Amelia W. Williams and Eugene C. Barker. Austin, TX: The University of Texas Press, 1938.

James, Marquis. *The Raven.* Dunwoody, Ga: Bobbs-Merrill Company, 1929.

Long, Jeff. *Duel of Eagles.* New York: William Morrow and Company, Inc., 1990.

Lord, Walter. *A Time to Stand.* Lincoln: University of Nebraska Press, 1961.

Moulder, Marsha. "Women Played Key Roles in Texas History, Others Fought Own Battles." *Victoria (TX) Advocate,* 8 July 2003.

O'Connor, Kathryrn Stoner. *Presidio La Bahia*. Austin, TX: Von Boeckmann-Jones Co., 1966.

Pruett, Jakie L., and Everett B. Cole, Sr. *Goliad Massacre— A Tragedy of the Texas Revolution*. Austin, TX: Eakin Press, 1985.

Roell, Craig H. *Remember Goliad! A History of La Bahia*. Austin, TX: Texas State Historical Association, 1994.

Schoelwer, Susan Prendergast, with Clifton H. Jones. *Alamo Images: Changing Perceptions of a Texas Experience*. Dallas: DeGolyer Libary and Southern Methodist University Press, 1985.

Wharton, Clarence. *Remember Goliad*. Glorieta, N.Mex.: The Rio Grande Press, Inc., 1968.

Yoakum, H. *History of Texas from Its First Settlement in 1685 to Its Annexation to the United States in 1846*. New York: Bedfield, 1855.

Online Sources

British Battles.com. Online. 1 March 2006.
http://www.britishbattles.com/bunker-hill.htm

Calliope Film Resources. "Shays' Rebellion." Copyright 2000 CFR. 1 April 2006.
http://www.calliope.org/shays/shays2.html

Handbook of Texas Online, s.v. 29 June 2006.
http://www.tsha.utexas.edu/handbook/online/articles/

Mexico Connect. Online. 1 April 2006.
http://www.mexconnect.com/mex_/history.html

Mexican Independence. Online. 1997-2006.
http://www.tamu.edu/ccbn/dewitt/mexicanrev.htm

Presidio LaBahia. Online. 1 March 2006.
http://www.presidiolabahia.org/

Sons of Dewitt Colony. Online. 1 March 2006.
http://www.tamu.edu/ccbn/dewitt/dewitt.htm

Texas State Library and Archives Commission. Online. 1 June 2006.
http://www.tsl.state.tx.us/exhibits/presidents/houston1/

The Galileo Project. Online. 25 June 2006.
http://galileo.rice.edu/sci/observations/longitude.html

Index